DANGER ON THE LINE

DANGER ON THE LINE

STANLEY HALL

LONDON

IAN ALLAN LTD

Contents

First published 1989

ISBN 0 7110 1872 3

Published by Ian Allan Ltd, Shepperton, Surrey; and printed by Ian Allan Printing Ltd at their works at Coombelands in Runnymede, England

Dedication

To all those railwaymen who, day in and day out, by day and by night, in summer and winter, and in fair weather and foul, do their best to get you to your destination safely and on time.

Half title:
Clearance operations proceeding in Clapham cutting on Tuesday 13 December 1988, the day after the tragic accident which claimed 35 lives. *Brian Morrison*

Previous page:
Aftermath of the Purley crash of 4 March 1989. *Brian Morrison*

Introduction and Acknowledgements

My first book on railway safety standards, and accidents to trains on British Rail, published in 1987 under the title *Danger Signals*, was concerned mainly with the operational aspects of railway work, under the control of drivers, guards and signalmen. This second book ventures into the realms of civil, mechanical and signal engineering and explores the technical aspects of accidents of which the driver is often an unwitting and unwilling victim or observer. However, as in *Danger Signals*, it also attempts to look beyond the obvious cause of an accident, and explores the way in which the conditions necessary for accidents are created, such as the impact of new technology, errors made by technical staff, the effect of management action or inaction, and the influence of the changing railway environment. It is, however, not a technical treatise, but is aimed equally at the professional and the layman, at the railwayman and that large body of people interested in railway activities.

Chapter 10 discusses the accidents at Purley, on the Southern Region's main line from Brighton to London, and at Glasgow Bellgrove, which happened within two days of each other in March 1989. The causes of accidents such as these where drivers pass signals at Danger were fully explored in *Danger Signals*, but they are of such significance in safety terms that it was felt to be essential to include an examination of them in this book.

I have taken as my starting point the nationalisation of railways on 1 January 1948, with only an occasional reference to events or accidents before that date, therefore the book is essentially concerned with the modern railway. Because of my background as a railway operator it is also an operating view of the railway scene, concerned with trains and the general running of the railway, as influenced by technical matters, such as the track, bridges, rolling stock, and the conveyance of dangerous goods.

Technical innovation is often a two-edged sword. It removes previous causes of accidents but may easily create other, new, and sometimes unforeseen hazards. Technology pushes at the boundaries of knowledge and experience, indeed that is how progress comes about, but the act of venturing into the unknown can have a downside so far as safety is concerned.

The theme of the book is safety, and it explains how today's very high standards have been achieved. I am writing these very words as I travel in High Speed Train comfort and safety through thick fog at 125mph, confident that the skill and care of engineers of all disciplines will get me to my destination on time and in one piece. By contrast, tonight's newspapers may well contain reports of multiple pile-ups on motorways, of people being trapped in their burning cars, and of the general mayhem which seems to afflict our motorways and trunk roads during fog and frost.

Accidents by their very nature indicate that something has gone wrong, or that someone has made an error, but the ultimate responsibility may well lie with the management of British Rail, because it is they who decide how the railways should be operated, and the extent to which the effects of human error should be guarded against. Accidents are almost bound to result in criticism but I hope that my comments are always fair and take account of the constraints, whether financial, political or legal, which often bear harshly upon BR. The views expressed in this book, and the criticisms, except where otherwise attributed, are mine alone, and I have striven to achieve an objective and dispassionate viewpoint.

In my descriptions of certain accidents I have attempted to give the reader a feeling of what it must have been like to have been involved, whether as passenger, driver or guard, and this necessarily entails a degree of dramatisation. I make no apology for this — accidents *are* dramatic and they *are* frightening.

This book would not have been possible without the enormous help I have received from the officers of the Railway Inspectorate of the Department of Transport, and from their Accident Reports, also from the Annual Reports of the Chief Inspecting Officer. I am also very grateful for the help and encouragement given by my family and friends, and to those of you who were kind enough to buy my first book *Danger Signals*, because that has encouraged me to write this book. I must also express my gratitude to those of my friends and former colleagues who have kindly read the drafts and given me their helpful comments.

Finally, I would like to acknowledge the help I have received from the following in the provision of material and with help in research:

The British Railways Board
British Timken, Duston, Northampton
British Transport Police
Chartered Institute of Transport
Cowans Boyd, Carlisle
Dorman Traffic Products Ltd, Southport
Graviner Ltd, Slough
National Railway Museum, York
National Union of Railwaymen
Procor (UK) Ltd, Horbury Junction.

1
Fires on Express Passenger Trains

Imagine that you are a passenger on an express train. Perhaps you are reading, or chatting, or just looking out of the window enjoying the view of the countryside. You catch a faint whiff of something burning. You do not recognise it but you think it might have come from outside, and you dismiss it from your mind. A few minutes later the smell intrudes into your consciousness again, only this time it is a little stronger and more acrid. You look round to see if you can detect where the smell is coming from, and you notice that one or two of your fellow passengers are also looking round in a concerned sort of way. In the rest of the coach life is going on as usual — family parties playing games, people eating and drinking and chatting happily. Some just sleeping.

Suddenly you get a definite smell of something burning, and a feeling of alarm starts to rise within you. You begin to wonder whether you should do something, but what? Go for the guard? No, you decide that would be futile; it would take too long, and in any case you don't want to fetch the guard on what might turn out to be a wild-goose chase if nothing can be found when you return. Pull the communication cord? You look to see where it is and spot a red handle near the ceiling on the opposite side. But suppose it is a false alarm? Would you have to pay £50? Perhaps it would be better to move away further down the coach, just in case. After all, you don't want to make a fuss, and look a fool when it turns out to be nothing. But even whilst these thoughts are chasing each other through your mind you notice a definite puff of dark smoke. Others do too, and the normal chatter of the coach is replaced by a more agitated hubbub. Voices are raised. People start to move away. Someone calls, 'fetch the guard'. Someone else shouts, 'is there a fire extinguisher?' Then, a small tongue of reddish-yellow flame licks up the wall. Passengers nearby start to move away in a hurry, but their way is impeded by the throng of other passengers blocking the aisle. Within seconds thick black suffocating smoke and fumes begin to curl down the coach along the ceiling, flames shoot up the wall to the roof and a mad scramble breaks out to get away from the fire. But the train is full. There are over 70 passengers in that coach. Some are elderly and not very agile and there's only one way out — through the door at the far end. But that door is blocked with a huge press of bodies jammed together in their panic and anxiety to escape. However, the train is slowing down because the communication cord has been pulled, but the flames are now rapidly advancing down the coach towards the

Below:
London & North Eastern Railway prewar third-class open saloon coach, with bucket-type seats. Six schoolboys lost their lives in a fire in a coach of this type in 1941, when a lighted match lodged between a seat and the side of the coach.
Ian Allan Library

Above:
Class A3 Pacific No 60035 *Windsor Lad* at Edinburgh Waverley on a train for Perth. This was the locomotive on the train involved in the fire at Penmanshiel Tunnel on 23 June 1949.
Eric Treacy/Millbrook House Collection

terrified trapped passengers, who can already feel the intensity of the heat. There is only one way of escape left — through the windows. People are already hammering on them but the windows are tough and double-glazed. Fortunately, someone remembers that there is a hammer provided for just such an emergency, fixed to the wall in a glass case. This is no time for standing on ceremony. A fist smashes the glass and the precious hammer is plucked from its housing. There is now a desperate race against time. Can sufficient windows be broken in the remaining few seconds before people are burnt to death or become unconscious from carbon monoxide poisoning? And how many people will be able to escape before being overcome?

It is a fearful scenario. And yet it takes only a few seconds for a small, smouldering fire to become a sheet of flame, if conditions favour it; therefore it is obviously vital for designers and builders of railway coaches to have full regard for the possibility of fire. Their success may be measured by the fact that, with the single exception of the Taunton fire in 1979, no passenger has been killed in a train on fire since 1951. Before that, fires were more prevalent, especially in the earlier days when coaches were built entirely, or mainly, of wood, and lit by gas, which was housed in tanks underneath the coaches themselves.

By the beginning of World War 2 steel was in general use for coach underframes, and the use of steel sheet for sides and roofs was becoming prevalent, but the body framing and the interior fittings were still generally of wood. However, throughout all the perils of World War 2 there was only one case where passengers were killed in a train fire, and that was at Westborough on 28 April 1941. Boys were returning to their public school at Ampleforth near York after the Easter holiday, and about 100 of them were travelling in two reserved open third-class coaches with bucket-type seats attached to the rear of the 12.45pm King's Cross to Newcastle express. Some of the boys were indulging in the stupid boyish prank of flicking lighted matches about and one match lodged between the seat and the side of the coach. The seats had roll-round foam rubber cushioning, which was very inflammable, and there was a small initial fire which within seconds was out of control. The communication cord was pulled and the train stopped near Claypole, about 10 miles north of Grantham. Both coaches, and the rear brakevan, were all burnt down to their underframes and six boys lost their lives.

In view of the conditions which existed in Britain in April 1941, when night after night whole city centres were set on fire by German air attacks, it is not surprising that the Westborough fire attracted little attention. In more normal times it might have led to action being taken to reduce the likelihood of such fires developing so quickly, but in the event little was done and it is surprising that eight years were to pass before there was a further serious fire.

Thursday 23 June 1949 was a fine, dry, warm day. The 7.30pm express from Edinburgh to King's Cross left on time, with 'A3' Pacific No 60035 *Windsor Lad* hauling 12 coaches, the last four of which were:

Corridor third No 1498
Corridor brake composite No 1148
Buffet car No 9124
Corridor brake third.

The train was about half-full and it passed Cockburnspath, 35 miles from Edinburgh, at 8.31pm with speed down to about 25mph on the 1 in 96 gradient. The signalman there watched it pass his signalbox and saw nothing wrong. About 5min later a passenger in the fifth coach went to the buffet car at the rear of the train and noticed no trace of fire in coach 1148 next to it. However, only a few moments later when he re-entered the brake compartment of coach 1148 on his way back from the buffet car, he saw passengers running into it from the corridor, with clouds of thick, black smoke following them. The guard was already putting the brake on and the train stopped quickly, enabling the passengers to jump out.

Coach 1148 was built by contractors for the London & North Eastern Railway (LNER) in 1947. It had a steel underframe and sheet steel external panelling, with wooden framing and interior fittings. It was of the latest LNER postwar design, with a small guard's-compartment, two first-class compartments, three third-class compartments, and two transverse corridors with outside doors. The transverse corridors were unusually located towards the centre of the coach instead of at the ends, a feature of the design which was intended to reduce the distance a passenger had to walk from an outside door to a compartment. On the evening of the fire the coach conveyed one first-class passenger and 14 third-class. One of the third-class passengers suddenly saw flames about a foot

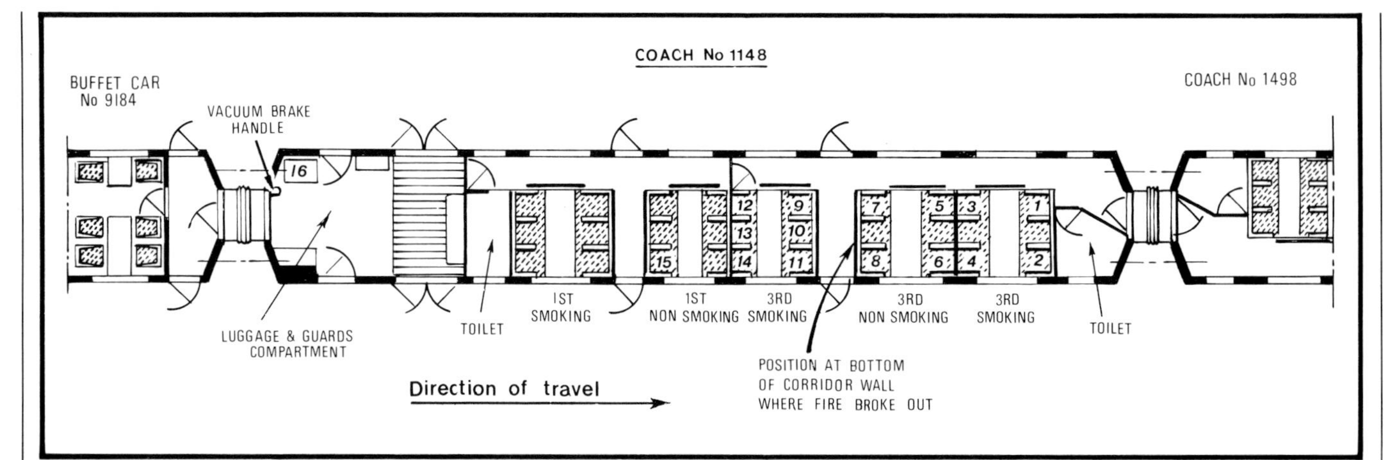

Top:
Coach No 1148 and the Penmanshiel fire

Above:
Postwar LNER third-class corridor brake coach of the type involved in the Penmanshiel Tunnel fire on 23 June 1949. It was built in 1947 and has an oval toilet window, which was distinctive of the period. *Ian Allan Library*

deep, accompanied by black smoke and a roaring sound, moving along the top of the corridor towards him. He at once pulled the communication cord, shouted to his companions, and ran into the corridor, through the flames, to safety. The flames immediately entered the open doorway of the compartment, blocking the escape route for the three other occupants. They were thus trapped and had no alternative, if they wanted to avoid being roasted alive, but to break the window and jump out. One of them was severely injured in doing so. All the other passengers were able to escape from their compartments in time, although some were burnt in doing so and suffered from the effects of smoke and fumes.

The astonishing feature of this fire was the rapidity with which it spread. Within little more than a few seconds it had raced along the corridor ceiling from end to end, down to the floor and into the compartments. The coach and the one next to it, No 1498, were swiftly burnt down to the underframes. If the train had been full, and travelling at express speed, there would almost certainly have been a heavy death toll, but in the event no one was killed. The cause of the fire was probably a carelessly discarded cigarette end.

The train stopped with the first eight coaches already inside Penmanshiel Tunnel and the train crew quickly split the train next to the burning coach. The front portion was taken forward to Grantshouse, where it arrived at 8.50pm, only 10min after the train had first stopped and with many passengers possibly unaware that there was anything amiss. It is an interesting comment on the emergency arrangements in those days that the first ambulance did not arrive until 9.45pm, over an hour after the train had stopped, closely followed by the fire brigade, despite the fact that the scene of the fire was immediately alongside a main road, but, as it happened, the injured had already been taken to hospital by cars and buses.

Tests were subsequently carried out to discover why the fire had spread with such rapidity, and some remarkable evidence emerged. A small twist of paper was placed on the floor of a similar coach, against the wall of the transverse corridor, and lit. The effect was astounding. In less than 10sec the whole transverse corridor was filled with flames and the test had to be abandoned to avoid the coach being completely destroyed. In the next test a lighted match was thrown into a corner of the corridor. Nothing happened for 10sec, then the surface of the wall suddenly burst into strong flames 2ft long. Some 15sec later the flames had reached the ceiling, and within another 10sec the entire corridor was in flames, and the fire had to be extinguished immediately.

When built, the interior woodwork of this type of coach had been sprayed with three coats of clear cellulose lacquer, and a panel taken from one of the coaches was sent after the fire to the Fire Research Organisation for tests. They found that the inflammability of the surface was, by a very large margin, the worst in their records. The LNER, in its specification to the contractors, had given details of the various paints to be used, which were all of the ordinary oil-bound kind. How cellulose came to be used was never discovered, but passengers in that coach during its two-year life had been travelling unwittingly in a time-bomb. When it exploded into flame they were lucky not to have been burnt to death, or asphyxiated by smoke and fumes.

The lessons of this accident were taken to heart and the cellulose coating was quickly removed from all the LNER coaches which had been sprayed with it. However, even whilst this remedial work was being done there was another train fire, in which lacquer containing nitrocellulose was a factor, although not the main one.

Thursday 8 June 1950 was also a fine, warm, dry day. The 11.00am express from Birmingham to Glasgow was making its way laboriously up Beattock Bank, 40 miles north of Carlisle, and as it passed Greskine signalbox at 4.53pm the signalman there watched it go past at about 30mph. Everything appeared to be normal. Ten minutes later he noticed from the track-circuit indicators in his signalbox that the train had not yet passed the Harthope Intermediate Block Home signal 2½ miles ahead, then 5min after that he received a telephone call from the signal to tell him that the

Above right:
One of Eric Treacy's favourite locations — Harthope, on the climb to Beattock Summit, and the site of the tragic fire on 8 June 1950:

1. **'Royal Scot' class 4-6-0 No 46157 *The Royal Artilleryman*, shedded at Edge Hill, on a short train of six ex-LMS coaches.** *Eric Treacy/Millbrook House Collection*
2. **'Princess Coronation' class Pacific No 46224 *Princess Alexandra* on the Down 'Royal Scot', with a complete rake of 15 ex-LMS coaches in early British Railways livery.** *Eric Treacy/Millbrook House Collection*

Right:
Trains at Greskine — before and after electrification:

1. **'Clan' class light Pacific No 72005 *Clan Macgregor* on a Carlisle-Perth parcels train, on 1 August 1964.** *Paul Riley*
2. **1S19 Bristol-Glasgow sleeper, with Class 40 diesel-electric No 40016 hauling dead electric No 81015, on 4 June 1978.** *Derek Cross*

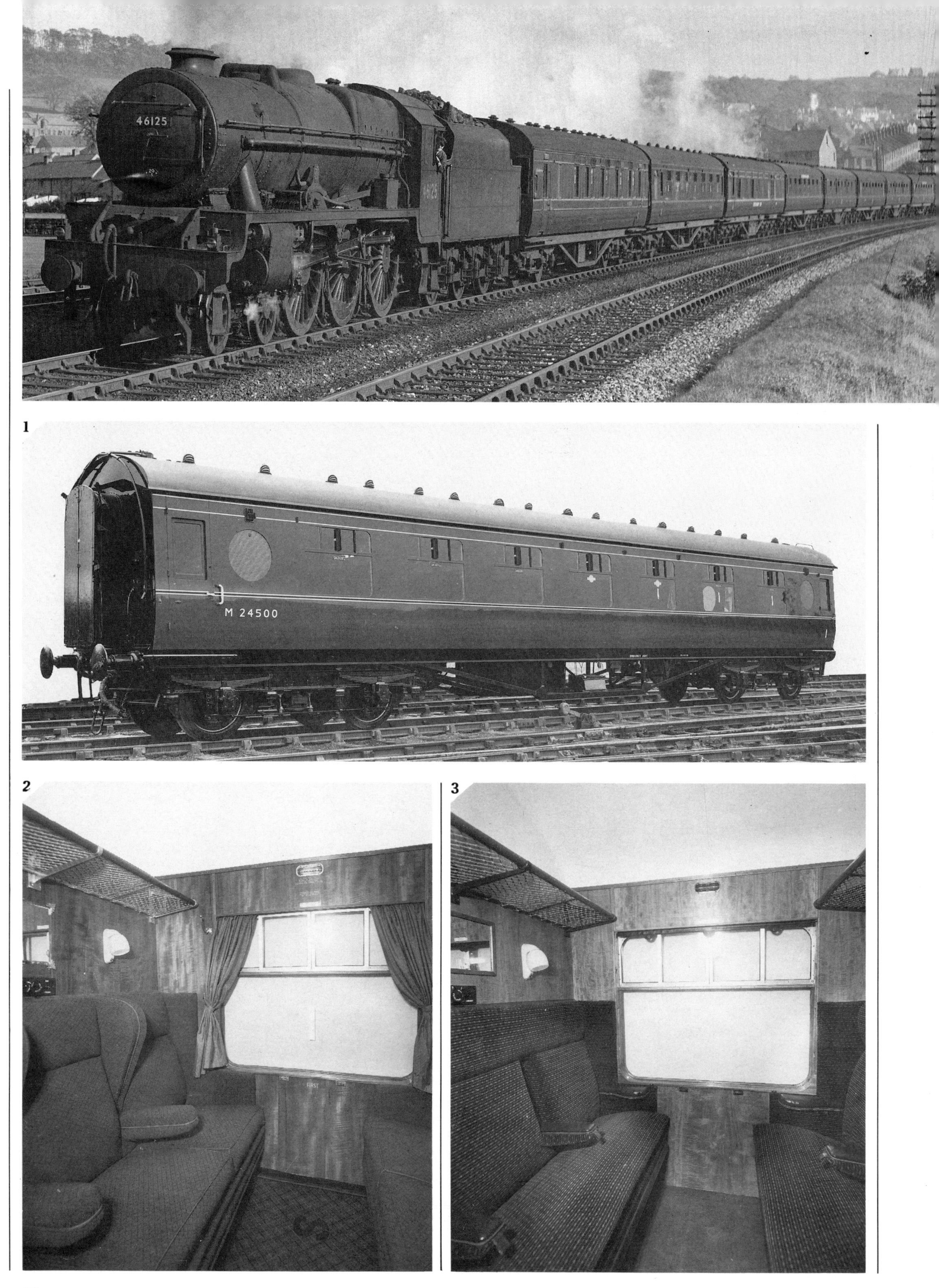
46125
1
M 24500
2
3

Left:
A typical London Midland & Scottish Railway express, in very early BR days, with a 12-wheeled dining car. The train is the Down 'Thames-Clyde Express', headed by rebuilt 'Royal Scot' class 4-6-0 No 46125 *3rd Carabinier* bearing a 20A shedplate (Leeds Holbeck), and is seen approaching Marley Junction between Bingley and Keighley. *Eric Treacy/Millbrook House Collection*

train was on fire and had been stopped. There were 10 coaches on the train, the first four being:

Corridor brake third
Corridor composite No 4851, in which the fire broke out
Corridor first No 1073
Dining car.

Coach No 4851 had three first-class compartments and four third-class. There were only five passengers in the coach — a mother and two young children in one compartment, and two ladies in the next one.

The train had left Carlisle at 4.02pm on the final part of its journey. In coach 4851 everything seemed normal. The restaurant car attendant brought a tea tray to the young family, and half an hour later he called to collect it. One of the ladies went to the toilet. All were unaware of the fearful events about to engulf them, although some had noticed a vague smell of something burning since the train left Carlisle.

When the train passed Greskine signalbox the signalman had had a clear view of the left-hand side of the train and was certain that there was no sign of smoke or flame coming from his side of it. At the same time the fireman had looked back from the engine along the right-hand side and had seen no signs of fire. And at this precise moment the lady in coach 4851 had gone to the toilet. All were unaware that the 'fire-bomb' which had been ticking away quietly for hours was about to explode.

At 4.56pm, 3min later, normality had changed dramatically into terror and death. The lady who had gone to the toilet came out into the corridor, and to her amazement found that it was full of smoke. She could also feel the heat of the fire, but she had chosen a fortunate moment to go to the toilet because it was next to an outside door through which she was able to escape. Her companion was not so fortunate. A few moments after being left alone she was suddenly horrified to see dark smoke pouring down the corridor. She grabbed her handbag and started to make her way towards the end door, then she saw the young mother with two small children trapped and helpless in the next compartment. Compassion overcame self-preservation and she went in to help to carry the children to safety. She was joined immediately by a man from the next coach who reached across and pulled the communication cord. It was his last act. A huge fireball of flame and hot gases erupted into the compartment and killed all five of them instantly. The man and lady had paid for their compassion and gallantry with their lives.

Left:
An LMS-pattern composite corridor coach, built in 1949; the type involved in the Beattock Summit fire:

1. **Exterior view**
2. **First-class compartment**
3. **Third-class compartment**

The exterior body panels and the roof were of steel, but the body frames, partitions and linings were of wood. *BR*

On the engine, the driver had just passed over Harthope Viaduct, travelling at about 30mph, when he noticed from his vacuum brake gauge that the vacuum was falling. He concluded at once that the communication cord had been pulled and looked back along the left-hand side of the train. He saw dense smoke pouring out of the second coach (4851) and immediately made a full brake application, which stopped the train in about 15sec. By now flames were shooting from the windows of coach 4851. With great presence of mind, and assisted by his fireman, he uncoupled behind the third coach (which by this time was also on fire), drew forward the front portion of the train including the two burning coaches, uncoupled again in front of the burning coaches and drew forward again, thus isolating them and preventing the fire from spreading along the rest of the train. The rear portion of the train was now standing without an engine on the 1 in 74 gradient falling back towards Carlisle, with only the vacuum brake and the guard's handbrake to hold it. The vacuum brake would slowly leak off, so the following train, the 'Royal Scot', was brought up behind for safety reasons.

Among the many acts of gallantry that afternoon might be mentioned that of Ganger Moffat. He was on duty on the line checking expansion joints in the rails, when he heard a train approaching and, looking up, he saw smoke and flames coming from the second coach (4851). The driver was already making an emergency stop and the train came to a stand with the blazing coach only a few yards away. He assisted two ladies from the rear door of the first coach (next to 4851), then, learning that there was another lady at the end of the coach on fire, he climbed up into that coach and found her standing in a dazed condition in the corridor against the lavatory wall. Having helped her out he re-entered the coach, went into the lavatory and seeing no one there, he entered the three first-class compartments.

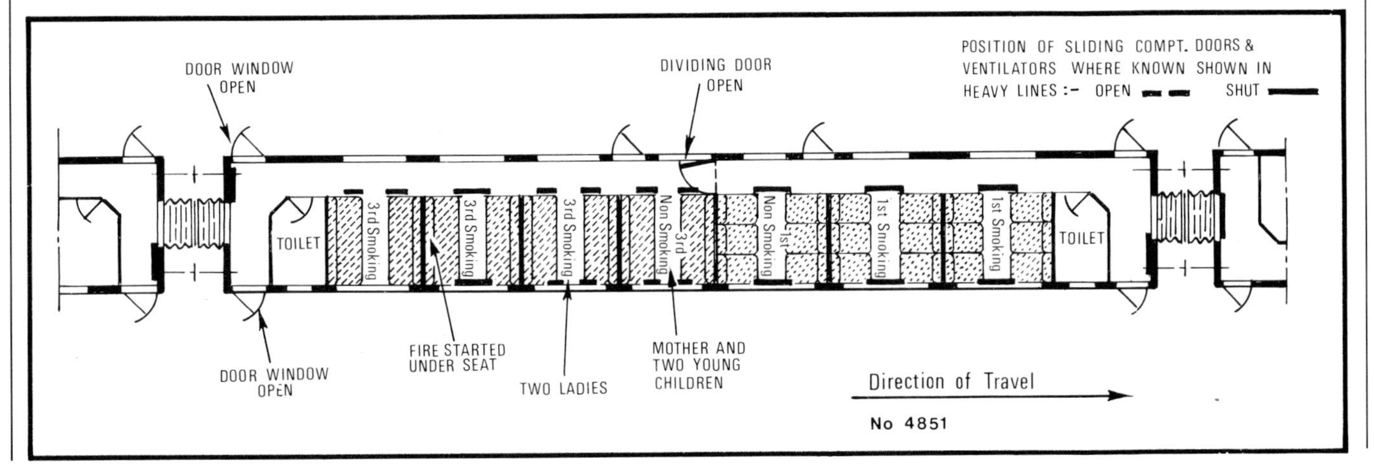

Below:
Coach No 4851 and the Beattock fire

The smoke was now becoming so thick that it was difficult for him to see anything at all, so he groped about on the seats but did not find anybody. His breathing had by now become badly affected but he pressed on and reached the next compartment. The smoke suddenly cleared and there was a burst of flame which swirled round the whole compartment. In that instant Ganger Moffat caught a momentary glimpse of the still figure of a woman seated, almost in repose. She was already dead. It is an oddity that those who lose their lives in a fire are often found in quiet and natural attitudes whereas one might expect at least some sign of panic or frantic attempt to escape. After all, if you were trapped in a compartment with a wall of fire rapidly advancing towards you, you would hardly sit quietly waiting for it to consume you like a latter-day Joan of Arc. What had happened is what happens in so many cases of fire — the victims are struck down in an instant by hot gases or carbon monoxide poisoning and that is what had happened in this case.

Ganger Moffat tried to enter the compartment but was forced back by the heat. He was rapidly losing consciousness but managed to crawl along the corridor and escape. He too almost lost his life attempting to rescue others, an act of gallantry for which he was awarded the British Empire Medal. Indeed, the train crews in both this accident and the one at Penmanshiel Tunnel acted with great presence of mind and promptitude in dealing with a difficult situation which they had never previously encountered. They deserved, and received, great praise.

The sad deaths of the young family, together with those of the two passengers who had tried to help them to escape, naturally aroused a great deal of public interest and concern. Anxiety was expressed in Parliament, not only on the subject of fire precautions on trains but also on the whole question of fire considerations in the design of passenger coaches. The public inquiry into this fire was held by Col R. J. Walker of the Railway Inspectorate, Ministry of Transport. In his report he concluded that some time before the train reached Carlisle a lighted match or cigarette end had been carelessly thrown down on to the floor by someone travelling in the compartment next to that one occupied by the two ladies. It found its way under the heater beneath the opposite seat, into a collection of dust and bits of paper behind the heater in the space between the heater and the partition wall separating the two compartments. The partition was made of plain softwood. A small smouldering fire started in the rubbish, spread to the partition and the seat, and continued to smoulder for an hour or more. All that time the fire was using up the available oxygen in the compartment, the doors of which were closed, and forming carbon monoxide and other gases. The temperature was also rising quickly.

Before gases produced in this type of fire will ignite they require both oxygen and the right temperature, but because the gases were produced in a closed compartment they would not ignite, whatever their temperature, because there was insufficient oxygen. However, the smouldering fire eventually burnt a small hole through the partition, allowing gases and smoke to escape into the next compartment, which was empty, and into the corridor. This probably happened a minute or so after one of the ladies left her compartment to visit the toilet, an act which fortuitously saved her life.

The man who died had been travelling in the next coach and, noticing the smoke, went forward to investigate. He came upon the lady in coach 4851 who was now alone, then the two of them moved forward to escape, without realising the potential danger of the situation and the high temperature of the gases inside the closed and empty compartment. They immediately saw the young family and entered their compartment to help to evacuate the two young children. At this precise moment the burning hole in the partition wall reached such a size that the correct conditions of temperature and air mixture were produced, and the gases ignited. The temperature in the closed compartment shot up, breaking a window in the corridor side. The main volume of gases rushed into the corridor, mixed with the air, and burst into flame with a huge ball of fire. It was in effect a slow explosion and the heat which it generated was enough to kill instantly anyone within range. It was this fireball which killed the five passengers, and it also set the whole of the coach on fire.

In 1950 much thought was being given to the detailed design of the new British Railways standard coach, known subsequently as Mk 1, and there were plans to build 1,189 of them in 1951. All the circumstances of the fire in coach 4851 were therefore examined in great detail, to see to what extent they could be guarded against in the new coaches. These factors were as follows:

1. The location of the heater underneath the fixed seats made it difficult to clean behind the heater, and allowed fluff and odd bits of paper, etc to accumulate. To overcome this problem the seats in the new coaches were made removable and wire mesh grilles were fixed underneath the front of the seats to prevent rubbish from finding its way through to the back. Although this was a good idea in theory it made it harder for the cleaning staff to clean behind the heaters and could even have led to increased danger if the cleaning were not carried out conscientiously.

2. The partitions between the compartments were of plain deal boarding. It was decided to protect the boarding in new coaches by covering it with asbestos millboard.

3. The interior finish used in coach 4851 was a special lacquer which had been used for the previous 13 years. It had a matt finish and required only a very thin coating, and one of the reasons for its use had been to reduce the fire risk. However, it contained a certain amount of nitrocellulose and as a result had a fairly high flammability. It was decided not only to discontinue its use but also to remove it from existing coaches.

4. If inflammable materials such as wood and furnishings were to continue to be used in coach construction it was felt to be important to provide additional doors away from the ends of the corridors. This feature had already been incorporated in the design of the new BR Mk 1 side-corridor coaches by the provision of a central transverse corridor, with an additional door in the corridor side (two in the case of composite coaches), but the Railway Executive had considered it unnecessary to provide them in open-type coaches.

5. Fire extinguishers. Up to 1948 fire extinguishers on the London Midland & Scottish Railway and the London & North Eastern Railway were only carried in restaurant cars and guard's vans. In both the Penmanshiel and Beattock fires, extinguishers would have been useless because the fires were far too big when discovered, to have been capable of being put out by hand-held extinguishers. However, the Railway Executive felt that it ought to be seen to be taking some positive action, and provided them in all coaches, but in fact,

Left:
LNER prewar streamlined express formed of articulated twin-sets: Pacific No 2510 *Quicksilver* on the Down 'Silver Jubilee' at New Barnet. *Eric Treacy/ Millbrook House Collection*

Below left:
A typical prewar LNER streamlined express, formed of articulated twin-sets: 'A4' No 4492 *Dominion of New Zealand* passes Grantham with the Down 'Coronation' on 4 July 1939.
T. G. Hepburn/ Rail Archive Stephenson

Below:
Class A3 Pacific No 60058 *Blair Athol*, the locomotive which hauled the Down 'West Riding' on the day it caught fire near Huntingdon.
David J. Dippie

> fires on trains were so rare that if these two fires had not happened it would have been difficult to justify the provision of extinguishers in every coach.

Two serious fires in two years was much more than the statistical average, but railway accidents are no respecters of statistical averages. But three in three years was highly unlikely. However, fate thought otherwise.

The famous 'West Riding' train from King's Cross to Leeds, which had covered the distance prewar in 2hr 43min hauled by one of Sir Nigel Gresley's equally famous streamlined Pacifics, had become by 1951 the 3.45pm from King's Cross to Leeds, taking 3hr 45min, although with a much heavier train. On Saturday 14 July 1951 the train consisted of 14 coaches hauled by a Class A3 Pacific engine No 60058 *Blair Atholl*, marshalled as follows:

Twin open brake third, Nos 1738 and 1737
Twin open first
Twin restaurant open third
Corridor composite
Corridor third
Corridor brake third
Corridor composite brake
Corridor composite
Two corridor thirds
Corridor brake third.

Seating capacity, excluding the restaurant car, was 96 first-class and 316 third-class, and the train was actually carrying 10 first-class and about 340 third-class passengers. The first six coaches were articulated twin-sets

Above:
'Coronation' set, ex-works, with beaver-tail observation car at the rear. Twin articulated coaches of the type in this trainset were involved in the fire at Huntingdon on 14 July 1951. *BR*

Left:
Interior view of a third-class twin coach, showing the high standard of luxury and fittings. Prewar, there was a supplementary charge for the use of these trains, for example King's Cross to Leeds 2s 6d third-class. *LNER*

specially built by the LNER in 1937 for its high speed trains the 'Coronation' and the 'West Riding'. The coaches were designed to a very luxurious standard, with seats at tables, arranged with two seats at one side of the centre gangway, and single seats at the other. The only exit doors were in the vestibules at the extreme ends of each twin-set. The underframes were of steel, and the bodywork consisted of steel exterior panels with teak framing and softwood interiors. The whole of the interior was covered with a leathercloth fabric known by the trade name of Rexine. Significantly, the fabric was coated with nitrocellulose.

With two such serious fire hazards — the location of the doors and the presence of nitrocellulose — the question arises as to whether the railway administration, which in 1948 had become the Railway Executive, should have allowed such coaches to continue in service, now that the risks had been pointed out so dramatically and forcefully at Penmanshiel and Beattock. However, the railways were short of coaches. They had lost a lot during the war from German bombing, and new building had been restricted since 1939. After the war the shortage of steel had restricted the number of coaches which could be built. Many of the express coaches in use in 1951 had fire hazards of one sort or another, indeed some still had wooden bodies, and to have taken them all out of service would have made it impossible to run an adequate train service. What is more, the railway's record of fire safety was excellent — there had been only three serious fires on trains since 1939. One wonders whether any of the passengers in the three twin-sets felt any qualms about their safety, and whether any, more knowledgeable or more cautious, chose to travel in the ordinary coaches, hoping that they had had any nitrocellulose removed. The decision by the Railway Executive to allow these twin-sets to remain in service, or, to put it more accurately, the failure to consider whether the twin-sets should be allowed to remain in service or not, was severely criticised by Col Walker in his Report.

However, to return to the events of 14 July 1951. About 40min after leaving King's Cross a passenger who was sitting in the rearmost seat on the left-hand side of the second coach of the twin-set next to the engine (coach No 1737) noticed a wisp of smoke rising up the side of the coach near the armrest. She called the attention of a passing pantry boy, who returned to the fifth coach, the restaurant car, and informed the conductor. This man went to have a look, then went back to tell the guard, who was riding in the ninth coach. The guard went forward and, lifting the seat, saw that smoke was coming from the corner of the floor, between the edge of the carpet and the side of the coach. He at once jumped to the conclusion that the smoke was coming from an axlebox running hot. Incredibly, instead of stopping the train at once so that the axle did not have time to disintegrate, and derail the train, he decided to write a note which he intended to throw out of the train at Huntingdon, about 10min away, asking for the train to be stopped at Peterborough for examination. He even went to the dining car for a potato to act as a weight for his note. Being unable to find one he threw the note out anyway. It was found next day, and it was perhaps fortunate that the smoke was not from a hot axlebox, which might well have collapsed and caused a serious derailment, with many casualties.

After the guard had left to write his note, the smoke increased and the passengers became more uneasy. One of

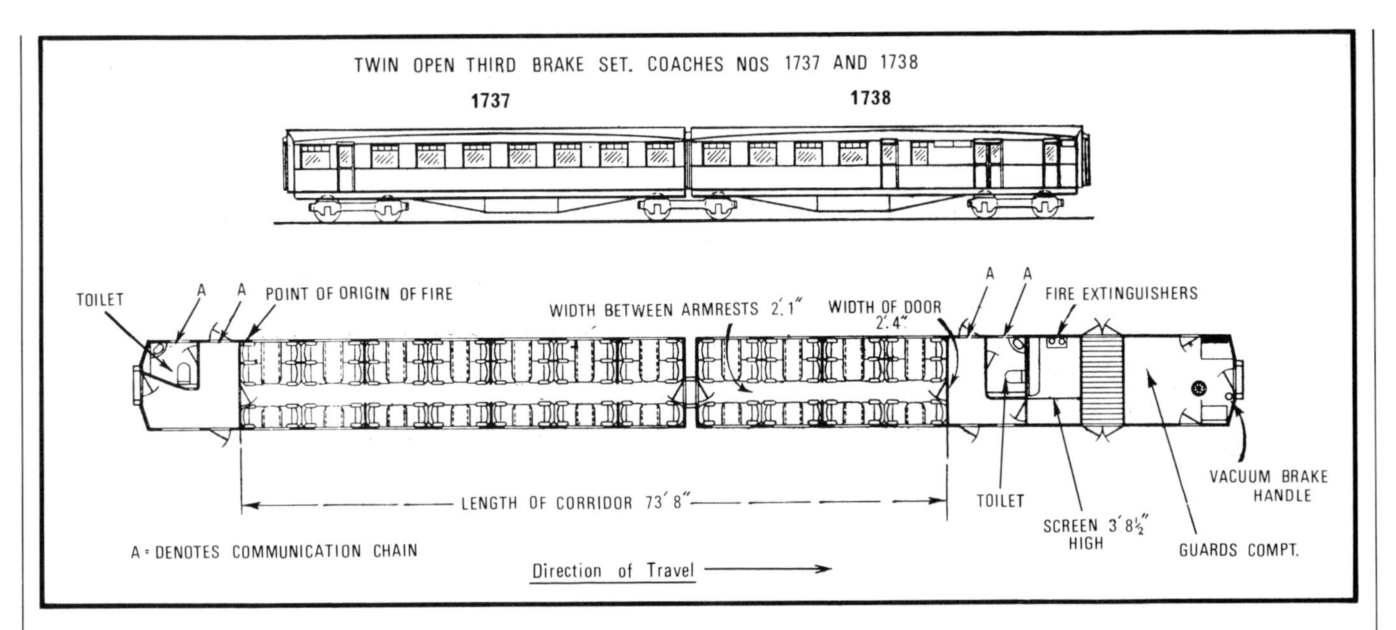

Above:
Twin-set Nos 1737 and 1738, the coaches of the Huntingdon fire

them decided to pull the communication cord, and as the train came to a stand just beyond Huntingdon flames appeared and suddenly spread with great rapidity up the sides and into the roof. In a matter of seconds the fire was spreading quickly forwards along the sides and roof of the coach. At once all the passengers tried to escape but the only available exit was through the intercommunicating door into the next coach and then through a single door into the vestibule at the leading end of that coach. Both coaches were full and in addition some soldiers and sailors were standing in the vestibule, so that there were probably about 75 people in the twin-set. The flames were accompanied by dense and choking fumes and smoke which quickly filled the coaches; and in the alarm and excitement the centre aisles of both coaches became blocked with passengers at once. Others were unable to leave their seats to get into the aisle at all because of the crush. People were therefore trapped between the solid crush of passengers at one end and the rapidly advancing flames at the other. There was only one way of escape left open to them — by breaking the windows and climbing through. It was literally every man (and woman) for himself. But train windows are not easy to break even in the haste and incentive of a fire breathing down your neck. The glass has to be tough, and it was only the efforts of the soldiers and sailors in helping to break windows that enabled some passengers to escape with their lives, but 22 passengers and the guard received burns and other injuries in escaping, including nine seriously hurt.

The cause of the fire was thought to have been a piece of live coal from the engine firegrate falling on to the track then bouncing up and lodging in a small hole cut through the floor of the coach to allow an air duct to be taken through. The space between the duct and the sides of the hole had been filled by asbestos at one time but it had fallen out unnoticed, as the carpet and underlay covered the hole completely. The floor was deal boarding.

After the Penmanshiel fire two years earlier the Railway Executive had set about examining all of its 25,000 coaches

Below:
Smoke and flames pour from the windows of the second and third coaches of the 3.45pm from King's Cross to Leeds near Huntingdon on 14 July 1951. *Times Newspapers Ltd*

for the existence of nitrocellulose. By the time of the Huntingdon fire all but 1,000 had been examined. Over 8,000 coaches were discovered to contain inflammable surfaces and almost 7,000 had been dealt with. Nitrocellulose-coated cloth presented a new problem, which had to be dealt with quickly to make it less vulnerable to fire, and this was done. It is difficult now to understand how such a dangerous material came to be used in the first place; it would have been easy to have tested it for flammability, when its latent defect would have immediately become apparent. There was perhaps some complacency in railway circles about fire hazards, based in part on an excellent safety record, although in mitigation it has to be said that the twin-sets for the LNER's streamlined services were designed to be staffed with attendants, similar to the practice on Pullman trains. It is clear that the fire hazards of using them as ordinary coaches without attendants had not been appreciated.

The need for additional external doors which had been demonstrated at Beattock was not accepted by the Railway Executive for its new open-type coaches, and even after the Huntingdon fire they were unconvinced, and suggested that the steps they had already taken would sufficiently reduce the risk of fire. They refused to budge from this standpoint at first, but finally gave way and agreed to incorporate additional doors in the new BR Mk 1 open stock. The additional cost was in fact negligible.

This issue of additional doors presents one of the few cases this century where the Railway Inspectorate has felt sufficiently strongly that some action ought to be taken, but which is being resisted by the railway authorities, that it has sought the help of the Minister. Strange as it may seem, the Railway Inspectorate had no powers to compel railways to adopt different methods or use different materials on existing railways, but could only recommend or apply pressure. The Minister supported the Railway Inspectorate and ultimately made a statement in Parliament that additional precautions were to be taken to minimise the risk of fires, and one of these was the provision of centre doors on the new open coaches. The Minister had the ultimate power, had the Railway Executive continued to prove obdurate, of sacking the chairman and appointing one who would carry out his wishes. The Railway Executive accepted the inevitable and gave in. Whilst it may be difficult to understand why it was so obstinate, the Railway Executive was strongly of the opinion that the measures it had already taken regarding the use of fire-resistant materials and finishes in the design of the new standard

Above:
BR standard Mk 1 second-class open coach, with centre doors. Seen at Bristol Temple Meads on 17 November 1984. *M. J. Collins*

Below:
BR Mk 2 second-class open coach, 1967 pattern, with centre doors. Exterior and interior views. *BR*

coaches would completely overcome any possibility of a repetition of the fires that had occurred at Penmanshiel, Beattock and Huntingdon. What is more, they were proved correct. There was no repetition, and there was never any need for the additional doors in open coaches to be used for the rapid evacuation of passengers in a fire, but the weight of public opinion, not always the best guide, and illogical on this occasion, was too heavy to be resisted. In later years, in the design of Mk 2 coaches, the additional centre doors were eventually dispensed with.

However, the saga was not yet complete. Railwaymen have long held a superstition that accidents always come in threes, but there was to be a fourth, near Fordhouses, about four miles north of Wolverhampton on the main line to Stafford of the former London Midland & Scottish Railway (LMS). Nor was there long to wait, as the fourth fire occurred as early as 14 March 1952, whilst the argument about additional doors was still raging. The circumstances were in many ways similar to those of the Beattock fire. It started in a pile of rubbish behind the heater underneath the seat, and began to smoulder. The passengers told the guard, who was in the same coach (a corridor brake third) and he directed a fire extinguisher as best he could on to the seat and the back, but it was difficult for him to deal with the area beneath the seat as it was fixed in position. When the extinguisher was empty and the fire was apparently out, the compartment was evacuated, the doors were closed, and the guard stopped the train by using his emergency brake valve.

The train came to a stand about 400yd from a station, and the guard and fireman examined the underpart of the coach for signs of fire, but could find nothing wrong. They decided to continue into the station so that passengers could be evacuated if necessary, and as the train stopped in the platform the compartment burst into flames, in a repetition of the Beattock fire of 1950. Fortunately all the passengers had already moved into other coaches or on to the platform and no one was injured. By chance, there was a wartime Supply Depot alongside, whose fire brigade was located next to the station. They quickly came into action and directed hoses on to the burning coach in a very short time, but despite this the coach continued to burn fiercely and was almost completely destroyed. The coach, moreover, had been built as recently as September 1950 to the previous LMS design. Incredibly, although nitrocellulose had been shown to be a highly dangerous substance when used in the interior finish of railway coaches, it was found to have been used in this coach, even though it was built 15 months after the Penmanshiel fire and three months after Beattock. What is more, the coach was one of those which had been tested for nitrocellulose and had been passed as safe. The Railway Executive found itself totally discredited.

Fordhouses proved to be the last serious train fire for many years, even though coaches built by the pre-

Below:
BR Mk 2c second-class open coach, without centre doors, but with a low ceiling incorporating ducts for air-conditioning.
BR

1

2

3

Above and left:
Further developments in BR coach design:

1. **First-class open coach, with wide doors.** *BR*
2. **Second-class open coach, Mk 2d, with air-conditioning.** *C. J. Tuffs*
3. **Second-class open coach, Mk 3. Neat, but rather spartan, seating arrangements.** *BR*

nationalisation companies continued in service for a long time. The new standard coaches, designated Mk 1, had a very good fire safety record, and this fine record was continued in subsequent series of coaches in Mks 2 and 3, to such an extent that over 30 years passed before another serious fire occurred (discounting for the moment the Taunton fire of 1978, which was an oddity, and which will be dealt with later).

British Railways Scottish Region operates an excellent express service of trains between Edinburgh and Glasgow — fast, frequent and comfortable, using very modern Mk 3 air-conditioned coaches built to a very high standard of fire resistance. On 22 August 1983 the 18.30 train from Edinburgh to Glasgow consisted of one of the usual push-pull sets and was being propelled by a Class 47 diesel-electric locomotive. It was marshalled as follows:

Brake open second-class, with driver's compartment
Open first-class, Mk 3
Three open second-class, Mk 3.

The train was well filled, and the weather was sunny and warm.

As the train neared the end of its journey a lady travelling in the fourth coach of the five-coach train went to the toilet at the rear of her coach. When she came out of the toilet she was amazed and horrified to see orange and yellow flames about 2ft high right across the gangway connection between the two coaches, so she went straight back into the toilet. Realising that if she stayed there she might well be trapped and burnt to death, she plucked up all her courage, opened the toilet door again, and rushed through the thick black smoke back into the coach. Luckily for her the automatic sliding door worked quickly but even so she felt the intense heat on her back and her hair was singed.

Meanwhile, other passengers in both coaches had seen the thick black smoke in the vestibules and the communication cord had been pulled. As the train quickly slowed down and stopped near Cadder signalbox, smoke and fumes began to pour into both coaches and passengers rapidly began to move away in fear and anxiety.

What happened then was almost a repeat of the Huntingdon fire. The fourth coach was quite full and people quickly moved towards the sliding door at the far end of the coach. Unfortunately it was defective and not working automatically, but could be opened by hand. However, in the haste and near-panic of the situation those passengers nearest the door failed to appreciate what to do and decided that they were trapped. The coach was rapidly filling with thick black smoke, making it difficult either to see or breathe. The only way out was through the windows, but fortunately there were sufficient passengers with the presence of mind to use the emergency hammers. Everyone was therefore able to escape with no more than cuts and bruises, but with the lasting memory of those awful moments of terror, although in escaping they had unwittingly put themselves in mortal danger of a different kind. Most of the passengers who jumped out of the windows landed on the opposite running line, where they stood around for some minutes whilst they recovered themselves. If another train had been coming on that line they would have been mown down.

Because of the materials used in the construction of the coach the fire advanced only slowly and was put out quite quickly and easily when the fire brigade arrived. One end of each of the two coaches was severely damaged, but significantly the seats themselves had not caught fire. The essential difference between Huntingdon and Cadder showed that the lessons had been well learnt. The fire at Cadder progressed much more slowly and burned much less fiercely than at Huntingdon, thanks to the use of fire-resistant materials.

The cause of the fire is thought to have been the same in four of the five fires examined in this chapter — the careless act of throwing down a burning cigarette end. At Cadder it eventually ignited the polyurethane foam used in the gangway end unit at the rear of the fourth coach, and it was fanned into flame by the draught of air in the speeding train. Both the fourth and fifth coaches had been built in 1975 with foam gangway units, but because the units had not stood up to the wear and tear of daily service they had been replaced as necessary by a later rubber bellows design introduced on all new stock a year later. Critically, the original foam bellows unit was still in use at the rear of the fourth coach. Foam ought not to have been used in the first place from a fire hazard point of view, and after a foam gangway had caught fire near Acton on a Paddington to Bristol IC125 unit on 5 July 1981, although causing little damage, they should all have been removed. Unfortunately they were not removed quickly enough, and the task was not completed until early 1984.

The fire in a sleeping car train at Taunton on 6 July 1978 was in one way the worst of all. It claimed 12 lives. But the cause was almost stupidly simple. The main store for the supply of clean bed linen to Western Region sleeping cars was at Old Oak Common, the coaching stock depot near Paddington. Clean linen was sent down each night in the sleeping car train to Plymouth and Penzance for use the following night on the return journey. Before May 1977 it had been loaded in the guard's van of the Plymouth portion of the train, but the formation of the train was then changed, and as there was no longer a guard's van in the Plymouth portion it had to be sent in the sleeping cars themselves. There was no suitable accommodation in the sleeping cars for bags of linen so they were merely stacked in one of the vestibules — a practical but unsatisfactory solution. Practical because the sleeping car attendants only used one of the vestibules in each coach to receive intending passengers, being the one nearest their cubicle. Unsatisfactory because it tended to block one of the limited number of exits in case of fire or other emergency demanding rapid evacuation. It was the first mistake of several.

The second factor was the construction of the sleeping cars themselves. The one concerned in the fire was vehicle No W2437 and had been built in 1960 by Metro-Cammell Ltd to a British Railways design. It had been fitted with a heating system worked by steam supplied by the locomotive, but with the changeover from steam to diesel locomotives, and the difficulty of finding a design of oil-fired boiler which could withstand the rigours of being installed on a vibrating diesel locomotive (plus the expense of carrying a second man on the locomotive merely to oversee the boiler), a decision was taken to change over from steam to electric heating. Sleeping car W2437 was modified in 1976, and as part of that modification an electric heater was fitted on the vestibule wall outside the attendant's cubicle. Significantly, it was not provided with a protective wire mesh guard, because it was thought that luggage would never be stacked there. This was the second mistake.

The third factor in the lead-up to the disaster was the method of heating and ventilating the individual sleeping berth cubicles. Air could be drawn either from outside the vehicle, or from inside through an opening in the end wall of the vestibule next to the attendant's cubicle — the one with the electric wall heater. Some of this air was then blown through ducting along the roof of the sleeping car and into each individual cubicle.

Above and above right:
BR Mk 1 sleeping cars, exterior and interior views. The single berth compartments were first-class, and the double berth second-class. *BR*

The stage had now been set for disaster and it is only surprising that it had not happened sooner. There had in fact been a potential disaster a few years earlier when a smouldering laundry bag containing linen had been discovered against a vestibule heater in a sleeping car on a Glasgow to Euston train, but it was quickly dealt with. The obvious lesson was not taken to heart.

On the evening of Wednesday 5 July 1978 the two sleeping cars forming the Plymouth portion of the 21.30 from Penzance to Paddington (including car No W2437) were platformed at about 22.30 so that the passengers could join the train and go to bed without having to wait for the arrival of the main train at about midnight. The five or six bags of clean and dirty bed linen were already in their deadly position in the vestibule next to the heater, which at this time was cold. The main train arrived at 23.50. It coupled up to the two Plymouth sleepers, and set off for Paddington on time at 00.30. The heating was now on and the bags of linen began to warm up. The electric wall heater began to overheat because it was covered by the bags of linen, and the linen itself began to smoulder. Smoke and gases, including deadly carbon monoxide, began to be given off, and were then sucked into the heating and ventilating system, along the roof ducting and into the sleeping-berth cubicles, where most of the unfortunate occupants never knew what killed them. A small number awoke and managed to escape with their lives. The train was stopped at Silk Mill signalbox, about half a mile short of Taunton station, at 02.41, by the communication cord being pulled. Car W2437 was now on fire but the disaster was over. Death had already taken place. It had all been so deadly simple.

One question that might be asked straightaway is — what were the sleeping car attendants doing? How could so much smoke and heat be given off without the attendant knowing about it? Each attendant looks after two coaches and the attendant in the Plymouth portion had been travelling in the sleeping car next to W2437. After Exeter he had had a wash and brush up in an empty berth, had gone to the lavatory, and on emerging he saw smoke coming from W2437. He knocked on a few doors in the sleeping car next to W2437 and shouted something about fire, then passed out. It was the attendant in the next pair of sleeping cars who pulled the communication cord. But there is no way of guaranteeing that attendants will be in the right place, or will stay sufficiently alert, to detect a fire as soon as it starts to give off smoke.

So far as the Taunton fire was concerned the means of preventing a repetition were very simple and staightforward. A wire mesh grill over the vestibule heater would have been sufficient; but Taunton was looked upon as merely the tip of the iceberg. Sleeping car fires had been

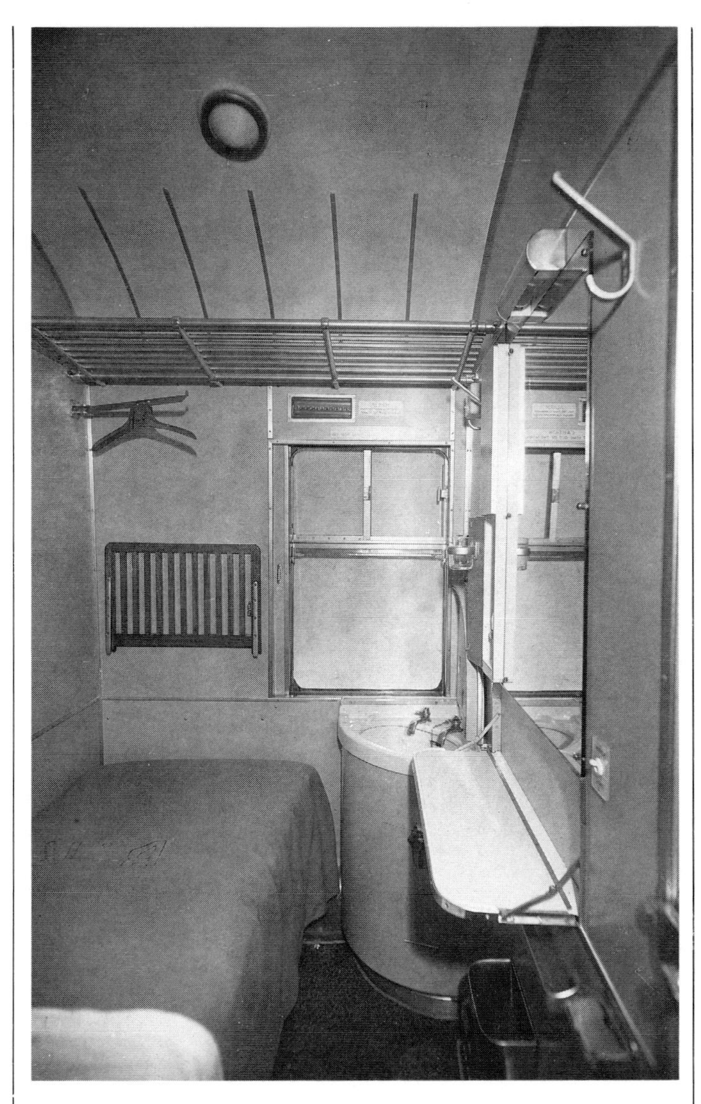

happening two or three times a year, mainly caused by electrical defects, but had been extinguished before they got out of control. Also the Taunton fire had revealed a number of unsatisfactory features. But its worst feature was that it provided a convenient stick with which to beat BR and a number of prominent people, including MPs, were not slow to use it. One or two managers within BR, who ought to have known better, also jumped on to the bandwagon. Red herrings abounded and a state of near-panic gripped British Railways. Certainly, after the disaster things needed to be tightened up but, perhaps inevitably, there was an over-reaction, culminating in a shopping list of 'things that needed to be done'. BR felt impelled to take every conceivable action that could be devised, despite the fact that before Taunton no one had been killed in a sleeping car fire since at least World War 1, and probably long before that. The sleeping car attendants suddenly found themselves a beleaguered species. They were required to explain to all sleeping car passengers as they joined the train, the action that the passengers should take in case of fire. Notices were posted in the compartments in three languages. Attendants were supplied with portable warning horns worked from a compressed-gas canister, with which they were supposed to run up and down the corridor, in case of fire. These might have been sensible measures if fires in sleeping cars had been a nightly occurrence, but they have to be viewed against a background of millions of sleeping car passengers conveyed safely without being disturbed by fires. One other illustration will suffice. The standing instructions in the Rules and Regulations said that all external doors were to be left unlocked, but it had long been the practice for attendants to lock the doors on the platform side at the far ends of the pair of coaches they were responsible for. This channelled the flow of passengers through the doors at the inner ends of the pair of coaches, enabling the attendant to deal with each passenger as he arrived, and to show him to his berth, in an orderly fashion. It also helped to keep out drunks and other undesirable people and provided security for the passengers' belongings. It was what is known in the trade as 'practical railway working'. It had no bearing on the number of casualties in the Taunton disaster but there were some complaints from the emergency services that they could not gain access to the train through some of the doors. As a result, the instruction was reissued and re-emphasised, but BR went even further. Previously the gangway door between the sleeping car portion of a train and the ordinary coaches had been kept locked to prevent ordinary passengers from passing through the sleeping cars and possibly causing a disturbance. Even this sensible instruction was revoked by BR. It was quickly reinstated however, when a senior Board member was disturbed one night shortly afterwards by a party of drunks. He learnt the hard way that railway conditions in the dark hours are often quite different from those which apply during office hours, and that there is usually a good reason for the Rules and Regulations being laced with a modicum of railway commonsense and practicality.

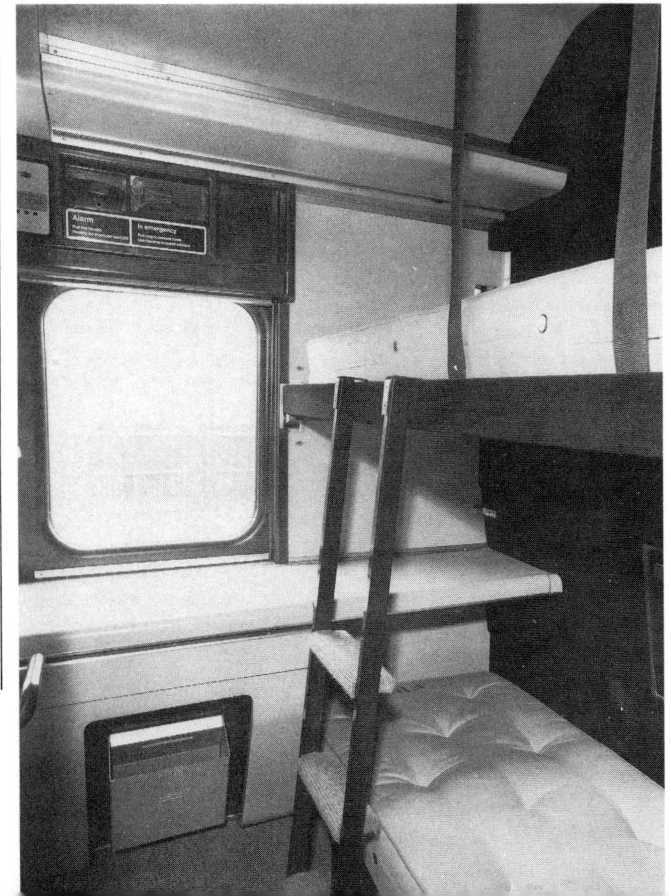

Above and left:
BR Mk 3 sleeping cars, introduced in 1981, exterior and interior views. The interior view shows the double berth mode. *BR*

Below:
Typical Graviner Fire Protection System

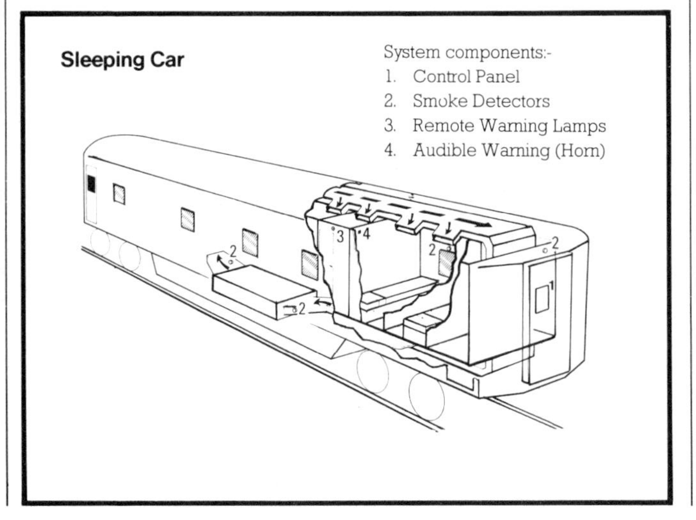

Above:
A presentation of certificates and cheques to a Banbury traincrew for their courage and resource in isolating a burning vehicle on their train, a Bescot to Eastleigh freight, at Tile Hill, near Coventry, in September 1975. BR takes a pride in specially marking such occasions. Seen in the photograph are (left to right) — the author (then Divisional Operating Superintendent, Birmingham); Vic Fuller, Banbury; John Pollard, Divisional Manager, Birmingham; Tom Callow, Banbury; Bill Bennett, Area Manager, Leamington; and Tom Jones, Banbury. *BR*

Taunton had a far more serious effect in a completely different direction. It occurred just at the time when BR was planning to replace its existing fleet of sleeping cars by the new Mk 3 version. Two hundred and thirty-six new vehicles were authorised in 1979 at a cost of £39 million but the design was extensively revised to incorporate the recommendations of the Railway Inspecting Officer. This increased the cost by several £ million and the order had to be reduced by no fewer than 26 vehicles to keep within the authorised cost. Graviner Ltd supplied a sophisticated and elaborate smoke detection system, to be fitted in every berth and in other sensitive locations. Warning horns were fitted in each berth, and elsewhere. Each berth is virtually a self-contained steel chest, and all decorative materials, furnishings and bedding were chosen for their fire-resistant qualities. In the event of smoke or fire, alarm horns sound, a warning lamp in the corridor is illuminated outside the berth concerned, and flashing arrows direct the attendant to the affected location. Internal doors are automatically closed. This is an impressive list of safety features, and shows what can be done to make sleeping cars safe against fire — but at a price. If Taunton had not happened would the Mk 3 sleeping cars have been any less safe in practical terms without all these features, and if the answer is 'yes' why had they not been incorporated in the original design?

Mention has been made several times of the actions of traincrews in case of fire. It is deeply ingrained in every railwayman's subconscious mind that if a vehicle catches fire the train should be split both in front of, and behind, the burning vehicle so that it is isolated, and the fire is prevented from spreading to the rest of the train. It is very pleasing to note how promptly and effectively this was carried out in the incidents that have been described, and it reflects great credit on the railwaymen concerned, particularly when it is remembered that most traincrews have no experience of trains on fire. One moment they are proceeding quite normally on an everyday journey. The next moment, without warning, they are faced with a grave and rapidly-worsening emergency and have to spring into action and deal with it as though it were a regular occurrence. Such occasions almost always bring out the best in railwaymen, often at some danger to themselves. One of the bravest acts took place at Soham, on the Ely to Newmarket line of the LNER, during the night of 1 June 1944. Driver Gimbert was in charge of 'Austerity' 2-8-0 No 7337, with a trainload of bombs. Looking back as he approached Soham he saw that the first wagon was on fire. Quickly he stopped his train, the fireman uncoupled behind the blazing wagon, then Gimbert set off again with the intention of leaving the wagon in open country in case its 10-ton load of bombs should explode. He didn't get very far. There was a tremendous explosion and the wagon simply disappeared. Fireman Nightall was killed instantly, and Driver Gimbert was seriously injured but survived. Both men did what they knew instinctively was expected of them, and both were honoured with the George Cross, the highest award for civilian bravery.

There is now a British Standard Code of Practice for fire precautions in the design and construction of railway passenger rolling stock (BS6853:1987) so there should be no more serious fires on InterCity trains, but Taunton and Cadder both showed just how easily events can conspire to create very hazardous situations. The code of practice was prepared under the direction of the Fire Standards Committee, with BR involvement, and is addressed to the designers of railway passenger rolling stock and those responsible for its maintenance, modification or refurbishment. It gives advice on the choice and testing of materials, the provision of fire barriers, and means of achieving safe evacuation from a train on fire. It owes its origins to the initiative of Lt-Col Townsend-Rose who, during his inquiry into the Cadder fire, was disturbed to find that no standards appeared to exist on this question. He therefore convened a working party to draw up such standards, and these formed the basis of the British Standard.

Fires are distinct from other types of railway accident. In a collision or derailment the passenger learns pretty quickly — in a matter of seconds — whether he is going to live or die (unless, as at Harrow in 1952, another train ploughs into the wreckage at high speed). In a fire, by contrast, the situation just gets worse and worse, and unless the passenger can escape, he's dead. And he dies in a particularly horrifying way too. So it is right that railway coaches should be as safe from fire as possible, especially as the fire brigade is unlikely to be able to reach the scene of a train fire quickly enough to be of value in rescuing passengers. This is no reflection on the efficiency of the fire service, but merely a recognition of the realities of the situation — it may be some time before the alarm can be raised, the nearest fire brigade may be several miles away, and there may be considerable difficulties of access to the train. By contrast, passengers will have escaped from the train, or met their death, within a very few minutes. Even at Taunton, where conditions were extremely favourable — the train stopped near a signalbox and therefore the alarm was raised straightaway; the fire station was nearby; and there was good road access — 15min elapsed between the communication cord being pulled and the arrival of the fire brigade. The railway situation is unique, and fire precautions have to be designed accordingly.

Below:
Locomotives frequently catch fire. Class 31 diesel-electric No 31256 was producing a lot of smoke and fumes near Hayes (Middlesex) on 10 September 1978. The other locomotive was No 31252. *D. H. Rayner*

2
Hot Axleboxes

Axleboxes are of two main types — plain bearing and roller bearing. Plain bearing axleboxes date back to the earliest days of railways, and consist simply of a whitemetal bearing underneath the springs of the vehicle or bogie, and resting upon the end portion of the axle, which is known as the journal. Bearing and journal are enclosed in a metal case (the axlebox), the whole being kept upright by axlebox guides attached to the wagon body, so that the wagon body can move up and down as the springs deflect under load or

Below:
10in x 5in Plain Bearing Oil Axlebox (cast steel, open-fronted)

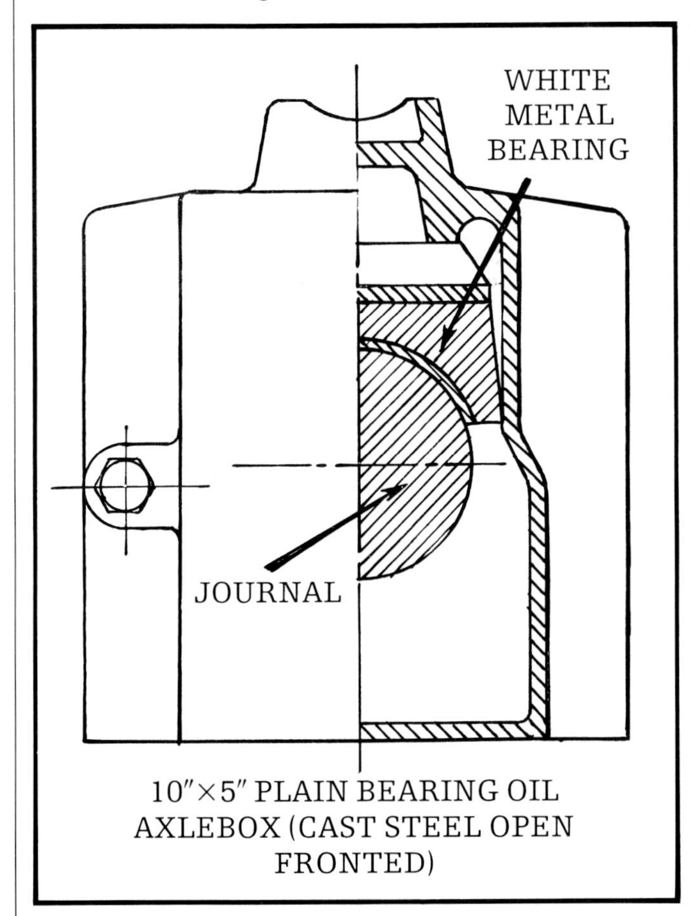

as a result of irregularities in track levels. This method of vehicle body suspension has been in use for many, many years, and hundreds of thousands of wagons were built to this design under the British Railways Modernisation Plan of the mid-1950s. Some of them are still in use, mainly by the Civil Engineer's Department.

It will readily be appreciated that the rotation of a dry, smooth axle journal underneath the plain whitemetal bearing will create friction and heat, leading eventually, if unchecked, to the journal becoming red-hot and breaking off, leaving one corner of the wagon completely unsupported and one wheel with no weight on it. At this stage, rapid derailment is inevitable. To avoid this happening, some form of lubrication is essential.

For many years grease was the normal means of lubrication, and a small army of men was employed, scattered throughout the length and breadth of the railway system, to refill the axleboxes. They were known, appropriately, as greasers, and could be found in every marshalling yard and goods yard of sufficient size.

In a later development, grease was replaced by oil as the lubricant, but it was not practicable merely to fill the axlebox with oil, as happened with grease, because the oil could not be prevented from leaking out at the point where the axle entered the box. The problem was overcome by placing a felt pad against the underpart of the journal, with the pad being supported on a spring mechanism, and a wick taking oil from the sump at the bottom of the axlebox, which thus allowed the rotating journal to carry around continuously a film of oil on its surface, and thereby providing adequate lubrication between bearing and journal. Needless to say, the axlebox needed constant

Below:
Traditional private owner's coal wagon, produced in hundreds of thousands, and equipped with grease axleboxes.
Ian Allan Library

Bottom:
A later-generation coal wagon, the standard British Railways 16-ton all-steel mineral wagon, with side and end doors, built at Derby in 1949. Equipped with oil axleboxes.
Ian Allan Library

examination and replenishment, and the army of greasers became an army of oilers and greasers. The pads required regular replacement to avoid surface glazing preventing the free flow of oil. The prevention of axleboxes overheating thus depended on every axlebox being examined regularly; easy enough to achieve with passenger coaches but not quite so easy with goods wagons unless an inordinate number of men were employed. And so the hot axlebox became a part of everyday railway life.

Regulation No 17 of the Regulations for Train Signalling required each signalman 'to be careful to notice each train as it passes to ascertain whether there is any apparent necessity for having it stopped at the next signalbox for examination, and if he observes or becomes aware of anything unusual in a train during its passage, such as . . . a hot axlebox, he must send to the signalman in advance the "Stop and examine train" signal' (seven consecutive beats on the bell communication between the two signalboxes). The signalman in advance, on receiving the bell signal, would then immediately put his signals to Danger, both to stop the approaching train and also to stop any train going in the opposite direction in case the train with the hot axlebox had in the meantime become derailed and wreckage was obstructing the opposite line.

Signalmen quickly learned how to recognise a hot axlebox, especially at those signalboxes where trains had already run long distances from a marshalling yard. The squealing of a dry axlebox running hot can be heard from quite a distance and is readily recognisable. It is a distinctive sound, unlike any other railway noise. When the oil pad becomes dry it warms up, and will eventually give off both smoke and smell; and the smoke is easily visible from the signalbox provided that it is on the same side of the line, and that there is sufficient light, either natural or artificial. The guard sitting at the back of the train might hear the axlebox squealing, or see the smoke as the train rounds a curve. He might also smell the smouldering pad. On a train fitted throughout with the continuous brake he can stop the train by the use of his emergency brake before any great harm is done, but on a loose-coupled train he would wait until his train passed a signalbox, and then, in the words of the Rule Book 'make every effort to attract the attention of the signalman', who would then promptly apply Regulation 17. The fireman would also look back down the train at frequent intervals.

Hot axleboxes were a frequent occurrence on goods trains, and, as might be expected an organisation developed to cope with them. The wagon with the defective axlebox was detached from the train and put into a siding at the signalbox at which it had been stopped for examination. Men known as carriage and wagon examiners visited such sidings regularly, or could be sent for specially if necessary. If the bearing and journal were undamaged, the wagon could have a new oil pad fitted and be sent on its way after being oiled, but if any damage had been caused the wagon would have to be sent on a slow train to the nearest wagon repair depot. In the worst cases special arrangements would have to be made to repair the wagon *in*

Below:
The type of goods train on which hot axleboxes were a frequent occurrence. Former Great Western Railway '28XX' class 2-8-0 No 2893 heads a goods train through Sonning Cutting, near Reading, on 16 May 1964. *Brian Stephenson*

Left:
Two diesel brake tenders, with Type 4 diesel-electric No D77 *Royal Irish Fusilier*, at Barrow Hill depot on 30 July 1967. The brake tenders are stencilled 'Return to Nottingham Division', and were mainly used on coal trains from Toton, although they frequently 'went astray' because they were so useful.
David Percival

situ, and it was often necessary first to tranship the load into another wagon. Special tranship gangs existed in some places but if they were not available the local permanent way gang was often glad to help out on overtime, or at the weekend, in order to supplement its rather meagre basic wage.

Wagon repair depots were established in all the bigger yards and depots. Quite often they were privately owned, as were many of the wagons prior to nationalisation in 1948, and some of the larger repair firms were nationwide, Wagon Repairs Ltd being one of the best known.

The organisation for detecting and dealing with hot axleboxes proved quite adequate for the task right up to the 1960s, but then several changes took place which considerably increased the hazard. Hot axleboxes have to run for several miles before they reach a critical stage, and as long as there were plenty of lineside signalboxes to maintain supervision there was little problem, but several factors were occurring simultaneously which had the effect of continuously reducing the amount of lineside observation. These were:

1. Minor signalling schemes, allowing intermediate signalboxes to be closed.
2. The automation of level crossings, allowing the staff to be withdrawn.
3. The abolition of signalboxes, when sidings or branch lines were closed permanently.
4. The abolition of signalboxes, no longer required owing to a reduction in the number of trains run, or the closure of such signalboxes during quiet periods.
5. Power signalboxes were being developed, covering ever-increasing areas, with little or no actual observation of trains.

The other main change taking place in the 1960s was the increase in the average speed of freight trains, brought about by the replacement of steam locomotives by diesel or electric traction, and the decrease in the number of trains run unbraked, ie without power brakes being operated on any of the wagons. Actually, the braking power of a diesel locomotive is less than that of a steam locomotive, and for some years during the transition period it was necessary for various stratagems to be employed to deal with the situation on unbraked trains, some costly, some inconvenient, and some both. The main ones were:

1. Shunting out all the available power-braked wagons in a train, so that they could be marshalled in the front portion, thus providing what became known as a 'fitted head', and considerably increasing the brake power available to the driver. There was a sliding scale allowing the train load to be increased proportionately to the increase in brake power. In practice the complicated calculations of train weight and brake power together with the nuisance and inconvenience of having to shunt out odd wagons from a train up to 60 or 70 wagons long meant that trains were rarely made up to their theoretical maximum load, and no amount of blandishments, threats and exhortations from higher management could ever achieve it.

2. An additional locomotive could be coupled to the train locomotive to provide extra brake power — an expensive solution and normally employed only over short distances.

3. A new vehicle, known as a brake tender, was designed. It was basically a short bogie wagon with heavy weights to increase adhesion, and power brakes on all four axles. The brake tenders were attached next to the locomotive, either singly or in pairs, and could be either propelled or hauled. As a stopgap they had their uses but were universally unpopular. They caused extra shunting and never seemed to be there when wanted. Locomen did not like propelling them, and eventually during one of their more intransigent periods refused to do so any more.

Below:
English Electric Type 3 No D6767, complete with brake tender, heads a freight train on the Up East Coast main line at Relly Mill, near Durham, in June 1967. *John E. Hoggarth*

Above:
Lineside hot axlebox detectors. They scan, and compare, the temperatures of the axleboxes at each end of an axle. If the difference is greater than a predetermined level, an alarm is given in the supervising signalbox. *Author*

The upshot of all this was that freight trains ran faster and faster, with less and less lineside supervision. A dangerous situation was developing, which had to be countered. Hot axleboxes had to be identified, and trains stopped, before disaster struck. Fortuitously, a similar situation had arisen in the United States a decade earlier and the railways there had sought a technical solution, resulting in a piece of equipment being designed known as a hot axlebox detector (HABD), which was installed in the track and scanned the two ends of each axle passing over it; then compared the temperatures and sounded an alarm in a monitoring signalbox if they were seriously different because one end was overheating. The signalman could then stop the train and deal with the defective wagon. Technically, all hot objects radiate heat energy, known as infrared, which is invisible but can be detected by an infrared camera (the scanner). The scanner always looks at the same point on the axleboxes of each passing train.

BR started to install lineside HABDs in the 1960s and by now there are about 200. They have never been entirely satisfactory. The level at which they are set has to be sufficiently low to detect an incipient hot axlebox, yet not so low as to give rise to false alarms triggered off by such things as locomotive exhausts. In practice it has not been found possible to strike the happy medium, in fact signalmen have been told to ignore alarms relating to ac electric locomotives, diesel-mechanical multiple-units and, as can well be imagined, steam locomotives in steam. HABDs were originally set for plain bearing axleboxes, but roller bearings (described later in the book) run warmer and to avoid false alarms the HABDs needed to be set very accurately, which stretched the capability of the equipment to its limits. Reliability was also a problem, as was the supply of spare parts. The whole subject demanded a great deal of management attention, which could not always be given when other more urgent or more important questions arose. There was a difficult learning curve for both management and technicians alike, and a number of unsatisfactory situations arose. Machines which had become unserviceable, or which had been switched off because they had generated too many false alarms, were removed from site to a workshop without being replaced and were often away for months waiting parts. During all this time there were loopholes in the safety defences. For example, on 20 September 1979, train No 8M79, the 03.40 Tyne Yard to Toton, conveying 38 wagons of coal with a fitted head of 16 wagons became derailed and caused considerable track damage and disruption about 1½ miles north of Thirsk when an overheated journal eventually became so hot that it broke off from the remainder of the axle. The wagon concerned was a 21-ton coal hopper. There should have been two HABDs between Tyne Yard and Thirsk — one at Croxdale, near Ferryhill, about 36 miles from Thirsk, and one at Danby Wiske, near Northallerton, about nine miles away. Both detectors were out of order waiting spares, the one at Croxdale since 1 July and the one at Danby Wiske since 21 July. Nor was the Thirsk derailment exceptional. Barely a week later, train No 8V63, the 02.10 Tinsley to Severn Tunnel Junction was derailed at Water Orton, approaching Birmingham, by a journal burning off. The hot axlebox had been picked up by the HABD at Lea Marston, a short distance away, and the signalman at Saltley powerbox, upon being alerted by the alarm, had put his signals to Danger, and the train was already slowing down. However, when the accident was being investigated it transpired that the previous HABD was no less than 36 miles away at Duffield, yet it was well known that 25 miles was the absolute maximum safe distance between adjacent HABDs. As at Thirsk, a casual observer might have been forgiven for concluding that BR had been gambling on safety, gambling that a wagon would not run hot and spread itself all over the tracks. It was not a deliberate gamble, of course; in the one case it was bad management, in the other a considered judgement of risk, but whatever it was it came off, although that was really just good fortune and one really ought not to pray good fortune in aid of safety. However, these were bad days for railways. Morale was at rock bottom, there was constant strife between BR and the trade unions, the financial squeeze was so severe that mere survival was counted success, and there was a lack of positive direction. Small wonder that HABDs did not receive enough managerial attention — they were well down the list of priorities.

One might ask what the nation's watchdogs were doing at this juncture. Perhaps the Railway Inspectorate of the Department of Transport was not fully in the picture, not aware of the extent to which safety was being hazarded day by day. The role of the Railway Inspectorate is a difficult one; on the one hand there is no point in its making unreasonable and impossible financial demands on BR, yet on the other hand it must not allow sympathy with BR's financial predicament to sway its judgement. It is a fine line but there are occasions when it must stand firm if it feels that the overall demands of safety are being neglected because money is tight. This was one of those occasions, because the sums of money involved were not large. It was the era of BR Chairman Sir Peter Parker's famous phrase — and he was a master of the elegant and persuasive phrase — 'the crumbling edge of quality'. BR assured the Railway Inspectorate that the phrase did not apply to safety, and that it would impose speed restrictions, or take equipment out of service, before dangerous conditions were reached, but it is clear that this weighed upon the mind of the Chief Inspecting Officer Lt-Col I. K. A. McNaughton, for in his Annual Report for 1979 he commented upon the increase in significant train accidents from 220 in 1978 to 243 in 1979 by saying that:

> 'In looking for an explanation of this increase . . . I would suggest that part, at least, arises from the direct or indirect effects of the continuing financial problems facing railway management.'

He was right. The problem continued to give cause for concern, and in his 1981 Annual Report his successor, Maj C. F. Rose, returned to the attack:

> '. . . so far at least, the Railway's policy of putting safety before operational or commercial considerations has prevented any serious erosion of their traditionally high safety standards.'

His use of the word 'serious' can hardly have been unintentional, and the inference is that he *did* consider that there had been *some* erosion of safety standards.

Maj Olver returned to the subject in his Report dated 30 April 1986, on the derailment at Birtley which occurred on 1 August 1984. After seriously criticising the civil engineering department, he concluded:

> '. . . with the ever-increasing manpower economies being introduced throughout British Railways, I consider it is essential that frequent checks are carried out at all levels to ensure that the new organisation is working efficiently and that it has not led to shortcomings . . . The slimming of the permanent way organisation, while not resulting in a detectable drop in safety standards, has no longer got the comfortable margins that it had of old.'

Worries about hot axleboxes are now largely, although not entirely, in the past, thanks to a simple but remarkable invention — the roller bearing. In a plain axlebox the bearing rests directly on the end of the axle (the journal) and friction between the two when the axle rotates is prevented by a film of oil. In a roller bearing axlebox a 'race' of rollers acts in the same way as, and replaces, the film of oil.

The advantages of roller bearings are that they require no maintenance between shopping and run hot very much less frequently than plain axleboxes. When they do run hot it is not due to lack of lubricant (except where there has been a failure to grease), but is usually caused by incorrect reassembly after shopping, or occasionally by mechanical failure, mainly where the 'cage', which holds the rollers in the 'race', breaks. In such circumstances the temperature of the axlebox rises very quickly indeed, to such an extent that the journal end can become overheated and break off within three to five miles. It will be seen, therefore, that HABDs provide only a slight defence against a roller bearing axlebox overheating — they would have to be positioned every two to three miles to provide effective cover, rather than the 25-30 miles which is the current practice.

However, when the use of plain bearings has been eliminated it will then be possible to set HABDs to act only for roller bearing axleboxes. HABDs located at 12 to 18-mile intervals will then give some degree of safety.

As the lineside hot axlebox detector is not a totally satisfactory solution to the problem, other answers have been sought. The West German railway network (DB) has considered the possibility of applying sensors to each

Below:
The essential parts of a Timken roller bearing, showing the race of roller bearings, and the cup. *Author's Collection*

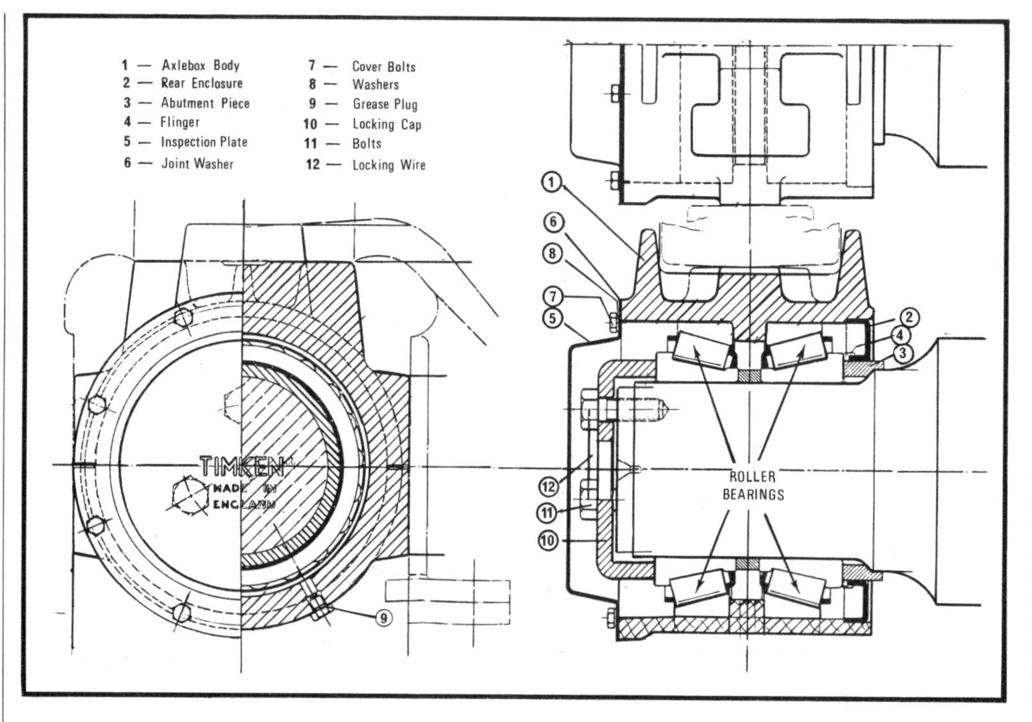

Left:
Side, End and Top Elevations of a Timken Roller Bearing

Below and bottom:
Insulated fish vans fitted with roller bearing axleboxes for use on the express fish trains between Aberdeen and King's Cross via the East Coast main line. The train is seen ready to leave Aberdeen on 20 January 1958. Note the two vans marshalled behind the brakevan for quick detachment en route. *BR*

journal bearing housing, but has found it costly. British Timken has experimented with a fusible plug incorporated in the axlebox, which emits dense smoke when running hot, but this is not entirely satisfactory as it depends on the smoke being seen, and the train being stopped, within a few miles — very difficult to achieve on most of BR's main lines.

Roller bearings were first introduced on Britain's railways in 1928, on the Euston-Watford dc service of the London Midland and Scottish Railway, but development was very slow and mainly confined to steam locomotive axles. It was to be 30 years before roller bearings started to come into widespread use on BR. On 20 January 1958 the first fish train to be composed of vehicles fitted with roller bearings left Aberdeen for King's Cross. Some 275 fish vans were provided for the Aberdeen fish trains, the vans being identified by a blue circle painted on the body side. The trains were known as Blue Spot fish trains, and because the vehicles had an unusually long wheelbase, they were allowed to travel at more than 60mph. In the 1960s roller bearings became the standard fitting for all new construction, both on freight and passenger vehicles, and with the rapid withdrawal of older types of vehicles in the 1970s and 1980s the great majority of vehicle axleboxes are now the roller bearing type.

Some of the plain bearing axlebox vehicles taken out of traffic use were adopted by Civil Engineers for departmental use, but in some cases the axleboxes were not changed to roller bearing because of the cost and the relatively short remaining life of the vehicles. However, some types of vehicle in departmental use may not receive the standard of maintenance which is given to traffic wagons, and as a result they occasionally run hot. On 20 July 1985 a wagon loaded with prefabricated track en route from Crofton depot, near Wakefield, to Newcastle triggered a hot axlebox detector near Thirsk and signals were placed to Danger ahead of it. At the same time, the axlebox burst into flames and before the train could be stopped the journal end had burnt off and derailment had occurred. Engineering Dept wagons are a source of worry even to the engineers themselves. One engineer, writing in BR's own house journal as recently as March 1988 expressed his fears that sooner or later there would be a major mishap with one of these vehicles. He was to be proved not far wrong.

Above:
Standard British Railways 21-ton coal hopper wagons, equipped with roller bearing axleboxes. These were a special batch of vacuum-braked wagons serving West Drayton Coal Concentration Depot. *BR*

Right:
A civil engineering department 'Grampus' wagon, fitted with oil axleboxes, off the rails at Redhill, Southern Region, on 13 October 1984. The cause in this case was not a hot axlebox. Its neighbour has already been fitted with roller bearing axleboxes.
Alex Dasi-Sutton

Below right:
Class 58 freight locomotive No 58004 heads a train of empty 32-ton coal hopper wagons through Nottingham station on a return merry-go-round working from Staythorpe power station (near Newark) on 1 November 1985. The entire fleet of 32-ton hoppers is equipped with roller bearings. *Gary Grafton*

Only a few months later, on 12 July, a departmental wagon loaded with concrete sleepers and being conveyed on the 16.58 freight train from Workington to Willesden became derailed at Hademore, on the West Coast main line near Lichfield, causing severe damage to several miles of expensive track. Fortunately, no other train was involved. The cause of the derailment was a hot axlebox. This particular wagon was fitted with FAG roller bearing axleboxes.

Failures of roller bearing axleboxes, though relatively few, can have dramatic results, but surely none more so than those which overtook train 6M08, the 01.40 Haverton Hill (Teesside) to Glazebrook (Lancs) on 20 December 1984. The train was conveying 13 bogie tank wagons loaded with a total of 835 tons of petrol, and was examined before the start of its journey. It ran quite normally to Healey Mills yard, near Wakefield, where a fresh traincrew took over for the next stage of the journey. Again the journey was quite normal as the train ran along the Calder Valley through Brighouse and Sowerby Bridge, heading towards the Pennines which in this area reach over 1,500ft on the bleak and boggy moorlands. The train climbed the gradually steepening gradient towards the 2,885yd long Summit Tunnel, with the final five miles at 1 in 182. The signalman at Hebden Bridge, seven miles from the tunnel, watched the train go by. He saw nothing untoward. The train looked just like all the other oil and petrol trains which passed his box. Little did he know that catastrophe was only minutes away.

In the driving cab everything was perfectly normal and routine too. The driver had applied full power to haul the heavy train up the gradient, then as the tunnel mouth loomed up and he reached the summit he eased off power and sounded his horn as he entered the tunnel. Tunnels, even those as long as Summit Tunnel, hold no fears for drivers these days. It is merely a bit darker in there than it is outside; quite unlike the days of steam locomotives when tunnels were stinking holes full of smoke, and loathed by traincrews. The train was running smoothly through the tunnel at about 40mph when the driver suddenly felt the locomotive shudder and noticed that the automatic air brake pressure gauge had suddenly dropped to zero. At the same moment he felt the brakes go on and immediately deduced that the train had broken in two.

As he climbed down from the locomotive in the inky darkness, lit only by the backglow of his headlight, he had little or no inkling that this was to be one of the most terrifying days of his life. He knew what he had to do — consult with the guard to see what was wrong, and then see whether the opposite line was obstructed in any way. If it was, it was then the driver's duty to go forward as quickly as he could, waving a red light to warn the driver of any train approaching the obstruction. What he failed to do, which in the event was of no consequence, was to place a track-circuit operating clip on the opposite line straight away. A track circuit is an electrical train-detection device which feeds a low current through the running rails. When vehicle wheels run on that section of track they short-circuit the electric current. The short circuit is detected by the apparatus, which places the last approaching signal to Danger, and illuminates an indicator in the

Above left:
A block trainload of 100-ton oil tankers, seen near Beattock with a Class 86 electric locomotive in charge. As a matter of interest, would the oil companies allow their road tankers to run about the country in such a disreputable state? *BR*

Above:
Sowerby Bridge West, in the Calder Valley, showing a Blackpool-Bradford train.
L. A. Nixon

Right:
Class 37 No 6942, at the head of a train of coal empties, descends the Calder Valley after leaving Summit Tunnel on 2 June 1971, and is seen passing through Todmorden.
J. H. Cooper-Smith

signalbox. It is a device which is at the very heart of the modern signalling and safety system, and can be operated equally well by a track-circuit operating clip, which is a simple device carried on all locomotives and multiple-units. It consists of two spring clips joined by a piece of wire. In an emergency the clips are placed one on each rail, and in an instant there is a short circuit and the signals are switched to Danger. It is certainly the quickest and most effective way of preventing a train in the opposite direction from running into an obstruction, provided that it has not already passed the last signal. If it has, no power on earth can save it because it will have crashed headlong into the wreckage in as little as a minute.

But to continue with our story. The driver climbed down on to the track and walked towards the other end of his locomotive, where the guard had already alighted. The scene was like something out of Jules Verne. There they were, in the middle of the tunnel, three-quarters of a mile from either end, with the back glare of the locomotive headlight eerily lighting up the surroundings, and clouds of dust and petrol fumes rolling towards them. They knew that they were carrying 835 tons of four-star petrol. They knew how even a saucerful of petrol could cause quite a blaze; then suddenly there was a 'whoosh' of flame down the train somewhere. What terror gripped them can scarcely be imagined. For all they knew, the whole 835 tons might explode into flames at any moment, and there was only one way the flames could go — along the tunnel. They ran for their lives, half expecting with every step to be overtaken by searing flames. The relief when they finally reached the tunnel mouth was enormous. Nor did they know what lay behind them in the tunnel. They had seen a whoosh of flame, they suspected that the train had become divided, but they did not know that most of the tankers had become derailed and that some of them were on their sides lying on the opposite line. If another train had been approaching, the resulting crash in the confined space of the tunnel among tens of thousands of gallons of highly-inflammable four-star petrol would have been too awful to contemplate. Luckily, the tanks lying on their sides on the opposite line had short-circuited the track circuit, so the vital signal at the tunnel mouth was already at Danger.

The traincrew used the telephone at that signal to raise the alarm, and immediately the whole emergency organisation sprang into action. On the railway, breakdown trains were alerted and arrangements were made to cancel trains or divert them from the blocked route. Key personnel were called out. Police, fire and ambulance services were at once notified, and they responded very quickly. The accident happened at about 05.50 and the alarm was raised just after 06.00. By 06.08 Greater Manchester Fire Service Control had received the call for assistance and had notified the West Yorkshire Fire Service Control at 06.13. Fire engines arrived at the Manchester end of the tunnel by 06.16 and at the Yorkshire end at 06.22 (the tunnel lies across the county boundary). Such promptness was most commendable, but thanks to the foresight of BR and the fire service a practice had already been held to test the response time, in view of the fact that the tunnel lies in two different fire service areas.

The firemen entered the tunnel from both ends to assess the situation, which could hardly have been more difficult or novel for them. They extinguished several small fires and appeared to have the situation under such good control that they felt it would be safe for the locomotive and first three tankers to be removed from the tunnel. The driver and guard were still there and they very bravely agreed to go back into the tunnel, even though the terror of recent events was still fresh in their minds. At last they reached the locomotive, but then found that the coupling between the third and fourth wagons was too tight to be lifted off the drawbar hook, the fourth wagon being derailed. At this stage they must have felt like calling the whole thing off but with great determination they stuck to their task. The driver reversed the locomotive and pushed the front three wagons against the fourth so that the buffers could be compressed and the couplings slackened. It was successful and the traincrew gingerly took the locomotive and front three undamaged tankers out of the tunnel into the open air. The relief they felt when they finally emerged into the daylight can be imagined, and the bravery they displayed was a great credit to the railway service.

Above:
The scene deep inside Summit Tunnel on 20 December 1984, just before the great fire erupted. The firemen are seen dealing with what were thought to be small and isolated pockets of fire. Their courage in such circumstances is greatly to be admired.
Brian Saville/ West Yorkshire Fire Service

By 09.45, 4hr after the accident, it appeared that everything was under control and that the railway breakdown gangs could soon move in to clear the line and reopen the route to normal traffic. In the event it was to be eight months before that happened. A fierce fire broke out with great fury and suddenness, and had the flames not been able to escape up two of the tunnel's 12 ventilating shafts it is likely that a number of firemen would have perished. The fire was so intense that flames shot out of the top of the two ventilating shafts to a height of 150yd, with great quantities of air being sucked into the tunnel to fan the fire. It burnt uncontrollably for 24hr, causing considerable damage to the tunnel lining.

The first people to enter the tunnel after the fire had a daunting experience. They had no idea what they would find. The tunnel might have collapsed, or it might be in a dangerously unstable condition ready to do so, but in fact the old tunnel had stood up to its ordeal remarkably well, especially as it had been built in the early days of railways as long ago as 1840/41, for the Leeds & Manchester Railway. George Stephenson had been Engineer-in-Chief and had done his job well. It was, incidentally, the first railway tunnel through the Pennines.

Major accidents often have minor causes and Summit Tunnel was no exception. Whilst the Inspecting Officer who conducted the subsequent inquiry, Mr D. Sawer, was examining the debris in the tunnel he discovered the journal end which had burnt off the leading axle of the

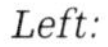

Left:
Smoke and flames shoot high into the air from the ventilating shafts of Summit Tunnel, fed by petrol from the derailed 01.40 Haverton Hill to Glazebrook train on 20 December 1984.
Steve Chapman

Below:
A Total Oil Co 100-ton bogie tank wagon of the type involved in the Summit Tunnel fire. This one was built by Chas Roberts & Co of Horbury Junction, Wakefield. *Chas Roberts & Co*

fourth tank wagon. The wagon had then become derailed, although the train actually parted between the sixth and seventh vehicles. The defective wagon was No PR82689. It had been built in 1968 by the Standard Railway Wagon Co for hire to Total Oil, and was purchased by Procor (UK) Ltd in 1971. It had originally been constructed to carry Class B heavy oil products but was converted in July 1984 to carry Class A light oil products before being hired to ICI. In November 1984 during the course of normal maintenance the wheelsets were found to require attention and the vehicle was despatched to Rail Car Services at Gloucester. Reconditioned wheelsets were fitted and on 10 December the vehicle was returned to traffic and sent to Haverton Hill. From then on it was only a matter of time before it fell to pieces. It had actually made one round trip to Glazebrook and was on its second when the accident occurred. Why it should choose to happen in the middle of Summit Tunnel is one of those quirks of fate.

The axlebox bearing which failed had been manufactured by British Timken and had been refurbished and reassembled by the British Steel Corporation. It is probable that the failure resulted from incorrect reassembly or incorrect fitting on the journal. Such a simple cause, costing millions of pounds! No doubt BR was relieved that it had insured itself against the cost of major accidents, but it has to pay hefty annual premiums to do so. At one time BR stood all its own losses arising from accidents, but the cost of the Britannia Bridge fire over the Menai Straits in 1970 seriously unbalanced BR's budget and it was felt to be better to even out the cost of major accidents (ie those costing several million pounds) by means of an annual payment of an insurance premium. Failures of roller bearing axleboxes on bogie tank wagons are quite rare, and the failure rate has been calculated at one per four to five million vehicle miles run.

Those who are opposed to anything with the word 'nuclear' in it were up in arms about the possibility of a train conveying a flask containing irradiated fuel rods being involved in such a fire as the one at Summit Tunnel. Whether the flask could withstand those temperatures over such a long period of time without the contents leaking is problematical. It has never been tested, nor is anyone likely to go to the trouble and expense of mounting such a test. The chances of a petrol train becoming derailed and catching fire in the middle of a tunnel are millions to one. So far as is known it has never happened before, not even a derailment, let alone a derailment and fire. And the chance of a train conveying a nuclear flask being so near that it had actually passed the last signal when the derailment occurred must be of such an order of magnitude that it is quite incalculable. Yet, the suggestion was seriously made that BR should timetable its trains so that nuclear flask trains are not planned to pass petrol trains in a tunnel. This is taking contingencies to extremes and is about as sensible as telling a pedestrian that he should not cross a road if a motor vehicle is likely to pass within the next three weeks. Fortunately BR took a pragmatic view — it agreed that it would avoid timetabling such trains to pass each other in a tunnel, but wisely made no stipulation about the actual day-to-day running.

Finally, it is interesting to speculate on what might have happened if neither police nor fire brigade had attended,

Above and Below:
Two views of the Britannia Bridge over the Menai Straits, after the fire in 1970. The sagging bridge and the smoke-blackened stone towers can clearly be seen.
John H. Bird/E. N. Kneale

Above left:
ICI liquid chlorine tank, registered in 1951. It has oil axleboxes and instanter couplings and is now on display at the National Railway Museum. *Author*

Above:
A 70-ton gross laden weight liquid chlorine bogie tank wagon, built by the Standard Wagon Co in 1970 and illustrating the considerable advance in wagon building technology. Equipped with roller bearing axleboxes and the airbrake. The two large stars on the tank barrel indicate that the wagon may be conveyed on fully-fitted express freight trains. The star rating system for tank wagons was as follows:
Three stars May be conveyed on passenger trains (eg milk tanks).
Two stars May be conveyed on express freight trains.
One star May be conveyed on partly-fitted freight trains.
No star May only be conveyed on slow freight trains.
Ian Allan Library

and if the whole incident had been dealt with by railway staff alone. After all, the fire brigade was unable to prevent the fire from burning itself out, although its action in keeping the fire under control during the early hours did enable the locomotive and three tank wagons to be rescued, which might not otherwise have been the case. But that is perhaps being unfair. Individual firemen acted with great bravery, and some might well have lost their lives. No one had experienced such a situation before and there were fears that the whole 835 tons of petrol might create a gigantic fireball, consuming everything in its path over a wide area, almost in the nature of an explosion. It was obviously sensible to take precautions, such as the evacuation of nearby residents. Police and fire services are very sensitive on this issue, following a number of serious eruptions and fireballs during derailments in North America. On 24 Feburary 1978 at Waverley in Tennessee a derailed tank wagon of propane exploded as it was being pumped out, and 12 people were killed. On 10 November 1979 at Mississauga, a Toronto suburb, a quarter of a million people had to be evacuated because of the danger that a tank wagon containing chlorine might rupture and release clouds of the poison gas which claimed so many lives on the Western Front in World War 1. Adjacent tank wagons in the derailed train were burning and exploding. The cause of the derailment was a hot axlebox of the plain bearing type. The Canadian Transport Commission recommended that, amongst other things, roller bearings should be fitted to tank wagons conveying inflammable liquids and that hot box detectors should be installed at 20-mile intervals in built-up areas.

To return to the subject of lineside hot axlebox detectors. Whilst they will detect an overheating roller bearing axlebox, such overheating can occur over a relatively short distance and may lead to catastrophic failure within a few miles. Obviously, HABDs located 25 to 30 miles apart do not provide continuous cover and consideration is being given to locating them on the approaches to long tunnels, viaducts and long bridges so that a train with a defective bearing can be stopped and be prevented from becoming derailed whilst actually in the tunnel or on a viaduct or long bridge. HABDs work best when they are located on straight and level track, and where the train has not recently been braking. It is also convenient to have a siding nearby into which a vehicle with an overheated axlebox can be detached. Whilst the first priority must be to identify an incipient hot axlebox, it is inconvenient if unsuitable siting gives rise to a lot of false alarms, and it is very inconvenient if an axlebox is discovered to be in such a bad state that it is not safe to take it forward yet there is no siding nearby into which it can be detached. These factors tend to determine the optimum location of HABDs but there is a need for some compromise here if safety is to be assured.

When the alarm sounds in a signalbox the instrument tells the signalman the number of the axle in the train, and whether it is the left-hand or right-hand side of the train. The signalman will then stop the train, and any other that may be approaching, in case of derailment, and inform the traincrew of the details. Driver or guard will then check to see how hot the particular axlebox is, but if nothing appears to be amiss the train may proceed forward at not more than 20mph to a place where technical staff are available. Alternatively the vehicle may be detached. If the axlebox is hot the vehicle must be detached, and no movement must exceed 10mph, but if there is any doubt about the wisdom of moving the vehicle at all it must not be moved until it has been examined by technical staff, who would authorise such movement if appropriate.

The frequency of false alarms on passenger trains, and the need to carry out these instructions, caused a lot of delay, and it was necessary to introduce some relaxation. Genuine hot axleboxes on passenger trains are quite rare, therefore if nothing can be found after an alarm the train may run forward at normal speed but an examination must be carried out within 50 miles either by technical staff or by the passage of the train over another detector. If neither is available, and everything seems to be in order, the train may run forward another 50 miles.

It will have been noted that in the discussion of the Summit Tunnel fire, all three parties (Railway Control, the police and the fire service) knew immediately that the train was conveying petrol. How this came about will be revealed in the next chapter.

3
The Transport of Dangerous Goods

The railways of Britain have been carrying dangerous goods ever since they were built, although it is interesting to reflect that they only did so on their own terms, in contrast to the general run of goods traffic for which the railways were common carriers and were obliged to carry anything that was handed to them, until freed from that obligation by the Transport Act 1962.

Reading through the old books of regulations, one is immediately struck by the way in which certain commodities have now passed into history, such as celluloid, calcium carbide, charcoal, saltpetre and oily waste; reminders of our industrial past. No mention then of some of today's hazardous commodities, such as liquefied petroleum gas and hydrocyanic acid, and the one that causes the most excitement of all — spent nuclear fuel. Our forefathers never dreamt of the marvels of the nuclear age, nor had any inkling of its dangers.

In this chapter we shall consider the problems surrounding the conveyance of certain types of dangerous goods, and the safety organisation which exists for dealing with the effects of an accident to a train conveying such traffics. One of the potentially most hazardous traffics is spent nuclear fuel, and it is certainly the traffic which appears to cause most concern in the public mind, mainly because the effects of an accident in Britain causing radiation leakage from a flask containing irradiated nuclear fuel are unknown. There is simply no experience of such an event because it has never happened, whilst the effects on the human body of radiation from other sources often take so long to manifest themselves, especially if the dosage is small. There is also the problem of the safe disposal of nuclear waste. These factors tend to make the nuclear power industry a focus of attack by pressure groups of all kinds.

There are a number of nuclear power stations around Britain's coastline, mainly of the Magnox reactor type, although there are some advanced gas-cooled reactor stations. Each fuel element for a Magnox reactor consists of a bar of uranium metal encased in a tube of magnesium alloy, called Magnox. Gas-cooled reactor fuel elements are made up of pellets of uranium oxide in stainless steel tubes, 36 of which are held together in a graphite sleeve.

Both types of fuel element are manufactured by British Nuclear Fuels at Preston, and are transported to the power stations by road. At this stage the elements are perfectly harmless and can safely be held in the hand, but after use in the reactor they are highly radioactive. A Magnox fuel element for the Sizewell power station is about a metre long and weighs 25lb. Each of Sizewell's two reactors contains about 26,000 elements, which remain in the reactor for up to 11 years. After use the elements are stored for three months, and then taken by rail in specially constructed containers known as flasks to British Nuclear Fuels' reprocessing works at Sellafield, on the line between Barrow-in-Furness and Whitehaven, in Cumbria. Each flask contains 200 Magnox fuel elements or 20 gas-cooled reactor

Below:
The result of inattention in the driving cab. Class 47 locomotive No 1614 had been hauling a train along the Up Goods line at King's Norton, near Birmingham, on 27 May 1970, but the driver failed to stop at the signal, and the locomotive ran into the buffers in the dead-end. The driver admitted having fallen asleep and there was no AWS on the Goods line to alert him. The accident, which happened in a built-up area, could have had disastrous consequences as there were five tank wagons of butane liquefied petroleum gas in the train, but fortunately the tank barrels were not ruptured.
Paul Cotterell

Above:
A propane/butane tank wagon, first registered in 1963 and built by Chas Roberts & Co of Wakefield. Gross laden weight 40 tons. Equipped with roller bearing axleboxes and the vacuum brake. *Ian Allan Library*

Left:
Class 25 diesel-electric No 25307 passes Cark signalbox on 28 July 1982 with a block trainload of nuclear flasks for Sellafield. *Noel A. Machell*

Above, left and below left:
A spectacular demonstration of the ability of a nuclear flask to withstand the impact of a 250-ton train at 100mph. Staged at Old Dalby, near Melton Mowbray, on BR's Research Department test track. The locomotive was No 46009.
Colin J. Marsden/
Colin J. Marsden/
Nicholas Sargeant

elements and is filled with water. A flask is essentially a massive steel box with 14in thick walls, which are designed not only to absorb radiation but also to be proof against breakage, heat or leakage. The flasks (which conform to internationally agreed standards) have to be capable of withstanding a fall of 30ft on to an unyielding surface; and to convince sceptics of the tremendous strength of the flasks the Central Electricity Generating Board arranged a spectacular demonstration in 1984 in conjunction with BR. The CEGB bought from BR a redundant Class 46 diesel-electric locomotive and three Mk 1 coaches, and equipped the locomotive with remote control (no one wanted to stay in the cab during the test!). They then positioned a flask, at its most vulnerable angle, on the line to simulate the worst derailment conditions, and drove the 250-ton train into it at 100mph, having carefully assembled the nation's press and TV beforehand. The locomotive was wrecked but the flask, to everyone's relief, was undamaged. Everyone, that is, except the anti-nuclear lobby who protested that it was not a representative test. What would happen, they said, if the flask was in a petrol fire for an hour (in what circumstances it is difficult to imagine, other than the Summit Tunnel fire, which in any case was a million to one chance), or fell off a high viaduct (when did a train last fall off a high viaduct on to an unyielding surface in Britain?). There has to be some regard to the balance of probabilities even when dealing with spent nuclear fuel. There have now been more than 10,000 safe journeys since flasks first began to be carried, with only one or two very minor derailments of no consequence whatsoever. Yet, the subject of the transport of flasks is a very delicate one and the consequences of radiation leakage are so unpredictable that it is quite proper and essential that all sensible and practical safeguards should be taken. But even if the flask were to be

Left:
On 19 April 1982 Class 25 diesel-electric No 25032 is seen leaving Blaenau Ffestiniog with a nuclear flask from Trawsfynydd power station. Note the guard's brakevan at the rear of the train — all trains conveying nuclear flasks must have one. *M. M. Hughes*

cracked in some way, and some of the water lost, the only effect would be to contaminate the ground in the vicinity, with no major threat to health. So long as the elements themselves remained undamaged, radioactivity would be contained; and in the worst case — damage to the fuel elements — many hours would elapse before there was any release of radioactivity which was not entirely confined to the vicinity of the flask. It is the objective of the emergency organisation to ensure that expert personnel and emergency services reach the scene during that period and take emergency action.

All trains conveying flasks have a brakevan at the rear, in which a guard must ride. In the event of an accident the guard and driver must not proceed along the train towards each other for the purpose of ascertaining the extent of the accident, but must immediately set off in opposite directions to protect the obstruction, to warn approaching drivers to stop, and to raise the alarm either by telephone or by going to a signalbox. The signalman will then inform the Area Operations Centre or Regional Control, which will call the fire brigade and notify the CEGB Alert Centre. The police, both British Transport and County, will also be called out, together with the railway breakdown service.

The CEGB Alert Centre is manned round the clock and would call out a Flask Emergency Team, supplemented if necessary by specialist advisers, and would also give advice on action to be taken in the meantime. Helicopters would be used where appropriate to enable the Flask Emergency Team to reach the scene of the accident with the least possible delay. If there was any suspicion of radiation leakage the police would arrange any necessary evacuation, but this is extremely unlikely as the Flask Emergency Team would have more than sufficient time to take remedial steps. To sum up, therefore, a train conveying a nuclear flask is very unlikely to have an accident in which the flask itself is directly involved; the flask itself is unlikely in the extreme to be dangerously damaged, and finally if it is, the Flask Emergency Team would have time to take remedial action. The danger area would be no more than a 50yd radius from the flask. Frequent exercises are held with the CEGB and the emergency services in order to test the emergency procedures.

Most railwaymen are more concerned with the dangers arising from the carriage of other commodities, such as hydrocyanic acid (hydrogen cyanide), known as HCN for short. This normally travels in block trainloads of tank wagons from Grangemouth, near Falkirk, to the ICI works at Haverton Hill, near Stockton-on-Tees. HCN is a liquid which is extremely poisonous by inhalation, by ingestion and by contact with the skin. It is also highly flammable and the vapour can form an explosive mixture with air. The tank wagons have additional protection at the sides and ends to minimise the damage in the event of a collision, and the tank barrels are painted white with a horizontal orange band round the barrel.

As with nuclear flasks, these trains convey a brakevan at the rear in which a guard must ride, and in the event of an accident the driver and guard must not proceed towards each other to see if the other line is obstructed but must immediately set off in opposite directions to raise the alarm and seek assistance. This instruction is designed to avoid the traincrew from having to pass near any tanks which may be leaking. Signalmen are aware of any train conveying HCN, because such trains are signalled by a special 'Is line clear?' bell signal 2-1-7. In power signalbox areas the train is known by its four-character identification code. Even when the tanks are empty they are considered to be dangerous because of the vapour they contain.

One of these trains was derailed near Ferryhill on 9 December 1975. The police and the fire services were called out, together with a specialist team from ICI at Haverton Hill. As it was not known initially how serious the leakage was the police decided to evacuate several nearby streets as a precaution. It turned out to have been unnecessary, but it was a sensible measure. The derailment was caused by substandard track, according to the Inspecting Officer, Lt-Col Townsend-Rose, in his Report.

Whilst nuclear flasks and HCN are relatively new traffics, the railways have been carrying explosives almost since they were first built. The regulations and instructions designed to ensure that explosives are carried safely have therefore been developed over a long period of time. Enormous quantities of explosives were carried safely during World War 2, with only two exceptions — the explosion at Soham in 1944, described in Chapter 1, and the

Above:
Ex-Midland Class 3F 0-6-0 No 43579, the engine involved in the Bootle explosion in 1945, is seen trundling a trainload of Barrow Ironworks empty coke hoppers through the cutting near Calverley & Rodley on 16 May 1951. *Leslie Overend*

Left:
Sister engine No 43585 is seen resting between duties outside Hellifield shed, on 29 June 1961. These simple, sturdy machines had a very long life. *G. W. Morrison*

Below left:
The gigantic crater at Bootle, after a wagon of depth-charges blew up on 22 March 1945. The first five wagons of the train are standing beyond the crater. This photograph was taken by a local railway inspector and may be the only one in existence of this disaster. *Inspector Redman, per Norman Stubbs Collection*

explosion of a wagon of depth charges at Bootle. Every 1,000-bomber raid needed eight complete trainloads of bombs, to say nothing of 28 trains of petrol.

The story of the Bootle explosion illustrates yet again the courage of traincrews when faced with a sudden emergency. Driver Goodall and Fireman Stubbs booked on duty to work the 5.55pm freight train from Workington to Carnforth on 22 March 1945. They had 58 wagons, including, next to the engine, seven wagons of 'government traffic' from the ammunition depot at nearby Buckhill, labelled 'Dangerous'. Their engine was an old Midland Class 3F No 3579. They were good engines for their size, but when worked hard they inevitably threw out sparks from the chimney. When passing through Bootle the fireman noticed the reflection of flames from the station buildings and when he looked back he saw to his horror that one of the ammunition wagons, the sixth from the engine, was burning furiously. The driver gradually brought the loose-coupled train to a stand and the fireman jumped off just before it did so. He quickly threw the coupling off behind the blazing wagon, despite the imminent danger, then ran back to the engine. Immediately the driver drew ahead with the blazing wagon then stopped again. The risk of a tremendous explosion was increasing with every second that passed. The fireman jumped down again and very courageously approached the blazing wagon, despite the great heat and the obvious danger that it might explode at any moment, blowing itself and him to smithereens. He managed to uncouple the blazing wagon and despite a natural inclination to put as much distance as possible between himself and the wagon he still had the presence of mind to apply its handbrake, lest it should follow them down the gradient — a nightmarish thought. Back to the engine he went again, heart pounding both from his exertions and from apprehension, then the driver took the remaining five wagons forward to what he thought was a safe distance. The fireman then considered his next duty, as though he had not done enough already. He knew that the 9.20pm passenger train from Barrow was due and he knew that he had to stop it before it reached the danger area. His devotion to the job saved his life. He grabbed the detonator case (detonators are small explosive devices which are intended to be fixed to the rail head in case of emergency and are exploded by the wheels of a locomotive passing over them, which alerts the driver and warns him to stop) and stuffed his pockets with them. Taking a lamp from the engine he ran forward along the line to warn the approaching train.

The next thing he knew was when he recovered consciousness, to find himself lying by the side of the track, temporarily deafened. A huge cloud of debris blotted out the moon. The blazing wagon had exploded, and the depth charges had blown a crater 60ft across and 45ft deep. The fireman returned to what remained of the engine to find that his driver had been blown to pieces, but he still remembered that he must stop the passenger train. Finding that the engine was still moveable he drove it forward to the next signalbox, at Silecroft, keeping a sharp lookout for any sign of the passenger train. To his relief he found it standing safely in the station at Silecroft. The signalman had kept it there, having received the 'Stop and examine train' bell signal from the signalman at Bootle, who had seen the wagon on fire.

It is pleasing to be able to record that Fireman Stubbs received the George Medal from King George VI for his outstanding bravery and resourcefulness. He not only lived up to the traditions of the railway service — he enhanced them.

Many years later, there was a rather frightening incident at Howe & Co's Sidings signalbox, near Armathwaite, just south of Carlisle on the line to Settle and Leeds, in 1969. Hot axleboxes were not uncommon on that line, in view of the sustained high speed achieved by freight trains on the long, falling gradients, and the distance which the trains had run since their last examination.

Signalmen were accustomed both to keeping a good lookout, and to detaching defective vehicles without fuss. One night a van containing high explosive shells was detached from a train with an axlebox on fire, but because the fire was thought to have burnt itself out the fire brigade and military authorities were not informed, as they ought to have been. Several hours later the signalman was greatly alarmed to see smoke and flames coming from inside the van, and he sent for the fire brigade. By the time it arrived the van was well alight, and shortly afterwards it exploded. This was the first explosion on the railways since 1945, but it was not the only explosives scare in 1969.

The conveyance by rail in peacetime of military ammunition and explosives is not as uncommon as might be imagined, particularly to NATO forces in Western Europe. On 22 October 1969 a special train left a depot in Hampshire en route to Felixstowe Docks. It consisted of 27 standard covered vans of 10ft wheelbase and conveyed 117 tons, mainly ammunition. The train left Temple Mills during the late evening, hauled by a Class 37 diesel-electric locomotive, and set off on the last leg of its journey. As the train was passing through Chelmsford the signalman saw sparks coming from it, and he realised straightaway that something was wrong. Almost immediately he heard the noise of a derailment, so he put all his signals to Danger and sent the 'Obstruction Danger' bell signal to the signalboxes at each side — Witham and Ingatestone. Luckily there was no train approaching from the opposite direction.

On the locomotive the driver had been running his train at about 45mph, the maximum speed allowed for 10ft wheelbase wagons, and had shut off power on the falling gradient approaching Chelmsford. He was just starting to reapply power as the train passed through the station, when he felt a slight snatch or jerk followed by the feel of the brakes being applied. Suspecting that something was wrong he looked back and saw sparks coming from the train, so he made a full brake application immediately. As soon as the train stopped both he and his secondman jumped down from the locomotive on to the track. After telling his secondman to go forward to protect the train and warn any approaching driver to stop, he himself went back to look at his train. He was quite horrified by what he saw — almost the entire train was derailed and four of the vans lay on their sides. If another train had been approaching and had ploughed into the wrecked vans at speed there is no knowing how the ammunition might have reacted. According to the Army authorities that would have been the most serious risk.

There was no single clearly identifiable cause of the derailment. As was the case with so many of the frequent short-wheelbase vehicle derailments of the time, the cause was a combination of minor imperfections in the track, worn springs and tyres on the wagon, and the speed of the train. The defects in the track and the wagon were all within the prescribed engineering tolerances and the speed of the train was no higher than the permitted maximum of 45mph. Up to 1963 such vehicles had been permitted to travel at up to 60mph, but following a disturbing increase in the number of derailments the limit was reduced to 50mph. Following further derailments the speed limit was reduced to 45mph in 1966. If safety had been the only consideration a speed limit as low as 35mph would have been imposed, but even at 45mph the effect on transit times was disastrous for BR's competitive position. Not only did express freight trains have to travel more slowly, but they had to be shunted out of the way of passenger and parcels trains more frequently. This reduction in speed could hardly have happened at a worse time. The backbone of the railways' overnight express freight services had always been the movement of large numbers of vans of mixed merchandise (known as 'smalls' or 'sundries') between the large goods stations in main centres. Under the Labour Government's 1968 Transport Act, which was genuinely designed to help the railways, the sundries business was handed over to a new body known as National Carriers, part of the National Freight Corporation. This quickly proved itself to be no lover of railways, and with express freight trains limited to 45mph, and of dubious punctuality, National Carriers quickly transferred the sundries business to road. It really had no alternative if it was to survive in the market place. And so the railways' sundries traffic, now carried on behalf of National Carriers, disappeared almost overnight. Some railway managers were glad to see the end of the railways' sundries business. It had long been regarded as a loss-maker, and had been subjected to numerous reorganisations in an attempt to reduce the losses, but which had sometimes resulted in greater inefficiency. The work was often concentrated on fewer depots, which then found that they could not handle the influx of traffic owing to shortages of staff, whilst the recruitment of sufficient numbers of suitable staff was very difficult at this period. Dissatisfied customers took their business away. But without the nightly flow of sundries vans the network of express freight trains between main centres could no longer be supported, and this immediately struck at the railways' competitive position for its full

Left:
Freight train derailments were commonplace in the 1960s, each one resulting in a pile of wreckage, like the one seen here at St Devereux, between Hereford and Abergavenny, after a diesel-hauled train of empty vehicles became derailed in running, on plain track. This was a typical short-wheelbase vehicle mishap, with no specific cause, but where speed, and the condition of both the track and the vehicles all played a part. Derailments of this nature caused great concern to both the railway authorities and Railway Inspectorate alike.
D. H. Cape

wagonload merchandise traffic, which at the time was quite profitable. It quickly ceased to be so — costs increased and transit times worsened. The long, slow decline in wagonload carryings accelerated. It is sad, but ironic, that BR had just produced a goods vehicle that would have knocked spots off the competition — a long-wheelbase two-axle vehicle with modern suspension, capable of travelling safely at up to 75mph with a very substantial payload, and equipped with roller bearings and the air brake. But it was too late. BR was destined to become largely a passenger railway in less than 10 years — one of the most astonishing transformations of the railway scene ever. In 1970 one could still stand at the lineside and see streams of freight trains pass by. By 1980 one could stand at the same lineside and hardly see any on many routes.

However, to return to our story. By the 1970s freight train operation was becoming more and more complicated, and hence potentially unsafe. In the late 1960s a new and very complicated method had been introduced of calculating the loads which could be hauled by different classes of locomotive on freight trains. It was an attempt to ensure firstly that every locomotive was loaded up to its maximum hauling capacity, and secondly that the train had sufficient brake power to enable it to be stopped safely on any falling gradient it might encounter on its route. It required the optimum permutation of:

1. Restrictions on falling gradients on the route concerned.
2. The hauling and braking characteristics of the locomotive.
3. The weight of wagons to be conveyed.
4. The power brake force of those wagons.
5. A factor representing the fact that, ton for ton, it is easier to haul heavily-loaded vehicles than lightly-loaded ones (less friction, less wind resistance).

An alteration in any one factor affected the others, and to arrive at the optimum solution required both concentration and mathematical skill — not matters that were taken into account to any great extent when recruiting new guards or shunters. They were given training, of course, as were existing staff, but not enough. However, BR was so short of

Above:
A 75mph high-capacity van, equipped with roller bearing axleboxes, special suspension, and the airbrake, being loaded with cartons of Kellogg's Corn Flakes. *(Both) BR*

guards and shunters that to have released them for more training would have meant cancelling trains. In those difficult days training was low down the list of priorities.

To add to the staff's problems, new types of train were being introduced such as freightliners and merry-go-round (MGR) coal trains, each with its own book of instructions. The vacuum brake was giving way to the air brake. Then TOPS came on the scene. Entitled in full 'Total Operations Processing System', it was imported from the Southern Pacific Railroad, USA, in 1970 and modified over the next three years to make it suitable for BR. It is a computer-based system which requires a completely new approach to the assembly and preparation of a freight train. Initially it was yet another complication for hard-pressed and short-handed supervisors to have to deal with, although now it has settled down to become an indispensable tool for the more efficient handling of traffic operations. However, in the 1970s it was looked upon with suspicion, as being yet another burden for the long-suffering staff to have to carry. Older staff looked back nostalgically to the 1950s, when freight train operation was carried on in much the same way as it would have been 30, 40 or even 50 years earlier. Now the pace of change had quickened, and was about to exact its price.

On Wednesday 6 August 1975 train No 4O68 set off from Coatbridge, near Glasgow, at 18.05 on its long overnight journey to Southampton. It was a Freightliner train, part of the new railway scene, and consisted of 15 vehicles, with a maximum speed of 75mph. On the first part of its journey it was electrically hauled, and it was well on its way when another train, No 6F52, left the sidings at Runcorn shortly before 22.00 on its journey to the ICI Works at Wallerscote, near Northwich. That train was hauled by a Class 40 diesel-electric locomotive No 40189 and conveyed 20 45-ton tank wagons, each one loaded with 30 tons of caustic soda liquor. The tanks had a maximum speed of 60mph but there was a particular complication that night, inasmuch as eight of the wagons were fitted with the vacuum brake, whilst the remaining 12 wagons had air brakes. The 1970s saw the transition from the vacuum to the air brake, and it had been the practice to equip air-braked wagons with a through vacuum pipe, so that they could run in a vacuum-braked train. The total weight of the train concerned and its locomotive was 1,033 tons and it had a vacuum brake force of 219 tons. The brake force available to the driver was insufficient, and either the load should have been reduced or the train should have been run at a lower speed. Neither was done, nor did the driver clearly understand that

Above and Below:
The scene of devastation at Weaver Junction after the sidelong collision between a freightliner train and a train of tank wagons on 6 August 1975.
(Both) Author's Collection

although his train was running as a fully-braked one, in that the brake pipe was connected up between every wagon, the power brake was only working on eight of the 20 wagons. Thus was the stage set for disaster.
The route of the train of tankers took it on to the West Coast main line at Weaver Junction, 16 miles north of Crewe, via a flyover with a falling gradient to the junction. In the signalbox there the signalman had been warned of the approach of both this train and the Freightliner train. He decided to give precedence to the latter and cleared all his signals for it. The train was approaching the junction at its maximum permitted speed of 75mph, when the driver glanced across at the Runcorn line and was alarmed to see a train approaching the junction on that line with sparks coming from its wheels. He immediately concluded that the tanker train would be unable to stop at the junction signal and would continue into sidelong collision with his own train at the junction. In a split second he decided to try to accelerate out of harm's way, a decision that may well have saved his life, but he was not completely successful, as the locomotive of the tanker train, running away at over 30mph, came into sideways collision with the fifth vehicle of the Freightliner train. It tossed aside the lighter Freightliner vehicles as though they were toys, whilst the heavy tank wagons piled up into each other. Caustic soda liquor began to gush out of the damaged tanks.

The signalman at Weaver Junction was a horrified spectator of all this. He had already cleared his Down main line signals for an express passenger train, the 16.39 from Poole to Liverpool, and when he realised that a collision between the two freight trains was likely he hurriedly put all his signals to Danger. He had a few anxious moments wondering whether he had acted in time to stop the express but luck was with him. The express had had to slow down to 20mph further back for track repairs and was able to stop well clear of the accident, thanks to the signalman's prompt action. If there had been no speed restriction . . . ! The consequences of an express crashing into the wreckage at 70mph with over 100 tons of caustic soda lying around in pools are too awful to contemplate. But accidents are full of 'ifs', and the fates were obviously satisfied with the extent of the existing wreckage.

The main line to Liverpool and the north was blocked for almost a week. The fire service attended and poured on millions of gallons of water to wash away the caustic soda liquor. Specialist teams from ICI also attended. They not only gave advice and provided protective clothing; they also arranged for unspilled caustic soda liquor to be syphoned off and tranferred to empty tankers, and they tipped over 100 tons of sodium bicarbonate to neutralise the 250 tons of spilled liquor, which was causing the water authorities great concern. ICI maintains a number of emergency centres round the country, one of which is at Runcorn, and all tank wagons are labelled with the emergency telephone number. The procedure worked well, but the fact that Runcorn was only a few miles away was helpful.

In the Report into the accident, by Maj Olver, the Inspecting Officer, responsibility for the accident was put on the yard staff and local management at Runcorn, and on the driver and guard of the tanker train. After all, they had made the mistakes or been negligent. Local management had failed to ensure that the yard staff at Runcorn knew what to do and then actually did it. The yard staff had made mistakes in not reducing the load or the speed of the train; the guard had not done his job properly, but he had only been a guard for a year and was inexperienced; and the driver had failed to brake soon enough for the signal at Weaver Junction. This was the measure of blame as apportioned by the Inspecting Officer who took the public inquiry. But was it fair? All the men concerned had transgressed in one way or another. But did management bear no responsibility for introducing complicated systems and for not ensuring that staff were properly trained? Or for not paying sufficiently high wages to enable good quality staff to be recruited and, just as important, retained? It seems a little unfair to have blamed local management and supervisors, because ever since the war they were the people who had borne most of the burden in keeping the railway running despite crippling staff shortages. They have rarely received the credit due to them. And does the government bear no responsibility? It is the government which has created the conditions in which railways have to operate, and which has then made it difficult for them to do so efficiently, by imposing crippling financial burdens and unfairly favouring the competition. And if the railway trade unions have been difficult at times, is it really any wonder?

Turning now to another hazardous commodity, the railways have been carrying petroleum products in tank wagons for many years, almost always in complete safety. Traditionally the vehicles used were tank wagons of 14-ton capacity, not fitted with the automatic power brake, and they were quite satisfactory when hauled by steam engines with their plentiful brake power, and at the low speeds which applied in those days. However, in the more competitive conditions after the 1953 Transport Act there was a general trend not only to improve payloads but also to enable tank wagons to run at higher speeds by equipping them with power brakes. The late 1950s saw the introduction of the 35-ton gross tank wagon, which was quickly developed to allow 40 tons to be carried by 1961, 45 tons by 1965 and finally 50 tons, which represents the absolute maximum that the track can bear on two axles. The next logical step was the bogie tank — the 90 tonner in 1965, then the now very familiar 100-ton tank wagon, which first appeared in 1967. One of BR's successes of the period was the signing of long-term contracts with the oil companies for the carriage of their products by rail in 100-ton tank wagons, built privately and owned by the oil companies, or leased by them. The contracts were very keenly priced, but at least they gave BR a guaranteed traffic which has lasted to the present day, and should now be more profitable to BR with the trains being operated

Below:
A traditional oil train, headed by Class K1 2-6-0 No 62001, between Darlington and Aycliffe in August 1964. Note the two barrier wagons, intended to reduce the fire risk.
John E. Hoggarth

1

2

3

4

Stages in two-axle tank wagon design:

1. **Shell-Mex Ltd 14-ton capacity, registered in 1929. Oil axleboxes, unbraked.** *Ian Allan Library*
2. **National Benzole Ltd 14-ton capacity, registered in 1954. Oil axleboxes, unbraked. One star (ie could be conveyed in partly-fitted trains).** *Author*
3. **Esso Petroleum Co Ltd 22-ton capacity, registered in 1957. Roller bearing axleboxes, vacuum-braked, screw couplings. Two stars (ie could be conveyed on express freight trains).** *Charles Roberts & Co*
4. **Esso Petroleum Co Ltd 45 tons gross laden weight, 1965.** *Esso*

Below:
The final development — the 100-ton tanker, put into service in 1967. Many thousands are in use today. *Ian Allan Library*

wherever possible by just the driver — with no secondman and no guard.

BR has carried millions of tons of petroleum products under these contracts with a high degree of safety, and with only occasional accidents to mar the record. Derailments are not unknown, partly owing to the stresses which 25-ton axleloads impose on the track, but serious fires are uncommon. One of the early incidents of fire took place on New Year's Day 1969 at Crich Junction, near Ambergate, on the main line from St Pancras to Sheffield via Derby. The train concerned was No 4M66, the 01.17 Teesport Refinery to Washwood Heath, Birmingham, and consisted of 10 100-ton tank wagons owned by Shell Mex & BP Ltd, and hauled by a Type 4 diesel-electric locomotive. As the train came out of Wingfield Tunnel on the approach to Crich Junction at about 08.15 the driver noticed a glow in the cutting and, looking back, he saw that the train was on fire. Considerably alarmed, and knowing the volatile nature of the contents of the tanks (Light Distillate Feedstock, a highly inflammable light oil used at the time by gas boards for gas production), he immediately made an emergency stop. Driver and guard both descended on to the track and the guard called to a man in a factory alongside to telephone for the fire brigade. The man lost no time in doing so, and the fire services responded promptly, the first appliances arriving at 08.30. Spilt oil was burning on and around the seventh and ninth tanks, on both of which the forward loading hatches were open. Flames were shooting from these hatches to a height of 10ft.

The traincrew, reacting with the bravery which is customary in such circumstances, divided the train behind the sixth tank and drew the front portion clear. Meanwhile the firemen were directing jets of water on to the blazing tanks to keep them cool, and managed to extinguish the flames which were shooting from the loading hatches, by smothering them with foam. Whilst the burning tanks may have looked as though they might blow up at any moment, there is much less risk of that happening when a tank is full than when it is nearly empty, with space for an explosive mixture of air and oil vapour to form, but the traincrew did not know that at the time, and it is possible that the firemen did not know it either. In the event, the fires were extinguished without too much delay.

The cause of the fire was quite straightforward. The loading hatches on the seventh and ninth tanks had not been secured at Teesport after loading had been completed. Then, as the train was braking heavily from almost full speed for a signal stop at Crich Junction, because the line ahead was not clear, oil surged forward in the tanks and some escaped through the unsecured hatches, to become

Below:
The scene at Blyton, Lincolnshire, on the line between Gainsborough and Northorpe, after the 11.05 from Preston to Lindsey Oil Refinery became derailed on 18 September 1981. These two-axle tank wagons are prone to derailment when running empty at maximum permitted speed on track with minor imperfections. *John M. Capes*

ignited by sparks from the brake blocks. Subsequently, modifications were made to the hatches, and a certificate was introduced to be handed over to BR at the starting point, confirming that all hatches were closed and secured.

A rather more serious accident occurred three years later on 8 May 1972 at Chester General station, just before 21.00. There were, luckily, very few people about on that part of the station, and the refreshment room on Platforms 10/13, which was badly damaged in the crash, was empty apart from the staff. The train concerned was No 8D66, the 19.31 Ellesmere Port to Mold Junction (between Chester and Rhyl) and was marshalled as follows:

Class 24 diesel-electric locomotive No 5028
Brakevan, piped only
Esso 35-ton tank wagon, vacuum-braked, containing kerosene
Esso 45-ton tank wagon, vacuum-braked, containing petrol
Three Esso 35-ton tank wagons, vacuum-braked, containing gas oil.
31 other wagons and brakevan.

The total weight of the train and locomotive was 981 tons.

Approaching Chester station from the Warrington direction there is a steep falling gradient of 1 in 100 for just over a mile. When train 8D66 approached the top of this gradient, prior to descending to Chester, it was only travelling at about 15mph, then the driver closed the power controller and applied the locomotive's air brake to gather together the loose-coupled train (ie to let all the wagons buffer up to each other to avoid shocks and snatches during braking). As he approached the station he could see that the Outer Home signal for Chester No 1 signalbox was at Danger, and he made a full brake application. To his consternation it had no effect. The train ran on out of control, with the driver sounding a series of blasts on the locomotive's horn; past the Inner Home signal, then past No 1 signalbox and No 2 signalbox. The driver could see that the points were set for No 11 bay platform and as there was nothing else he could do he jumped out on to the platform with the train still travelling at 20mph. There was a diesel multiple-unit standing at the buffer stops. The locomotive hit it head on and completely demolished the first coach. The second coach was hurled on to the platform against the refreshment room wall. Luckily, both coaches were empty. As the DMU had taken the brunt of the impact, most of the force of the collision was spent and only the first three tanks were derailed. However, fire — fed from the ruptured fuel tanks of the DMU and the locomotive — broke out at once and threatened to engulf the tank wagons.

The alarm was raised immediately by the station staff, and three fire appliances arrived at the station within 2min. They concentrated at first on trying to keep cool the three tank wagons by spraying jets of water on them, the remainder of the train having been uncoupled and drawn away; but the fire grew in intensity. Foam was applied to subdue the ground fires but by this time petrol and kerosene were leaking out of the tank wagons, adding to the fierceness of the fire which had by now engulfed some DMUs standing in adjacent platforms. The dangerous stage of the fire was now being reached. Could the firemen damp down the flames before the tank wagon bodies split at the seams, leading to a serious explosion with blazing petrol being hurled in all directions? Railway officers and fire chiefs were both aware that such a thing had already happened in Canada and the USA and were apprehensive that it was about to happen here. The petrol in the second tank wagon was already boiling and was being forced out of the pressure relief valve, where it ignited like a flamethrower. With great courage the firemen pressed on with their task, and to everyone's intense relief were finally successful in overcoming the fire.

The cause of the accident was exasperatingly simple. The five tank wagons next to the locomotive were all equipped with the power brake and the brake pipes should have been coupled up by the guard so that the driver could safely control his train on the falling gradient into Chester. The guard overlooked the need to do so. He was relatively inexperienced, having been a guard for less than a year, but no such excuse can be offered for the driver, who had been in the grade for 12 years. He failed to ensure that the brakes were tested before the journey started, an oversight that is all the more astonishing when one realises how vulnerable a driver is in his driving cab in the event of a head-on collision of the sort that one might expect on a runaway train. Were the complexities of the relatively new freight train loads and brake power calculation system a factor in the reckoning, which might have been put right by more thorough training, or was it just carelessness, which no amount of training could have overcome? It was probably both. The Inspecting Officer, Maj Olver, who held a Public Inquiry into the accident, records in his report that he had been assured that checks had been carried out throughout BR to ensure that all drivers had received adequate training in the freight train loading scheme, and that where necessary additional training had been given. He was misled on both counts. Drivers did not receive adequate training in the scheme either before the Chester accident or after it. Some were not greatly interested — they had always relied upon the guard to form his train correctly, and they continued to do so. Very few drivers actually checked the details of load and brake power that the guard gave them, to see that it was within the limits for the route they were to work over. Old habits die hard, and nowhere more so than on railways.

The Warrington area is one that is no stranger to railway accidents, and we have already met one at Weaver Junction. Indeed, Chester is less than 20 miles away. During the early 1980s there were no fewer than 22 accidents in the Warrington area, eight of which involved the carriage of dangerous goods. One of the worst occurred at 07.10 on 3 March 1983. The train concerned was No 6Z97, a special from the Shell Oil Refinery at Stanlow, near Ellesmere Port, to Bishopbriggs, Glasgow. It consisted of 14 45-ton and 100-ton tank wagons loaded with gas oil, and an empty van which was marshalled immediately behind the locomotive (a Class 47 diesel-electric) to act as a 'reach' wagon so that the tankers could be shunted into the Bishopbriggs Oil Terminal without the locomotive itself having to enter the siding (a fire precaution). The train was air-braked throughout, and had a maximum permitted speed of 60mph.

The train approached Acton Grange Junction on the approach to Warrington from the Helsby line, running at about 40mph, and was signalled across the junction on to the Down West Coast main line. Just as the train approached the signal the driver felt a snatch, and he looked back down the train to see if anything was amiss. It certainly was. His train was derailed and on fire. When the wagons came to rest a major fire broke out engulfing all the wagons in the middle of the train. Burning oil ran down the Up side embankment and one of the 100-ton tankers rolled to the foot of the embankment.

The guard was riding in the front cab with the driver, as often used to happen. It was against the Rules but the Authorities largely turned a blind eye to the practice. It was against the Rules because, when the use of brakevans on fully-braked trains was dispensed with in the 1960s, it was thought that if the guard were in the rear cab he could keep

ESSO
10 11

Above left and left:
Chester General station, after a freight train ran away approaching Chester and was diverted into bay platform No 11. The tank wagons caught fire, to add to the devastation. *Author's Collection*

Above:
The same location some years later, with a DMU waiting in bay platform No 11 on the left. The fire-damaged part of the station roof was removed. This photograph was taken on 1 September 1978. *Geoff Pinder*

an eye on his train just as well as he could from a brakevan, and raise the alarm if he saw anything wrong, for example a hot axlebox or a derailed wagon. The guard reported the derailment and fire to the signalman at Warrington power signalbox from a nearby railway telephone and the area supervisor telephoned the fire brigade. However, the fire service had already received a '999' call from a local resident and had already despatched four pumping appliances, a foam tender, an emergency tender and a Land Rover. Six more appliances were called, and later a further five. Clouds of dense black smoke blanketed the area. At first the firemen attacked the fire from the rear of the train to prevent those wagons not on fire from being engulfed, but they were driven back by a serious explosion, which they originally thought to have been a BLEVE, a Boiling Liquid Expanding Vapour Explosion, such as had been experienced in North America. It was later thought to have been due to the sudden release of inflammable vapour from a pressure relief valve, resulting in a fireball.

The fire was finally under control at 09.42. The fire service had responded very promptly to the '999' call and within 8min the initial fleet of appliances was already on site. Reading through the reports of the fires mentioned in this chapter one cannot fail to be impressed by the speed of the fire service's response; by its courage in tackling dangerous fires and by its skill in dealing with them. The speed of response is undoubtedly helped by its foreknowledge of the contents of the tanks. All hazardous substances have a United Nations Substance Identification number of four digits — for example anhydrous ammonia is 1005. These numbers are shown on special labels on the tanks, but under the BR TOPS system of traffic reporting and control the description of all dangerous goods on a train is entered into a computer before the train starts its journey, and details can readily be ascertained by a simple computer enquiry process, available both in local area offices and also at the Regional Control Office. Details are also shown on the Train List carried by the traincrew. Fire services know whom they should approach on BR for such information, and this is far more satisfactory than having individual firemen asking questions of BR employees on site, who may not know the correct answer and may unwittingly give misleading information.

The TOPS computerised system contains all the requirements for the correct marshalling and conveyance of dangerous goods. For example, it will only allow different types of dangerous goods to be conveyed on the same train if this is specifically provided for in the Regulations, and it will check that the marshalling of such traffic in the train is correct, and that any necessary barrier wagons have been provided. The instructions to the staff are contained in a publication known to railwaymen as the 'Pink Pages', because they are printed on pink paper in the Working Manual.

According to Lt-Col Townsend-Rose, who held a Public Inquiry, the cause of the Warrington derailment was the

poor condition of the track. It had recently been relaid on a bed of new deep ballast, but some of the rail joints had become badly dipped, causing the empty van between the locomotive and the tanks to become derailed. It then ran on in derailed condition for several hundred yards before striking the points and crossings at Acton Grange Junction, whereupon it led almost the whole train into derailment. If the guard had been riding in the rear cab of the locomotive as he was supposed to, he could hardly have failed to see the van become derailed. He would then have had time to take action himself to have the train stopped. He could have done one of three things:

1. Apply the emergency brake in the rear cab (against the Rules but probably very sensible in the circumstances). The guard need not have made a full brake application himself but just enough to have drawn the driver's attention to the emergency, so that the driver could use his braking skills to bring the train safely to a stand without causing the remainder of the train to pile up into a general derailment.

2. He could have gone through the engine compartment of the locomotive to the front cab, and warned the driver.

3. He could have given an unofficial code-ring on the firebell test button, which is one of those irregular but sensible practices used by traincrews to solve a problem in circumstances where railway management has failed to provide a solution. BR could quite easily have provided a buzzer connecting the two cabs, to be used in case of emergency, but chose not to do so.

However, the question of which locomotive cab a guard should ride in is now largely historical. Today most freight trains are worked without guards, and in any case the grade of guard has undergone a change. Where there is still a guard on a freight train he is likely to be called a trainman and can elect to enter the line of promotion to driver. His place now is in the front cab.

This accident is one of the first which we have discussed where the poor condition of the track was the primary cause. In the next chapter we will examine this question in more detail.

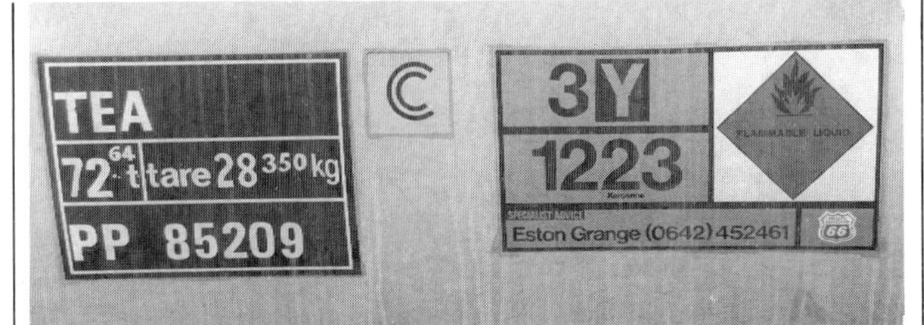

Above left:
Class 47 diesel-electric No 47163 leaving Redhill, Southern Region, with a train of Mobil two-axle tank wagons on 17 May 1980. *Les Bertram*

Below left:
On 8 April 1981, whilst negotiating a facing crossover at Hadfield on the former LNER electrified line from Manchester to Sheffield, five bogie tank wagons loaded with anhydrous ammonia became derailed, and one turned over on to its side. Because of the nature of the load a full alert, involving the emergency services, was called, but fortunately there was no escape of any of the liquefied gas. *David Maxey*

Above and Centre right:
Information panels on tank wagons:
Left-hand. TEA = Tank Type E, air-braked.
72t = carrying capacity
28t = tare weight
PP 85209 = fleet number
Right-hand — Hazard identification panel.
3YE is the Hazchem code for the information of the emergency services. 3 = foam fire-fighting equipment, Y = danger of violent reaction or explosion; use breathing apparatus for fire only. E = evacuation of people from the neighbourhood should be considered.
1223 is the UN No for kerosene; 1270 is the UN No for petroleum fuel.
Specialist advice can be obtained from the address given.
Author

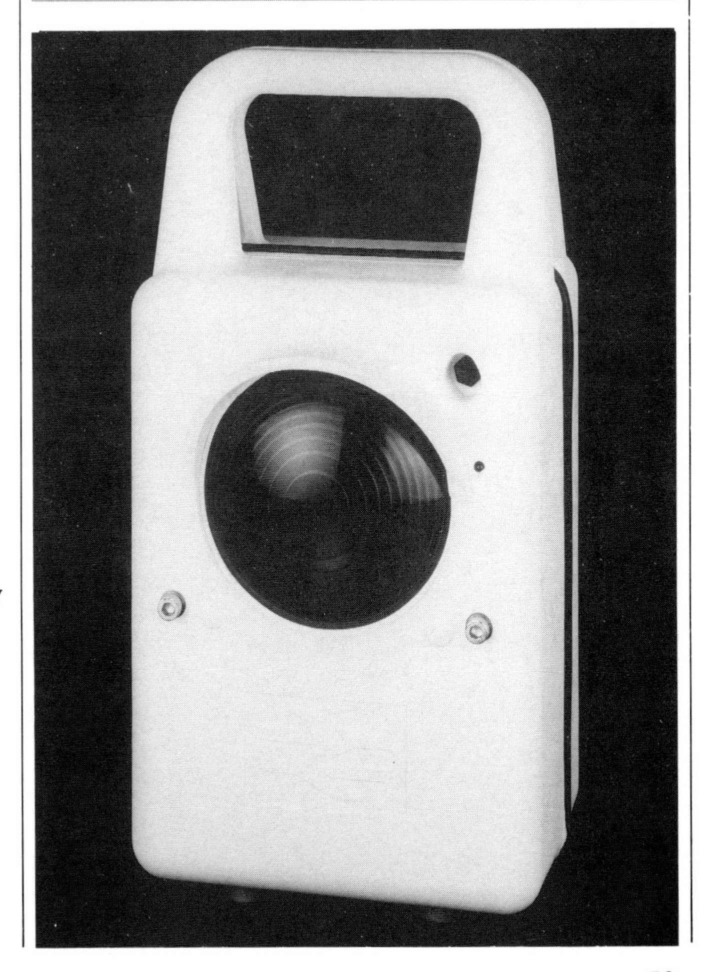

Right:
Dorman Traffic Products Ltd red flashing tail lamp, suitable for use on any type of wagon. The battery needs changing only once a year, and the light source is a light-emitting diode.
Dorman Traffic Products

4
Buckled Track Derailments

When schoolteachers were introducing a new class to the subject of physics, one of the early lessons was sure to be devoted to the expansion of metals, and it became imprinted upon every student's mind that the purpose of the small gap at the end of each piece of rail was to allow for the expansion of the rail in hot weather. If the gap was not there, it was explained, the forces of expansion in the rail were so great that they would cause the track to distort — this distortion being known as a buckle (one wonders how today's schoolteachers explain away continuous-welded track, but that will be dealt with later in this chapter).

It is not uncommon to have fine hot days in the spring, and 18 May 1948 was just such a day. Indeed, in the afternoon the temperature reached 75°F. The 11.45am express from London St Pancras to Bradford Forster Square was loaded up to 12 coaches that day, being Whit Tuesday, and was therefore double-headed with two '5XP' 'Jubilee' class 4-6-0s, Nos 5605 *Cyprus* and 5609 *Gilbert and Ellice Islands*. As there was also a relief train running, the parent train was not heavily loaded with passengers, and when it left Sheffield on its journey north there were fewer than 200 of them. Perhaps if they had known what was in store, some of them would have elected to travel in the relief train. Such trains, however, were never as popular as the parent trains — mainly because they usually had no restaurant car and were formed of older coaches.

The line between Sheffield and Leeds by the former Midland route via Cudworth would never have won any prizes in a competition for Britain's most scenic railway, but it would certainly have been among the contenders in a 'Most collieries per mile' contest. As a result the route suffered severely from colliery subsidence, although the Civil Engineer had managed to maintain the overall line speed at 75mph, which was very creditable in the circumstances. However, the maintenance of the track was a great problem, not helped by frequent changes of staff. Platelayers' wages were very low, and although there was plenty of Sunday work, not many people were prepared to work at weekends if they could earn as much by working a five-day week in industry. This problem of staff shortage, and frequent changes resulting in an inexperienced workforce, placed a great strain and responsibility on supervisors and junior managers alike.

Near Wath Road Junction, about five miles north of Rotherham, the problem of subsidence was dealt with by the use of large quantities of ash to maintain the line as level as possible, but the permanent way was not up to the standards demanded by a high speed main line. Furthermore, insufficient attention had been paid to the oiling of the fishplates, which joined the rails together at their ends. If the bolts which held the fishplates to the rails were too tight, and if there were no oil between the fishplates and the rail, a certain amount of resistance to the forces of expansion would be created. If the rail could not expand lengthways it would eventually do so sideways in the form of a buckle, especially if there was little resistance from the ballast. Dry ashes gave very little resistance.

1

2

The 'Jubilees' involved in the Wath Road Junction derailment on 18 May 1948, seen in happier times:

1. No 45605 *Cyprus* (the pilot engine on 18 May 1948), shedded at Leeds Holbeck, heads north from Leeds City with the 4.55pm to Morecambe Promenade, the 'Residential Express'. The girder bridge in the background carried the lines to Leeds Central station. *Eric Treacy/ Millbrook House Collection*
2. No 45609 *Gilbert and Ellice Islands* in repose at its home shed, Sheffield Millhouses, on 11 April 1955. *D. Marriott*
3. No 5609 is seen in its earlier form in LMS days, with domeless boiler and straight-sided tender. *L&GRP, courtesy David & Charles (814)*

3

Right:
'Royal Scot' Class 4-6-0 No 46133 *The Green Howards* passes Wath on Dearne signalbox and Wath Main Colliery on 20 June 1959 with the 10.30am Bradford Forster Square to St Pancras, and approaches the site of the derailment at Wath Road Junction on 18 May 1948. *D. Hellewell*

Below right:
Not a picture for steam buffs, but enough to make present-day civil engineers green with envy, not to mention drivers. Such neat and tidy permanent way has not been seen for many years. There is not a particle of ballast visible on any of the sleepers, and the neatness of the cess in the 10ft way is astonishing, even if it were specially done for the photograph, which was taken on 15 June 1949 to show the first standard 109lb flat-bottom rail in the North Eastern Region at Alne, on the East Coast main line 10 miles north of York. Note also the two-hole fishplates on the far lines. *BR*

At 3.29pm the St Pancras to Bradford express left Sheffield on time for its nonstop run to Leeds City. After passing through Rotherham Masborough speed built up to 60/65mph then, near Wath Road Junction, the driver on No 5605, the pilot engine, was horrified to see a pronounced kink to the left on the track ahead of him. There was no time for him to do anything about it, other than shout a hurried warning to his fireman, and both men hung on to their engine for dear life. They had no idea what would happen when the engine hit that awful kink but they were running on a 30ft high embankment and they feared for their lives. The engine gave a tremendous lurch, there was the squeal of steel tyres on the rails, and the footplatemen felt their engine drop on to the sleepers. However, they were lucky. The engine ran forward as they hung on grimly, and eventually came to a stand, still upright. In the train behind them everything was suddenly chaotic. One moment complete normality — the next moment the train engine No 5609 hit the kink and turned over on to its side. The first five coaches all turned sideways across the track, almost side by side with each other, but by absorbing the train's momentum in this way they did not telescope into one another. Nonetheless, seven passengers and the driver of the train engine lost their lives, whilst 33 passengers and a dining car attendant were detained in hospital. It was remarkable that the death toll was not much higher. When looking at the pile of wreckage, one wonders how anyone could have survived. The first and second coaches were on their sides and the body of the fourth coach had been torn from its underframe.

The relief express had passed over the same spot only 8min beforehand. Its driver saw nothing, but the guard, who was riding in the last coach, felt a lurch. He later described it as severe but it did not alarm him enough to cause him to stop the train with his emergency brake and raise the alarm. The line would then have been examined before any more trains were allowed to pass over it at speed. Lurches on the track are part and parcel of every railway journey. Some are more severe than others but it is not an easy matter for a guard to decide at what point a lurch becomes so bad that the train should be stopped and the alarm raised. It is a matter of individual judgement and experience, and some guards may fear that they will be reprimanded for stopping their trains unnecessarily if no cause for the lurch can be found. Guards, and drivers too, are reluctant to stop their trains from full speed unless the lurch is so severe, or is so far out of the ordinary, as to cause real alarm. It is clear, however, that the guard's

failure to report the lurch preyed on his mind. On 30 July he committed suicide by coal gas poisoning, the verdict at the inquest being that 'the balance of his mind was disturbed'. Drivers and guards carry heavy responsibilities for other people's lives, which are not always recognised, and certainly not in the rates of pay of the time. These tended to reflect the security of tenure which a job on the railway afforded, an important factor in prewar days, but largely irrelevant in the booming postwar labour market.

By 1948 British Railways was beginning to change over from bullhead rail supported in chairs and held with wooden or spring-steel keys, to flatbottom rail standing on baseplates and secured directly to the sleepers by spring-steel spikes. Trials had begun as early as 1936, and by 1948, 260 miles had been laid by the former companies. The new Railway Executive, formed only at the beginning of 1948 following nationalisation, decided almost at once that flatbottom rail would be the future standard. The new rails, weighing 109lb/yd, were considered to be much stronger than the 95lb bullhead rails and more suitable for higher speeds and heavier axleloads. Thenceforth, flatbottom rail became increasingly common, but the mixture of the two was to cause problems.

On 8 August 1953 it was a particularly warm, sunny day in the Scottish lowlands. The Down 'Royal Scot' that day consisted of 13 coaches, hauled by Class 8P Pacific No 46231 *Duchess of Atholl*, and was coasting down easily

Left:
Class 8P Pacific No 46231 *Duchess of Atholl* pulls out of Carlisle with the Down 'Royal Scot'. This was the engine involved in the Abington derailment in 1953. *Ian Allan Library*

Below:
***Duchess of Atholl* in LMS days, in its original form without smoke deflectors.** *Wethersett Collection/ Ian Allan Library*

from Beattock when it became derailed near Abington. The engine and first six coaches passed safely, then a buckle developed underneath the train and the last seven coaches became derailed. The damage to the train was remarkably slight and there were no serious injuries. The train was formed throughout with the new BR standard Mk 1 coaches and it is probable that the buckeye couplings fitted to these coaches held them together and in line, whereas in the Wath Road Junction derailment the coaches had all been of the former LMS pattern with screw couplings.

The initial derailment at Abington occurred on bullhead track, but only 32yd beyond the end of a section of 113lb flatbottom rail. Owing to a lack of appreciation of the situation, action had not been taken to remedy the 'creep' of the heavier and stronger flatbottom rails against the lighter and weaker bullhead section, and this, coupled with the strong expansive forces developing during the hot afternoon, caused undue stresses to be set up, which became released in the form of a buckle as the express passed. There had already been a number of incidents of this nature, and indeed they continue to occur even now where different types of track join each other.

Rail creep, which has been mentioned, is a phenomenon which occurs when trains pass over a length of track and cause it to move fractionally lengthways. From time to time, therefore, the rails have to be pulled back to avoid undue stresses developing. In the worst places special anti-creep fittings, known as rail anchors, are attached to the rails next to a chair or baseplate to try to minimise the problem but they are only partially successful.

By the late 1960s the use of flatbottom rail on main lines had become commonplace, and the practice had developed of welding the ends together to form one continuous rail. The advantages of doing this are many:

Above:
An illustration of the flexibility of long-welded rails, seen at Motherwell. *BR*

1. It eliminates joints in the rails, which have always proved troublesome. Rail-ends are a source of weakness and prone to cracks radiating from the bolt holes. If not detected, breakage of the rail may ensue. Many derailments have resulted from this cause, as we shall see in the next chapter.

2. The track is less firm vertically at a joint, and this gives rise to pressures on the track formation and bed whenever a train passes over. In wet conditions it may even give rise to clay slurry being pumped to the surface by the frequent downwards pressure and subsequent release as the wheels of a train pass over. Such places are known as 'wet spots', and if not treated can lead to an empty space or void beneath the sleeper, leading to considerable stresses in the rail ends and possible breakage. The dip in the rail level at a bad joint as a train passes over it can lead to derailment.

3. Less maintenance is needed when there are no joints, for example there is no need to pull rails back to equalise expansion gaps, no oiling of fishplates, no checking the tightness of fishplate bolts. Apart from the obvious economy in manpower it helps to overcome the problem of recruitment and staff shortage.

4. Continuously welded rail (CWR) is stronger than jointed track, more suitable for high speeds and heavy axleloads.

5. Continuously welded rail gives a smoother, quieter ride.

However, it must not be thought that all these advantages are achieved without other problems arising. We are now back to our schoolteacher and the physics class. If there has to be a gap every 60ft to allow for expansion, how big does the gap have to be at the end of a piece of CWR half a mile long? Schoolboys might attempt to answer that, by working out how many 60ft rails there are in half a mile, then multiplying the result by a quarter of an inch. The end product would be a gap of nearly a foot, which no train could leap safely even at 125mph. The fact is that all the expansive forces are contained in the rail itself, except for short portions at the ends, which have special joints. To achieve this it is necessary for the stresses to be contained in the track, and this requires:

1. A greater depth of ballast under the sleepers.
2. A full ballast section up to the tops of the sleepers and extending sideways well beyond the sleeper ends.
3. Extra ballast being placed beyond the sleeper ends, creating a ballast 'shoulder'.
4. The use of tight-gripping rail fastenings.
5. Ensuring that the rails will be free from stress in the mid-temperature range.

Stressing is a technique which is applied to track when it is laid, and is intended to produce an absence of stress at a rail temperature of 27°C/81°F. When track is laid at a rail temperature below 27°C it will have shortened in length through natural contraction, and must be stretched to the length it would have been at 27°C. This stretching is done by hydraulic rams, and when the rail has been stretched to the required length it is welded to the adjacent rail. It is now under tension in a stressed condition and can safely contain the compressive forces of expansion up to a rail temperature of 27°C, at which temperature it will be stress-free. It should be noted that rail temperatures can be considerably higher than air temperatures — car drivers will know how hot the roof of a standing car can become when a bright sun is beating down on it.

By 1968, there were 4,000 miles of CWR and considerable experience had been gained of handling the problems involved, but two accidents that year showed that things could still go wrong. On 12 June, a fine, dry day, train No 3E46 the 12.40 Freightliner from Ardwick, Manchester, to Harwich Parkeston Quay, consisting of 15 wagons, became derailed on buckled track when running on the Up fast line at speed just before reaching Berkhamsted station. The area had been relaid the previous December but had not been stressed. The actual work to be carried out had consisted of removing a redundant crossover, replacing it with new plain track, and stressing it. The work was planned to commence at 04.00 on Sunday morning, the quietest time of the week for closing the line, and needed two special cranes to work under the overhead electric wires. The works train was several hours late in arriving on site (not an uncommon occurrence when guards failed to turn up for duty, for example, and the source of innumerable acrimonious disputes between the operating and engineering departments) and as a result the work could not be completed in time. The general manager of the day was fed up with delays to the busy Sunday evening expresses caused by engineering work overrunning, and had laid it down that such work must end on time, being cut short if necessary. The problems that this caused to engineers can be imagined, especially if the cause was not of their making, but suffice it to say that the stressing work on the day was postponed. It was programmed to be done the following May but was somehow overlooked. And so the track eventually buckled and a train was derailed, although fortunately not an express passenger train.

The other derailment took place at Auchencastle on the descent from Beattock Summit, two days later on 14 June 1968. It was another hot and sunny day and the train, another Freightliner, was running down the bank at the maximum allowed speed of 75mph when the rear portion became derailed as the track buckled beneath it. The track had been relaid in 1965 and had been realigned and stressed in June 1967. Significantly, in the weeks preceding the derailment 170 sleepers had been changed, then on Sunday 9 June the section of line had been mechanically tamped by a new Plasser Duomatic lining and tamping machine (tamping is a process in which ballast is repacked under the sleepers to provide a firm trackbed). This derailment illustrated the dangers of disturbing a stressed section of line, especially when temperatures are higher than normal, because there is a possibility of inducing incorrect stresses. The whole question of stress is a complex one, and accidents were almost inevitable during the learning process.

If 1968 had not been a good year for the reputation of CWR, 1969 was to prove much worse and to demonstrate that the subject of track maintenance had progressed far beyond the school syllabus. It was now more appropriate to postgraduate research. On 13 June an express passenger train from Paignton to Paddington was derailed at nearly 80mph on CWR between Somerton and Castle Cary (Somerset), then 10 days later the 'Tees-Tyne Pullman'

Left:
Brush Type 4 No D1536 passing Marshmoor signalbox, near Hatfield with an Up East Coast Pullman express in March 1965.
P. Hocquard

Above:
Auchencastle, on the climb to Beattock Summit; the site of a derailment in 1968 caused by buckled continuously-welded rail. 'Jubilee' Class 4-6-0 No 45703 *Thunderer* pounds up the hill some years earlier with a Birmingham-Edinburgh express.
Eric Treacy/
Millbrook House Collection

Below:
Overlapping rail joint at the end of a section of continuously-welded rail.

express from King's Cross to Newcastle was derailed at over 90mph on CWR near Sandy. In each case the buckle in the track was seen by the driver as he approached. Although casualties were light in both cases a great deal of disquiet was aroused in the public mind, reinforced by two other CWR derailments — a train of empty carflats at Lichfield on 10 June and a Freightliner at Lamington, between Beattock and Motherwell.

Immediately a searching analysis of the forces set up in CWR was initiated. The Chief Civil Engineer quickly established an emergency programme to add extra ballast along the shoulders of the track. This was a very large-scale operation but it was given a high priority by both engineers and operators, so that by the onset of warm weather in 1970 virtually all the CWR lines had been strengthened, and there is no doubt that this relatively simple and unsophisticated measure played a major role in restricting the number of buckles the following year.

Simultaneously with the shoulder ballast programme a special exercise was launched in July 1969 to stress all lengths of CWR in which conditions were at all suspect. This was also a large-scale programme and the work continued until the summer of the following year. The Chief Civil Engineer incorporated all the lessons that had been learned, in a new Code of Practice issued in March 1970. This laid down strict conditions for the maintenance of CWR during hot weather. Arrangements were made with the Meteorological Office for weather forecasts to be supplied to local engineers during the hot weather months May to September. This enabled additional patrolling to be organised so that a special watch could be kept on rail temperatures during hot afternoons (especially when there had been a large temperature rise during the day). If there was any doubt about the safety of the track, speed reductions were imposed over the section of line concerned.

These measures in combination were highly successful. The number of track buckles on CWR (only a few of which resulted in derailment) went down from 48 in 1969 to nine in 1970. By comparison the number of buckles on ordinary jointed track was 55 in 1969 and 34 in 1970, for four times the mileage of track. It was found that almost half of the CWR buckles occurred on track less than a year old, and that almost half of all CWR buckles were caused by unsatisfactory ballast conditions.

By 1975 the mileage of CWR had doubled from 4,000 to 8,000, and the 'state of the art' regarding the maintenance of CWR had become very refined. However, on 28 July that year, another hot and sunny day, there was another derailment which re-emphasised the lessons previously learned, and the need to follow to the letter the instructions issued by the Chief Civil Engineer. The 08.20 Paddington to Fishguard express that day consisted of 12 coaches, hauled by a Class 47 diesel-electric locomotive No 47095. It had left Carmarthen and was on the last leg of its journey. Speed had risen to over 70mph by the time the train passed through Sarnau station, when the driver suddenly saw a bad buckle in the shape of an 'S' in the line ahead. He immediately threw on his brakes but there was insufficient

Above:
Sandy, on the East Coast main line, 23 July 1969. The last vehicle, a bogie van, of the Down Tees-Tyne Pullman has come to rest almost on its side after the train was derailed on buckled CWR whilst travelling at over 90mph. *P. R. Foster*

Centre right:
Yet another buckled-rail derailment in the Beattock-Carstairs area occurred at Lamington in 1969. English-Electric Type 4 No D301 is seen passing through Lamington station with the Up 'Royal Scot' on 8 April 1961, with a light load of eight coaches. *Derek Cross*

Below right:
Long-welded rail on concrete sleepers, secured by Mills clips. Photographed near Attleborough, Eastern Region, on 22 September 1960. *BR*

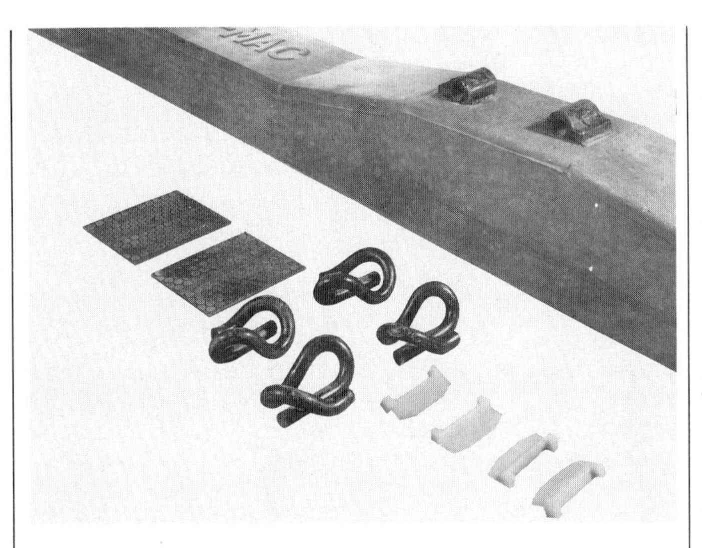

Above:
BR standard track components, showing Dow-Mac concrete sleeper and Pandrol clips. *Leslie Shipsides Ltd*

Below:
'Hall' Class 4-6-0 No 4962 *Ragley Hall* pauses at Clarbeston Road on 28 June 1962 with a train from Fishguard.
Rev T. R. Hughes

time to prevent the whole of the train from passing over the distortion, resulting in the 8th, 10th, and 12th coaches being derailed. Casualties again were light, and only eight passengers were taken to Carmarthen hospital. They were all discharged the same day and continued their journey. Maj King, who held the Public Inquiry into the accident, found that there was no clear cause of the derailment, but only a number of minor discrepancies, the most significant of which were that the line had been tamped five weeks earlier and that ballast had not been heaped on the shoulders.

Since 1975 the mileage of CWR has continued to rise and is now over 12,000. By contrast the mileage of ordinary jointed track in 60ft lengths has gone down to 7,000. Whilst all attention was being focused on CWR problems in the early 1970s, there was a serious accident on jointed track as a reminder that CWR was potentially much safer. Smethwick is not one of the more favoured areas of the West Midlands, and certainly not as wealthy as Sutton Coldfield or Solihull. A special train had been organised to take parties of schoolchildren from the area to the seaside at Rhyl for a day's outing, and it pulled out of Smethwick Rolfe Street station early on the morning of Friday 2 July 1971 with 10 coaches, filled with 32 adults and 380 children. As the mothers stood on the platform and waved the train away, with just the odd tear, they said to themselves 'Aren't the children lucky to have such a lovely

sunny day'. They were indeed lucky. It turned out to be the hottest day of the year so far.

The children enjoyed themselves enormously in the sunshine, then, in the late afternoon, they all trooped back to the station, tired and sunburnt. The sun had shone all day, to the great delight of holidaymakers, and it bestowed its gifts far and wide, on railway lines as well. Engineers anxiously watched over their CWR, little thinking that danger may also be lurking elsewhere.

The train set off on its homeward journey at 17.25. It was still very hot, 75°F, and everyone settled down eventually for the journey home. The train passed through the busy junctions at Chester and headed for Crewe. In Tattenhall Junction signalbox the signalman received the 'Is Line Clear for an Express Passenger Train?' bell signal of four beats. So far as he was aware the line was clear, therefore when he had received permission from the next signalbox down the line for the train to proceed he cleared all his signals for it and waited for it to appear. Although the signalbox still bore the name Tattenhall Junction, there was no longer a junction there, the cross-country line to Whitchurch having closed in 1964.

The patrolman whose job it was to examine the stretch of line at Tattenhall Junction regularly had become concerned about an area of rail creep some months earlier. Rail creep has been mentioned before — it gradually closes up the gaps which are provided at the ends of the rails to allow for expansion in hot weather. By the beginning of July the gaps were becoming smaller and smaller and the weather was becoming hot. The patrolman was uneasy. If the gaps could not take all the expansion there was only one way it could go — sideways. The patrolman had already reported the matter to his superiors but it seemed to have got lost in the bureaucracy. About an hour before the schools special left Rhyl on its homeward journey, the patrolman was examining his length of track. Near a bridge, No 50, about ¼ mile on the Chester side of Tattenhall Junction signalbox, he noticed that the rail joints were completely closed up, but otherwise the track appeared to be in good order. However, any compression stresses that might have been in the process of being set up in the track were invisible to the naked eye. It was a very warm afternoon.

It was now 18.00 but the temperature was still in the mid-70s. In Smethwick housewives were washing up after the evening meal and thinking to themselves that they would soon have to be making their way to the station at Rolfe Street to collect their children. What a lovely day they must have had at the seaside.

Below:
Class 40 diesel-electric No 40028 pulls out of Chester past No 2 signalbox on 18 June 1983. *J. Checkley*

Right:
Class 45 diesel-electric No 45140 threads its way gently into Chester General station from the Manchester line with the 07.44 Manchester Victoria-Bangor on 4 June 1983. The line on the right goes to Tattenhall Junction and Crewe.
Dave Hunt

At 18.03 the signalman at Tattenhall Junction received the 'Train entering section' bell signal from Chester No 1 signalbox for the schools special. On the Class 47 locomotive the driver started to accelerate, after threading his way carefully through the maze of points, crossings and signals at Chester; and approaching Tattenhall Junction he had almost reached 70mph. The Distant signal had been pulled off for him and he was looking ahead through Bridge 50 to get his first view of the Home signal and signalbox when he suddenly saw the signalman standing on the little platform at the top of the signalbox steps, holding his arms above his head as a warning of danger. He immediately sounded his whistle in acknowledgement and threw on all his brakes. 'What on earth is wrong?' he thought to himself. What had the signalman seen?

In the signalbox the signalman had been watching for the train. He saw it approaching at normal speed then, when it had nearly cleared Bridge 50 he noticed dust and rubble being thrown into the air near the back of the train, and one of the rear coaches veering out of line. He realised that it was derailed.

In the train the guard was riding in the brake compartment of the last coach. The journey had been perfectly normal, then suddenly the coach seemed to jump in the air and sway violently. He caught hold of the handbrake wheel to steady himself as the coach struck Bridge 50 and turned over on its side. He managed to climb out and made his way to the nearby signalbox where the signalman assured him that the lines had been protected in both directions.

There was no doubt about the cause of the derailment. The track had buckled under the middle of the train when the forces of expansion could no longer be contained. The 8th, 9th and 10th coaches were flung sideways, crashing into the brickwork of Bridge 50, but the first seven coaches were undamaged and the passengers in them had no idea at first that death and disaster had struck the rear of the train.

The accident happened at 18.08 and the emergency services were called out at once. The police arrived at 18.21, ambulances at 18.24 and fire engines at 18.35. Eight adults and five children were taken to Chester Royal Infirmary, and one adult and 12 children were taken to Wrexham War Memorial Hospital. They had had an awful demonstration of the elementary laws of physics which they would never forget. There was no lack of helpers on site — the WRVS, the Salvation Army, Girl Guides, local shopowners, taxi and coach firms and teachers from other schools gave whatever assistance they could.

At Smethwick word quickly got around that disaster had struck the schools special. Anxious parents rushed to the station for news, and waited for the names of those who

Below:
Class 47 diesel-electric No 47541 hauls the 09.30 from Crewe to Holyhead on 24 April 1982. Half a mile away, in the distance, is the bridge at Tattenhall Junction where the derailment occurred in 1971. *Paul A. Biggs*

Top:
A view of the buckled track at Tattenhall Junction after the derailment on 2 July 1971. *Author's Collection*

Above:
Electric locomotive No 87002, which hauled the 07.10 express from Glasgow to Euston on 2 July 1977, and whose driver stopped specially to report a track defect near Bletchley which eventually derailed a later train. *B. J. Nicolle*

had suffered in the crash, or who had been spared. The anguish of the long wait can hardly be imagined. A special train was arranged to take relatives to Chester and Wrexham hospitals, whilst the uninjured adults and children went forward in the first seven, undamaged, coaches of the schools special. When it finally arrived at Smethwick the scene of joyful, tearful reunion would have melted the hardest heart. Two children, a little boy of 11 and a little girl of 10, never returned home. They paid the price of a bureaucratic bungle, according to Maj Rose, who held a Public Inquiry into the accident. Repairs which ought to have been carried out to the track, were not. Local staff knew that the repairs were needed but somehow the urgency of the message was diluted as it passed up the organisational chain.

Six years exactly after the Tattenhall Junction derailment, Saturday 2 July 1977, was also a fine sunny day. By mid-afternoon the temperature was in the mid-70s, and it marked the start of a hot sunny spell.

The West Coast main line south of Rugby has always been very busy and its maintenance in tip-top condition has been a continuous preoccupation of the Civil Engineer, but the hammering it has received from a constant procession of trains passing at high speed and with heavy axleloads, to say nothing of the unsprung forces from the axle-hung electric motors on the Class 86 electric locomotives, has made it very difficult to achieve the desired standards; indeed, by 1977, 10 years into main line electrification, the quality of the ride was deteriorating and it was starting to become quite rough in places.

The 07.10 Glasgow to Euston express that day was hauled by a Class 87 electric locomotive, No 87002. About 11.40 the train passed through Wolverton and a couple of minutes later, when travelling at the maximum permitted speed of 100mph, the locomotive suddenly gave a severe jolt, bad enough almost to throw the secondman out of his seat. Drivers are accustomed to sudden lurches and know the bad places, but this was a jolt of unexpected severity and at a place where such jolts did not normally occur. Both driver and secondman looked back out of their cab windows to see if the train was safe, and were relieved to find that it was. However, the driver felt that the lurch was so severe that it could cause a train to be derailed, therefore he stopped his train and telephoned the signalman at Bletchley from an instrument at the foot of a signal post (all signals have a telephone in power signalbox areas). As far as he could remember he told the signalman that the bump had occurred at about 400yd on the approach side of signal No BY157.

The signalman at Bletchley immediately arranged to divert all Up trains from the fast line to the slow line, and sent for the local permanent way supervisor. However, he was on leave, so the signalman then called out the supervisor from the next section, who knew the area well. This supervisor immediately went to the site of the reported bump and found that there were dips in each rail of the CWR, voids under the sleepers, and signs of 'pumping', where wet clay slurry had been forced to the surface by the weight of passing trains. Satisfied in his own mind that these conditions were the cause of the reported bump, and that they were not sufficiently serious to cause any danger of derailment to trains passing over them, he asked the signalman to send one more train over the Up Fast line so that he could observe the behaviour of the track as the train passed over it. The next train happened to be an express from Llandudno to Euston. Its driver had not been warned and he came at full speed. His locomotive was No 85018, a rather rough-riding machine given to jerks and lurches, but about two miles south of Wolverton the driver felt a quite exceptional lurch. He was so alarmed by this that he made a full emergency brake application, and reported the facts to the signalman.

This information was relayed to the permanent way supervisor, who collected a gang of men to 'fettle up' the defective track. He asked the signalman to send one more train along the Up Fast line so that he could decide precisely what needed to be done. As it turned out, the next train was an express parcels train. South of Wolverton, travelling at 90mph, its driver was horrified to see a severe

Above:
A tamping and lining machine, seen at Midgham, near Newbury in 1980. *D. E. Canning*

distortion, like a snake, in the line ahead. He threw on his brakes, shut off power, and hung on as best he could. The lurch threw him first against the window, then right out of his seat on to the floor. The locomotive managed to cling to the rails but the entire train became derailed.

The permanent way supervisor had positioned himself to watch the train pass over the section of defective track which he had firmly fixed in his mind was the cause of the bumps that drivers had stopped to report. He saw the parcels train approaching in the distance, then it disappeared in a cloud of dust, and stopped. He was nonplussed. No wonder. He had been looking at the wrong track defect. There was a much worse section of defective track half a mile to the north. Had it been his regular section he would have known that men had been working on it there all week, dealing with a severe wet spot. They had left it with insufficient ballast, and the sun had done the rest. A serious distortion was just waiting to happen.

Maj Rose's Report, following his Public Inquiry, traced the derailment to a number of causes — bad management, poor supervision, wrong reporting of the location of the bump, people jumping to conclusions, and of course those two demons which are present at most accidents — coincidence and chance:

1. The signalman had not been told that the usual permanent way supervisor was on leave, and who his deputy was to be during that period.
2. The repair job carried out during the week had been left short of ballast.
3. The man in charge of the repair job was only a Leading Trackman. He had not been properly supervised.
4. Both drivers who stopped to report bumps had given wrong or vague locations.
5. The permanent way supervisor had been misled by the drivers' vague reports of location and he had found the wrong piece of bad track. He then jumped to the conclusion that that was the source of the trouble.
6. He should not have asked for a third train to pass over the bad piece of track. The fact that two drivers of express passenger trains had stopped specially to report a bump should have put him on his guard.

The signalman was in a difficult position. He was uneasy when the permanent way supervisor asked for a train to be sent over the suspect line at full speed. He was even more uneasy when he was asked to send another one, knowing that he had now had two reports from drivers of very bad bumps, and that drivers did not stop express passenger trains unless there was something really wrong. Yet what could he do? The technical expert on site had assessed it as being safe.

In a perfect world no work would have been done on CWR during hot weather, to avoid the dangers of setting up incorrect levels of stress in the rails. Yet, so far as the Civil Engineer was concerned he inhabited a very imperfect world. He was expected to maintain the track in fine condition suitable for 125mph speeds and 25-ton axle-loads, yet on the one hand the Operating Department would not give him enough opportunities to get to work on the track (known as 'possessions' or 'occupations'), and on the other hand mechanical engineers designed electric locomotives that bashed his track to bits. Just to add to his troubles the General Manager told him to cut his staff numbers, so he took his cheque book to Plasser Theurer's and bought millions of poundsworth of shiny new track-maintenance machines only to find to his chagrin that they spent nine-tenths of their time standing idle because the Operating Department insisted on running trains instead of giving him possessions.

Was the operator, then, the stumbling block? Not at all. He had every sympathy with the Engineer. Nothing would have pleased him more than to have given the Engineer all the track possessions that he wanted. And why did he not do so? Because the railway would have lost half of its customers. If track maintenance work were to have been done during the daytime, the result would have been, on some lines at least, that streams of expresses would have had to be cancelled, or diverted with appalling delays. The train service would have deteriorated and the railway would have gained a reputation for unreliability — not a good selling point. The Passenger Manager would soon have been hammering on the operator's door to complain. Would it have been easier to have given possessions at night? Up to a point. But engineering gangs do not think it is much fun to work permanent nights. And some of the railway's freight and parcels customers would not have been very pleased if their trains had often been cancelled or delayed. The newspaper men valued punctuality and reliability very highly. So did the Post Office, which was often very critical of BR's unpunctuality, and threatened more than once to take its business elsewhere when it became weary of persistent train delays, often caused by possessions. Was weekend work the only answer? In many cases it was. The staff liked it, naturally, because of the extra pay, but even at weekends engineering work played havoc with the train service and BR was not really in the Sunday passenger market until after 4pm, thus denying themselves a wide range of business opportunities.

Was the situation of BR's own making? The answer has to be, partly, yes. Did the Civil Engineer make his needs sufficiently known? Did he emphasise the huge waste of money in having expensive machinery standing idle for much of the time? Did he protest loudly enough when alternative routes were closed, or additional running lines taken up, or sidings ripped out, making it more difficult for him to be given worthwhile possessions, or the facilities to make the most productive use of those possessions? Did he make his voice heard when remodelling and resignalling schemes were carried out, so that they incorporated the facilities that would allow the operators to give him more possessions, such as reversible working on both lines, or signalled high speed facing crossovers, or refuge sidings where he could temporarily shunt his machines clear of the main line?

Was the operator then to blame? Partly, yes. Certainly in the early days he did not appreciate the Engineer's needs,

Diverted West Coast main line expresses:

1. **The Down 'Royal Scot' approaches Hellifield off the Blackburn line on 4 August 1968.** *D. Cross*
2. **English Electric Type 4 No D214 approaches Dent with the 11.30 from Glasgow Central to Manchester Victoria on 1 May 1966.** *M. S. Welch*

and when he did start to appreciate them he found that the planners and accountants were very reluctant to allow him to provide them, because of the cost involved. Now that Sector Management has arrived things may improve, if it is not too late. At least we shall now have a corporate business approach, something which has been sadly lacking in the past.

The biggest mistake of all, so far as track maintenance is concerned, would have been the closure of the Settle to Carlisle line. How was the Engineer to maintain the line between Preston and Carlisle, 90 miles of heavily-used trunk route, nearly all double-track, without a reasonable diversionary route? And was it an indication of the diminishing degree of importance which BR seemed to attach to the West Coast main line north of Preston?

Sir Josiah Stamp, Sir William Wood, and Sir Ernest Lemon must be turning in their graves at the long, slow decline of the premier line that they bequeathed to British Railways on nationalisation in 1948. And to the decline of the former Midland route from St Pancras to Scotland via Leeds, Settle and Carlisle, which started with nationalisation when the route was split into no fewer than five sections under four different Regional managements, each already with its own favourite main line. How could any route prosper under such a cumbersome, negative organisation? Yet it could prosper under the new business organisation in BR, either as a Provincial route or an InterCity route. BR had already cut its marginal capacity so fine that it could hardly deal with any increase in traffic, and it was in danger of compounding the error with the proposal to close the Settle to Carlisle line. In 10 or 20 years' time BR may have regretted its actions, especially if the hoped-for increase in traffic resulting from the opening of the Channel Tunnel actually materialises.

And let not governments feel that they are free from criticism in this direction. During the whole lifetime of the railway they have interfered with its management. It is governments that have created the financial, legal, organisational and competitive conditions in which BR and its predecessors have had to operate.

The behaviour of CWR can still be unpredictable, even after all the studies that have been made, and all the experience that has been accumulated. The civil engineer is still often working at the boundary of his knowledge, as was demonstrated on Sunday 15 June 1986 when the 16.10 express from Glasgow to Euston became partly derailed as it was approaching Motherwell. The locomotive and first two coaches ran on and finally came to a halt half a mile beyond the station. The CWR had buckled as the train was passing over it. When the CWR had been laid, a section of points and crossings had been used as an 'anchor' when the CWR was stressed. During the winter some work had been carried out on those points and crossings and it is thought that incorrect stresses were then set up in the adjoining CWR, which finally buckled as the express was passing over. Fortunately there were no fatalities but it was an expensive lesson!

The Leeds-Settle-Carlisle line when it was still being properly used as a trunk route:

1. **LMS Standard Compound No 41119 pilots a Stanier Class 5 4-6-0 into Skipton with the Down 'Waverley' on 10 September 1958.** *R. H. Short*
2. **'Jubilee' No 45562 *Alberta* passes through Gargrave with the Up 'Waverley' Edinburgh to London St Pancras.** *J. Davenport*
3. **The 'Thames-Clyde Express' speeds through Kirkby Stephen in March 1973, on the long descent from Ais Gill.**

5
Derailments on Broken Rails

When a child receives his first trainset he soon realises that the two essential components are the train and the track. He also discovers fairly quickly that unless he lays his track level and joins the ends of the rails accurately and firmly, derailments will occur. And he soon learns to examine the line frequently, so that any breaks are discovered *before* he runs his train. It is the same with the real railway.

Thirty years ago, there were about 200 broken rails per year, nearly all of which were discovered before derailment took place. By 1970, that figure had gone up to over 400, with a considerably reduced track mileage, and in addition there were well over 200 breaks at welded joints in continuously welded rail. In 1987 there were still over 350 broken rails, but the number of broken welds had risen to over 250, although with a much greater total number of welds in the track than in 1970.

One does not have to seek far for the reasons behind this rather alarming increase. Train speeds are higher — up to 125mph in the case of the IC125 units (HSTs) and up to 60/75mph for heavily loaded freight trains with 25-ton axle-loads. Locomotives and multiple-units with axle-hung nose-suspended electric motors severely punish the track, owing to their heavy unsprung weight.

There are three main types of rail break. On jointed track, which is the name for track laid in 60ft lengths joined together with fishplates, the most common break results from fatigue stresses at the fishbolt holes, resulting in cracks radiating from the hole in the form of a star, known appropriately as star cracks. If they are not detected and dealt with, the cracks will eventually extend until they reach the rail head, and at this stage a piece of the rail will become bodily detached from the rest of the rail.

Below:
On a misty Sunday morning in February 1975, breakdown cranes set to work to rerail several loaded 100-ton tank wagons which fell on to their sides following a derailment caused by a broken rail near Fosse Way, between Lichfield and Walsall. The operation is being watched with keen interest by Water Board officials, who had to intervene and stop the rerailing when oil started to gush out of one of the tanks whilst it was being turned to an upright position. *Author*

Below:
Very high standards of permanent way are required for IC125 units, one of which is seen passing through Newport with a Paddington train on 3 July 1977. *L. A. Nixon*

Right:
The permanent way needs to be strong to withstand 25-ton axleloads, imposed by trains such as the one seen here, at Langley, near Stevenage, on 31 January 1970, headed by Class 47 diesel-electric No 1872. *J. H. Cooper-Smith*

Below:
This derailment, at Stoulton near Pershore on 30 November 1984, was caused by a broken fishplate. The first six coaches of the train, the 07.05 Hereford to Paddington, which was travelling at about 75mph, remained coupled to the locomotive, Class 47 No 47500, but the last four became detached and were completely derailed. There were no serious injuries.
S. Widdowson

The second type of break occurs away from the rail end. Usually a fatigue crack develops, which will spread in time until either the rail breaks in two or a piece of the rail head breaks off. Sometimes the crack develops from a wheel burn, caused by a locomotive wheel spinning under power whilst the train is travelling at low speed. During a wheelspin, a portion of the rail head surface becomes heated very rapidly to a temperature as high as 700°C, and as soon as the spin ceases the area rapidly cools, causing a change in the nature of the steel, from which small cracks may grow. Sometimes the damage causes shelling of the surface, resulting in a shallow depression, which has to be restored to its former level by welding and grinding. In severe cases it may be necessary to replace the rail.

Sometimes rail breaks are caused by metallurgical faults arising during manufacture, and may be of the tache ovale type, which is a slowly growing internal flaw originating in an area of high stress concentration in the rail head, probably due to the presence of hydrogen trapped in the metal during the steelmaking process.

The third type of break is the defective weld, which has caused so much concern in recent years. The subject will be examined in detail when we look at the accident which occurred at Bushey on the West Coast main line on 16 February 1980.

Each broken rail is a potential cause of derailment, which may have the most serious consequences. The highest death toll in an accident on British Railways in the last 30 years was caused by a broken rail at Hither Green, on the electrified South Eastern Division main line of the Southern Region, on Sunday 5 November 1967, when 49 passengers were killed. In view of such possible calamity the detection of defective rails is obviously a matter of great importance. There are two main systems for achieving this.

The first is the time-honoured system of visual examination by a track patrolman. All lines are patrolled regularly, either daily or every two days, so far as the busy lines are concerned. The patrolman is concerned with many aspects of track maintenance, particularly the security of track fastenings, but he is also looking for cracks and breakages. However, he can only really see cracks when they are so big that they are reaching the dangerous stage, and they need to be discovered before that if possible.

To enable cracks to be discovered before they have grown to the extent that they can be seen by the naked eye, a scientific apparatus was devised known as an Ultrasonic

Top:
A typical wheel burn. *BR*

Above:
A view of the wreckage in the Hither Green derailment on 5 November 1967. *Author*

Flaw Detector. This is a hand-held apparatus which sends ultrasonic waves into the rail, and the operator can distinguish, for example by a variation in the pitch of an audible signal, whether the waves are being reflected from the base of the rail or from a bolt hole or hidden flaw. The use of hand-held equipment is slow and laborious, and to overcome this disadvantage BR brought into service in 1971 an ultrasonic rail flaw detection train, which is a converted two-car diesel multiple-unit and travels at 20mph whilst testing.

A third way of discovering a broken rail arises quite fortuitously through the use of track circuits. As has already been explained, a track circuit is an electrically-operated train detection device in which a weak electric current is fed through one of the running rails of a section of track, and then back along the other running rail. Adjoining sections of track are insulated from each other. At the opposite end of the section of track from the power source is a relay, held open by the current passing through it. When a pair of vehicle wheels enters the track-circuited section of line the electrical current takes the shortest way back, which is through the wheels and axles of the vehicle. There is then no current flowing through the relay, which closes and operates other equipment, such as placing signals to Danger or locking the movement of points. The track circuit in this state is referred to as 'occupied'. However, if an empty track circuit suddenly becomes occupied when there is no train in the vicinity, the signalman will become aware of this from his indications panel, but he will not yet know the cause. It may be due to an obstruction on the line short-circuiting the current (for example a lorry may have fallen on to the track from an overbridge), or it may be due to a failure of the apparatus, or it may be due to a broken rail. If the rail is completely broken and there is a gap between the two pieces, the electric current will not be able to flow and the relay will close, putting the protecting signal in rear to Danger and alerting the signalman. Unfortunately on some lines the track circuit only uses one rail, therefore the equipment will not detect a break in the other rail. To convert all track circuits to two-rail operation would be a costly process, especially in skilled man-hours, which BR is not prepared to undertake.

It might be appropriate at this stage to examine the actions of the signalman when he notices that a track circuit is showing 'occupied' when there is no train nearby. At this stage he does not know the cause, and one of his first acts will be to ask the signal technician to find out if there is a fault in the equipment which can quickly be put right. If not, the signalman must arrange for the section of line to be examined. This is normally done by using a train, and the driver will be told what has happened, and that he is to proceed cautiously through the affected section and to report at the next signal ahead. The driver must pass the protecting signal even though it is showing Danger, and travel at a speed low enough to enable him to see what is wrong and to stop before hitting any obstruction. In the great majority of cases the cause will be either an equipment failure or a broken rail. If the driver travels through the section and notices nothing, subsequent trains may be allowed to pass through at low speed after the drivers have been cautioned by the signalman, and this procedure will continue until the cause has been found and remedied. However, if the driver notices a broken rail, or feels what he suspects is one as his locomotive travels over it, it will be necessary to call out the civil engineering staff to deal with the defect. In the meantime, trains may be allowed to pass over the break at walking pace under certain safety conditions, among which are:

1. The break must be in CWR.
2. The break must be nearly vertical.
3. The gap must be not more than an inch.
4. A supervisor or other authorised member of staff must watch the train pass over the break, so that it can be stopped instantly if necessary.

When the engineering staff arrive on site they will put a clamp on the rails at the break, rather like a pair of fishplates, so that trains can pass over safely, then at a convenient time they will cut the rails a few feet to each side of the break, and weld in a new piece of rail cut to the precise length of the gap. When that has been done trains may be allowed to proceed normally.

Above:
Class 8P Pacific No 46250 *City of Lichfield* is seen heading the Up 'Royal Scot', just south of Carlisle, on 22 December 1963.
Peter J. Robinson

There is yet another way in which broken rails are detected. Drivers are accustomed to lurches and bumps and bounces as part and parcel of everyday life on the footplate. They also know the rough spots on any particular route and can quite easily distinguish anything out of the ordinary. In the latter case they should stop at the next signalbox or telephone and inform the signalman, so that he can call out the civil engineering staff and arrange for other drivers to be cautioned. The cause of the unusual bump felt by the driver need not be a broken rail. It might be a bad wet spot or a buckle in the track, as we saw in the last chapter. It might be an obstruction on the line, or a body on the track.

There is of course the ultimate way in which a broken rail is discovered, and that is when it derails a train. History is littered with such cases, and some of them have interesting features, or have happened to famous trains. The 'Royal Scot' has had quite an eventful career and it was destined to add another page on 3 February 1954. The Up 'Royal Scot', 10.0am Glasgow to Euston express, that day consisted of 10 coaches, and was hauled by a Class 8P Pacific locomotive No 46250 *City of Lichfield.* It was travelling through Watford Tunnel at about 65mph when a broken rail derailed the last pair of wheels of the eighth coach. The train travelled on like this for a mile and a half until the derailed wheels hit the points and crossings at Watford No 2 signalbox, whereupon the last two coaches became completely derailed. They broke away from the remainder of the train and came to rest leaning against the platform at the station. The 4.37pm Euston to Wolverhampton express was just leaving the station on the next line when its driver saw the derailed vehicles approaching him. He immediately stopped his train but the sides of some of its coaches were grazed as the two derailed coaches scraped past them. The first eight coaches of the 'Royal Scot' were brought to a stand when the brakes were automatically applied by the parting of the train. No one was seriously injured.

An interesting feature in this accident is that the communication cord was pulled by a passenger in the ninth coach as soon as he realised something was wrong, and although the brakes were partly applied and speed was reduced slightly the driver was unaware that the cord had been pulled, and had no idea that anything was wrong until the brakes went on fully when the train broke in two. The passengers at the rear of the train were terror-stricken. They suddenly heard a banging and clattering underneath the coach and their hearts momentarily stood still. Anyone who has travelled on a train when it has thrown up pieces of ballast on to the underside of the coach will recognise the sudden feeling of alarm at the unusual noise, then the relief when the noise subsides. On the 'Royal Scot' that day the noise did not subside, and the pulling of the communication cord did not seem to have worked. The apparatus is designed so that the pulling of the cord (on the coaches then in use it was actually a chain) causes a rod, mounted transversely at the end of the coach, to rotate and lift a valve to allow air into the vacuum brake pipe, thus causing a partial application of the brakes. The amount of vacuum

Above:
A scene of track maintenance in years gone by, when labour costs were lower and recruitment easier. *LMS*

in the pipe is shown on a gauge in the locomotive cab. When the brakes are fully off it will register 21in and a normal brake application will reduce it to 12 or 13in. When the communication cord is pulled and air is allowed into the brake pipe the gauge on the locomotive will start to fall, and when the driver notices this he is told to infer that the cord has been pulled and that he must stop the train with as little delay as possible, but that he must use his discretion in stopping, it being undesirable to bring the train to a stand on a bridge or viaduct, or in a tunnel. In order that he can exercise such discretion most effectively a driver will normally look back down the train to see what is wrong. If he sees smoke he will stop as quickly as possible, but if he sees that part of his train is derailed he will apply the brake more gently to keep the train upright and in line as far as possible. The guard also has a responsibility — if he has reason to think that the cord has been pulled but has not been noticed by the driver he must apply the brake from his van. In the case of air-braked trains the method of operation is very similar. When the brake is off, the brake pipe pressure gauge reads 72lb/sq in of air pressure. A normal brake application will reduce the pressure to 48lb/sq in, and an emergency application will reduce it to zero.

The equipping of trains with an apparatus which the passenger can use to stop the train, or to have it stopped by the driver, is a legal requirement under the Regulation of Railways Act of 1868. Section 22 states that 'All trains travelling a distance of more than 20 miles without stopping are to be provided with a means of communication between the passengers and the servants of the company in charge of the train. The apparatus provided is to be approved by the Board of Trade'. The duties of the Board of Trade have now been taken over by the Ministry (or Department) of Transport. It will be noticed that the Act does not specify that the passenger must be able to stop the train, but merely to 'communicate', and that was precisely what was done at first. A cord ran down the length of the train at roof level outside the carriages, and pulling it rang a bell on the locomotive. The modern form of apparatus was introduced later in the century when the use of the automatic vacuum brake became standard (the continuous brake itself became a legal requirement under the Regulation of Railways Act 1889), but the name 'communication cord' has survived until the present day.

On older coaches the actuating rod referred to above was fitted with a red disc at each end. The disc is horizontal when the equipment is normal, but when the rod rotates upon the cord being pulled, the disc turns to the vertical position. The guard can then tell in which coach the cord has been pulled.

At the Public Inquiry into the accident Lt-Col Wilson, the Inspecting Officer, commented upon the failure of the passenger communication apparatus (the cord) to alert the driver, and there were discussions with the British Transport Commission as to whether the brake application when the cord is pulled should be made automatic and outside the control of the driver, but the railway authorities felt that this was an isolated case and that discretion should remain with the driver. The Inspecting Officer also commented upon the difficulty of maintaining the track in tunnels and mentioned, significantly, that the quality and quantity of labour had been insufficient for a long time to maintain the track to the standard required. This was a problem that was to dog the London end of the West Coast main line for many years; indeed it affected the standard of performance in both the civil engineering and operating departments throughout most of Britain until the labour market eased in the late 1970s. It is easy to forget how difficult those days were for local managers, with the constant daily struggle just to keep the job going in the face of staff shortages, the poor quality of some of the new recruits, and the rapid turnover of staff.

Further north on the West Coast main line there is a delightful spot where the line descends from the bleak moorlands of Shap to the fields and pastures of Morecambe Bay, where on a clear day the mountains of the Lake District provide an attractive scenic backdrop, and it is possible to pick out the shipyard cranes at Barrow-in-Furness 20 miles away. At Hest Bank the line actually runs along the coast for a few hundred yards, the only place on the West Coast main line where it does so. There was a small station here, half a dozen camping coaches, and a junction to Morecambe

Below:
Hest Bank, on the West Coast main line between Lancaster and Carnforth, and the site of the derailment of the 22.10 sleeper from Glasgow to London on the night of 19/20 May 1965. The photograph shows a Fowler Class 4P 2-6-4T on an excursion from Barrow to Morecambe on 18 September 1954. The sleeping car express was derailed when passing over the water troughs, just beyond the tail lamp of the excursion train. *H. Armitage*

Euston Road station. There were also water troughs just to the north of the station level crossing. During the winter at high tide tens of thousands of birds can be seen from the train, feeding on the shore line.

Not long after midnight on 19/20 May 1965 the 22.10 sleeping car express from Glasgow to London (Kensington Olympia) set off from Carlisle on the next stage of its long journey south. It consisted of 12 vehicles, including seven sleeping cars, and carried 114 passengers. The locomotive was No D1633, a Type 4 diesel-electric. After running down easily from Shap and Grayrigg the driver was passing through Hest Bank station at about 70mph and was just closing the power controller to slow down for Lancaster when he felt a pull and saw that the needle on his vacuum brake gauge had fallen to zero. When the train stopped he sent his secondman forward to protect the other line and warn the drivers of any approaching trains to stop whilst he himself went back. He could hardly believe his eyes. There were only three coaches attached to his locomotive, then nothing for 250yd. He hurried along in the darkness with mounting apprehension and then came upon the next four vehicles, three of which were sleeping cars, lying on their sides between the platforms. Reaching the signalbox, he was assured by the signalman that both lines had been protected and that the emergency services had been sent for. He could dimly make out to the north the shape of two more sleeping cars on their sides. Ambulances arrived quickly at the level crossing and the injured were taken to hospital. There were only 11 of them, all with minor injuries or shock, and only two were detained for a few days. There were no fatalities, the reason being partly that five of the six overturned vehicles were sleeping cars, whose occupants were cushioned to some extent from the effects of the derailment. A very rude awakening was all that most of them suffered, apart from the memory of those awful moments when the derailed train bounced along then turned over onto its side, which will stay with them for ever.

The cause of the derailment was a broken rail. The line had been relaid 10 years earlier, using 60ft flatbottom rail welded into 300ft lengths. The rails had been wheelburnt in a number of places and a transverse crack had started from one of them, spreading horizontally for a length of several feet, leading eventually to a whole section of rail head breaking off. Wheelburns were a problem at this location, wheelspin being aided by water spilt from the troughs, and salt spray from the sea, borne on the prevailing westerly wind. The rail had been examined for cracks six months previously but fatigue cracks underneath wheelburns are almost impossible to detect with an ultrasonic flaw detector.

Across on the other side of northern England the East Coast main line also runs close to the sea at places north of Newcastle. Given the present flourishing state of Anglo-Scottish traffic on the East Coast main line and its relative stagnation on the rival West Coast route it is odd to recollect that in the 1960s it was intended to downgrade the line north of Newcastle, and actually to single it from Alnmouth to Dunbar. Anglo-Scottish passenger traffic would have been concentrated on the West Coast main line and freight traffic would have been routed via Newcastle and Carlisle. Planning for the future has been a notoriously difficult exercise on BR ever since it was created and the record is not a good one, in fact some of the planning assumptions and decisions that were made with apparent great confidence now appear to us quite astonishing. The fact is that it is quite impossible to plan with any degree of accuracy 20 years ahead or to forecast the changes that might take place. All the more foolish, therefore, would it have been to jettison the Settle to Carlisle line, just as it

Above:
The scene at Amble Junction after the Up 'North Briton' was derailed by a broken rail on 15 July 1967. *Author*

Below:
The pieces of broken rail reassembled afterwards. The star crack can be seen running from the bolt hole. *Author*

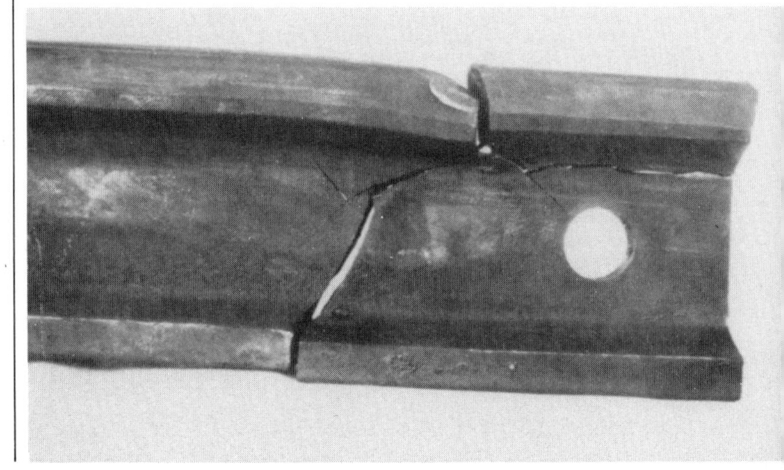

would have been reckless to have singled and downgraded the Newcastle to Edinburgh line.

These difficulties of long-term planning are the background to the next accident to be examined. On the evening of 15 July 1967 the 'North Briton' express from Edinburgh to Leeds was running at about 75mph between Acklington and Chevington when it became derailed on a broken rail. Fortunately all 12 coaches remained upright and fairly well in line, and only nine of the 160 passengers required hospital treatment. All were discharged within a few days. Prompt action was taken to summon assistance but as the site was not easily accessible by road the ambulances were sent to the nearby RAF station at Acklington and the injured passengers were airlifted by helicopter; perhaps an additional fright for some of them but a good example of initiative, and certainly an effective way of getting them to hospital with the least possible delay.

The rails in the line were of the 95lb bullhead type and had been laid as long ago as 1941. Their weight had been reduced over the years to 84/88lb/yd and that section of line was programmed to be relaid in the following October. The rails were drilled with only one fishbolt hole, a common practice at one time. A star crack had developed from the bolt hole at the running-on end of a rail, and eventually a piece of the rail had broken off, leaving a gap which caused the derailment. The LNER had adopted the two-hole fishplate in some areas because it allowed the sleepers at each side of the rail joint to be brought closer together, thus providing better support for the joint, but the practice was not thought to yield sufficient benefits and it was later abandoned.

The incidence of rail breakages at joints was causing concern both to the Railways Board and to the Railway Inspectorate, even though the derailments that were occurring were not causing fatalities. However, that was to change dramatically a few months later, and the concern felt was seen to be well founded.

Trains on the Southern Region's electrified lines often seemed to give a rougher ride than trains on other Regions' lines, although it was difficult to tell whether it was the rolling stock or the track which was at fault, or indeed a combination of the two. It would be easy to understand why the track may have been less than perfect — the punishing effect of electric multiple-units, the frequency and the speed of trains, the lack of opportunity to carry out maintenance, and the difficulty in obtaining a sufficient quantity of good quality labour, are reasons which spring readily to mind. Couple all those with restrictions on staff numbers and expenditure imposed by the Railways Board and it becomes easy to understand why the quality of the ride from Paris to Calais on what was not one of SNCF's front-rank main lines was so vastly superior to the ride from Dover to Victoria.

The Chislehurst to Hither Green section of line was considered by passengers to be fairly rough in the 1960s, especially after the Southern Region raised the speed limit from 75mph to 90mph in July 1967. Local permanent way staff had some misgivings about this, firstly as to whether the track was in a good enough condition for 90mph running and secondly whether they had sufficient resources to maintain it to the standard required for such speeds. However, they certainly did not imagine how quickly defects in the standard of the track would lead to one of Britain's worst postwar railway disasters.

On Sunday, 5 November 1967, the 19.43 from Hastings to Charing Cross, composed of two of the six-coach diesel-electric 'Hastings' multiple-units was approaching Hither Green under clear signals on the Up fast line, running at about 70mph, when the leading pair of wheels of the third coach struck a small wedge-shaped piece of rail that had broken away from the end of the running rail, and became derailed. The train ran on in this condition for about a quarter of a mile, to the mounting alarm of the passengers in the coach, an open second-class, until the derailed wheels struck some points and crossings. The impact caused the coach, together with the one in front and the two behind, to fall over and slide along for 250yd; the sides of two of the coaches being torn off as they did so, precipitating the passengers on to the rails, sleepers and ballast below to be mangled or crushed to death, or to suffer severe injuries, as the disintegrating coaches grated

Below:
Hither Green, on Monday morning 6 November 1967, showing the wreckage of the 19.43 Hastings to Charing Cross, which had been derailed by a broken rail the previous evening. The ease of accessibility to the site, for the emergency services, was fortunately very good. *Author*

Left:
The broken rail at Hither Green, subsequently re-assembled, showing the triangular portion of the rail-head which broke away and caused 49 deaths. *Author*

Below left:
The 07.30 IC125 unit from Leeds to Edinburgh was derailed near Tyne Yard, Gateshead, as it ran along the Down Slow line at about 40mph on 1 August 1984. It had been diverted from the Down Fast line owing to the presence of a failed train, and was derailed by a defective point assembly. Three passengers were seriously injured. Maj Olver, the Inspecting Officer, in his Report severely criticised the local civil engineering organisation and management. *Author*

over them. The train was well filled, with some passengers having to stand, and altogether 49 of them were killed and 27 seriously injured. It is significant that the number of serious casualties in an accident in which coaches overturn is almost always related to the extent to which the coach bodies retain their integrity, even though the bogies may be torn off and the ends battered. Provided the coach body sides remain intact and the body remains whole, so that passengers are not thrown out or dropped on to the ballast, the number and severity of casualties remains low, but as soon as the coach body is breached or torn open the number of casualties rises considerably. This is a lesson which has not been lost on coach designers, and it is rare to see modern coaches being breached, even when thrown on to their sides at high speed. The passengers inside may be bounced around, and suffer bruises and broken bones, but they rarely receive the serious injuries which occur to passengers thrown out of a coach, who are harmed not only by the impact with the ground but also from the mauling they receive bodily as the train or wreckage passes over them.

The emergency services reacted very promptly indeed. The accident happened at 21.16 and the Metropolitan Police were on the scene within 5min, just a minute before the first ambulances. The first casualty reached hospital only 18min after the accident. Fortunately, road access to the site was good.

One of the features of this accident was the behaviour of the first coach. The driver was just preparing to apply the brake lightly for the 60mph restriction in the inner suburban area beyond Hither Green, when he felt a drag on the train, which became progressively more severe with much snatching. The brakes came hard on and the coach stopped in a short distance. The driver concluded that his train had become divided, and he opened the cab door and prepared to climb down on to the track. As he looked back along his train he could scarcely believe his eyes. His coach was standing alone on the rails, undamaged, but the other coaches were scattered in all directions. It is a situation that we have met before, where a derailment occurs part of the way along a train.

Col McMullen, the Inspecting Officer who held the Public Inquiry into the accident, found that the rail end had broken off owing to stresses which had been set up in it by the unsatisfactory manner in which it was supported by the sleeper and track bed. He considered that the general standard of maintenance of the section on which the derailment occurred was inadequate for the speed at which trains were being run, and he attached the responsibility for this to the entire permanent way organisation, all the way up from the local staff to the Chief Civil Engineer.

One of the 'Hastings' units was tested on the East Coast main line to see how its 'ride' compared with that on its home ground. It was markedly better, to no one's surprise. Passengers on the East Coast main line are accustomed to having a comfortable ride, although a Great Western supporter might maintain that the ride from Paddington is superior. He may well be right — the Western Region seems to have been rather more adept than the other Regions at squeezing money out of the British Railways Board. The London & North Western Railway (LNWR) used to pride itself on the condition of its main line from Euston, and it was widely regarded as being among the best in the country. That was long before the days of main line electrification, and by 1980 the ride on the West Coast main line at its southern end was definitely lively. It was almost unbelievable that a line could have deteriorated so much in such a short time. Part of the reason was the hammering it received from electric locomotives, but when the effect became apparent remedial action should have been taken.

Below:
High Speed Trains have been a major commercial success on the East Coast main line. The 07.45 King's Cross to Edinburgh is seen passing Ouston Junction, north of Chester-le-Street, on 5 April 1978. *I. S. Carr*

The fact that it was not is surely a criticism of the management of the London Midland Region, and not just of the civil engineering function but of general management as well. It is also surely a criticism of the Railways Board, which changed the General Manager frequently. Between 1970 and 1977 there were no fewer than four changes of General Manager at Euston. There were also no fewer than five Chief Operating Managers at Crewe! In such circumstances, how could any proper control and direction be exercised or any continuity be given? And this on BR's biggest Region!

The London Midland Region's attitude to its most important line seemed to be that as long as it was not unsafe the passenger would just have to put up with a rough ride, and an uncharitable observer might remark that that more or less encapsulated the Region's attitude to its passengers, as though they were a nuisance to be tolerated. How else can one explain the declining popularity of the West Coast main line, compared with King's Cross and Paddington? In 1989 for example, the express service from King's Cross to Edinburgh has become so popular that the hourly service has had to be augmented to half-hourly at certain times of the day, and the average journey time is down to about 4½hr. By contrast, the rival West Coast service to Glasgow has declined to two-hourly, with an average journey time an hour longer than the East Coast.

It seems incredible that there are more trains from London to Plymouth than there are from London to Glasgow, which is three times bigger. Part of the West Coast malaise can be attributed to the long-drawn-out Advanced Passenger Train fiasco, but its roots go back much further. The fact is that the East Coast companies always fostered and nurtured their passenger traffic. So did the Great Western, which was held in immense esteem by its passengers. The LNWR and its successor, the London Midland and Scottish Railway, were quite content to pay lip service to the passenger business but the main interest of these two companies was in the freight business, which provided much more of the revenue and the profits. From a business point of view, that was a perfectly proper attitude, and any other would have led to the bankruptcy courts, but today the relative size of the passenger and freight businesses has been completely reversed. The passenger business is absolutely dominant, yet the old attitudes seem to have persisted to this day at Euston, which is incredible 40 years after nationalisation. It is almost as though the Eastern and Western Regions were determined to prove

Below:
The East Coast companies always fostered their passenger traffic. They were the first to use Pacifics on their expresses, the first to use streamlining, and they ran crack high speed services such as the 'Elizabethan', pictured here behind Class A4 Pacific No 60024 *Kingfisher* at Grantshouse, on its 6½hr run from King's Cross to Edinburgh. *Eric Treacy/Millbrook House Collection*

Right:
Class 86/2 Electric No 86247 approaches Bushey with the 09.00 Euston to Carlisle on 30 June 1976. *Brian Morrison*

Below right:
Bushey station, on the West Coast main line just south of Watford, showing one of the derailed coaches of the 20.25 Euston to Manchester on 16 February 1980, caused by a broken weld in the rail. The strength of the coach bodies helped to prevent any fatalities. This photograph was taken from the Up Fast platform, looking north. The coach body is lying across the Watford dc lines. *Daily Telegraph*

0000

that they could be better than the London Midland when the latter was favoured to be the first long-distance electrified main line. The other Regions were put on their mettle and were determined to prove that they could do better even without electrification. The LMR was content to rest on its laurels.

The West Coast main line, especially its southern end, has seen many accidents, and it was to be the scene of yet another on the evening of Saturday 16 February 1980. A regular passenger on the 19.40 express from Euston to Birmingham was relaxing in the first coach of the train as it settled down on its 100mph run to the first stop at Rugby. Approaching Bushey, just south of Watford, he was startled by a bad bump underneath the coach. Other people felt it too, but none of them thought that they ought to tell the guard, or do anything about it, and they felt reassured when the train immediately resumed its normal progress. Perhaps they thought that if there was anything wrong the driver or guard would have taken the necessary action. However, the driver felt nothing.

Just as the train was slowing down for the Rugby stop, and the passengers had put the bump near Bushey out of their minds, another express was approaching Bushey. This second train was the 20.25 Euston to Manchester, consisting of nine coaches hauled by a Class 87 electric locomotive No 87007 *City of Manchester*. It carried about 150 passengers. The driver was sitting quietly at the controls watching the succession of green signals ahead, and keeping his eye on the speedometer needle, which was hovering around the 100mph mark, the maximum speed allowed. At this speed even the excellent Class 87s bounce around a little, and when he felt an irregularity in the ride approaching Bushey he dismissed it from his mind as just another wet spot. It was to prove nothing of the sort.

Top and above:
Site welding in progress, and the finished weld. *BR*

Above:
The last two coaches of the 13.50 from York to Liverpool rolled down an embankment into a field near Ulleskelf after the train was derailed by a broken weld on 8 December 1981.
Yorkshire Post

Almost immediately the driver felt the brake go on, and he noticed the 'line light' go out, indicating that the locomotive was no longer receiving power from the overhead electric wires. He lowered the pantograph to save any damage, then got down on to the cab floor to avoid any bits and pieces of the overhead equipment that might be flying around. When the locomotive stopped he sent his secondman forward to telephone the signalman from the next signal, whilst he himself placed track-circuit operating clips on the next line, the Up fast, to put the signals on that line to Danger. In the darkness and mist he could only see two coaches, but the second was leaning at an angle of 45°. He could not see the rest of his train and he would have been horrified if he could have done. The next three coaches were strewn on their sides across the track, and torn from their bogies, but the coach bodies remained structurally intact and very few of the windows, all of which were double-glazed, were broken. The passengers inside those Mk 3 coaches owe their lives to the integrity of the coach bodies, and there were no fatalities, although 19 passengers suffered serious injuries. The Inspecting Officer Lt-Col Townsend-Rose, commented that the derailment had had a more serious effect on the behaviour of the coaches when they were running along derailed because the buckeye couplers became disengaged vertically. He felt that if the couplers had been so constructed as to prevent vertical disengagement the coaches might have been held together and in line, instead of becoming uncoupled and falling over on to their sides. It seems an excellent idea, and yet eight years later a solution has not been found by BR, which might indicate that very little effort has been applied to find one.

The track in the area of the derailment was originally laid in 1965 using flatbottom rail but in October 1979 the cess-side rail was found to be worn and contain serious flaws. It was therefore replaced on 16 October 1979 by two 720ft lengths of CWR, which were welded in, and it was the site weld between this new rail and the old rail which failed. The weld was not up to the required standard and there was little supervision of the work. The organisation was faulty — the welding supervisor was almost fully occupied in the office doing administrative and clerical work, and could rarely get out to exercise supervision. After the accident more welding supervisors were appointed, and were relieved of some of their office duties.

Broken welds are not a rare occurrence. Several had been found in the Watford area previously by patrolmen, and some had been reported by drivers or brought to light by track circuit 'failures'. However, to keep the matter in

Above:
The rear coach of the 13.50 from Aberdeen to Inverness on 3 February 1983, lying on its side near Elgin after the train had been derailed by a broken rail-end. *Northern Photos*

perspective, there were at this time approximately 150,000 welds of this type in track on the LM Region and the failure rate was no greater than on the other Regions. At the end of 1979 there were very nearly 10,000 miles of CWR and there were 550 broken welds that year, a rate of 5.5 every 100 miles. In the Watford area the rate was almost the same at 5.4. By the end of 1987 there were 12,000 miles of CWR and the failure rate had gone down to 2.18 every 100 miles, a welcome improvement.

However, defective track continues to cause derailments, which are invariably expensive and occasionally cause fatalities. On 8 December 1981 the 13.50 York to Liverpool express, consisting of seven coaches hauled by Class 47 diesel-electric No 47409, was derailed by a broken weld near Ulleskelf, between York and Church Fenton. The locomotive remained on the track as usual but all the coaches were derailed and the last two rolled on to their sides down a steep embankment. Twenty-four passengers were taken to hospital, nine of whom were seriously injured, and one subsequently died. The weld which broke was situated between the first two sleepers following the ends of the waybeams over a steel girder bridge spanning the River Wharfe, and was thus subjected to additional stress.

A broken rail-end caused another fatality when the 13.50 train from Aberdeen to Inverness, consisting of a Class 27 diesel-electric locomotive No 27007 and five coaches, was derailed at Llanbryde, two miles east of Elgin, on Thursday 3 February 1983 when travelling at 60mph. The last three coaches were derailed, and the rearmost one turned on to its side and slid for 100yd. Three other passengers were seriously injured. The break in the rail started as a fatigue crack from a fishbolt hole and developed into a brittle fracture.

Derailments continued to occur but year by year the situation improves, which must give the Chief Civil Engineer and his staff much satisfaction. It is also worthy of comment that in none of the derailments we have looked at in this chapter was a second train involved. It is partly a matter of luck, but is also partly due to the widespread use of track circuiting, which allows protecting signals to be put to Danger instantly either because derailed wreckage short-circuits the track circuit or it is done by the traincrew using a track circuit operating clip. The Engineer deserves a bit of luck. He has had to cope with the demands for heavier and faster trains, the pounding of electric-motored traction units, shortages of staff and a tight purse. He also has other responsibilities, such as thousands of bridges; a subject which we will look at in the next chapter.

6
Bridges Under Attack

The River Towy in South Wales is not a long and mighty river. It rises in the bleak moorlands to the north of the pleasant market town of Llandovery and is joined by many tributaries, then it flows down the peaceful and pastoral Vale of Towy to Llandeilo and Carmarthen, gaining in strength and size all the time. In dry spells of weather the flow of water is very much reduced, but even at such times a glance at the nature of the river bed and the banks, together with the width of the watercourse, betrays the fact that the river is not always benign and somnolent. When storms break, up in the mountains and moorlands, and the rain lashes down hour after hour, the tiny tributaries become torrents and the river becomes a raging brown flood, strong enough to uproot fully-grown trees and carry them miles downstream. Such storms are not unknown in South Wales, in fact they are quite common, and to be told that the Towy is in flood would excite no special interest, except among the fishermen, who regularly line its banks.

There is also a railway in the Vale of Towy, just a single track, which sticks fairly close to the river and changes sides every now and then. It is a railway with an interesting history. The line was opened on 1 April 1858 by the Vale of Towy Railway, but it was worked from the outset and leased by a neighbouring railway company known as the Llanelli Railway & Docks Co, which had reached Llandeilo the previous year. Meanwhile, the mighty LNWR had its eyes on the lucrative traffic in the Swansea district and Southwest Wales and pondered upon how it might obtain access to the area. It had already reached Shrewsbury and owned jointly with the Great Western the railway which joined that town to Hereford via Craven Arms. It therefore resolved to project lines through central Wales via Knighton and Llandrindod Wells to Llandovery, which it reached in 1868 and where it joined the Vale of Towy Railway. The LNWR then took over a share of the Llanelli Co's lease of the Vale of Towy Railway, and a few years later gained the lines from Llandeilo to Carmarthen, and from Pontarddulais to Swansea Victoria. The LNWR had achieved its objective, and for the next century or so the line saw a fair amount of long-distance freight traffic and some passenger traffic, including the legendary York to Swansea mail, which ran nightly in both directions. The Great Western also ran a local service from Llanelli to Llandovery over the Vale of Towy line, which it jointly owned as successor to the Llanelli company. For many years after World War 2, the former LNWR services were worked mainly by standard Fowler parallel boiler 2-6-4 tanks and Stanier '8F' 2-8-0s, which came to epitomise the line.

Between Llandeilo and Llandovery the line crosses the river three times — near Glanrhyd, five miles from Llandeilo; between Llangadog and Llanwrda, about seven miles from Llandeilo; and at Llwyn Jack, 10 miles from Llandeilo and a mile or so from Llandovery. The maintenance responsibilities of the Vale of Towy Railway were divided between the LNWR and the Great Western, the boundary point being Milepost 24.

Sunday 18 October 1987 was a very wet day in South Wales. The driver of a light locomotive returning from Craven Arms to Pantyffynnon after weekend engineering work on the Central Wales line noticed that floodwater was near the track at Milepost 26 between Llandovery and Llanwrda. He resolved to report it to the signalman at the first opportunity and continued on his way. At the Glanrhyd Bridge he stopped for a short while out of curiosity to see how high the river was and how fast it was flowing. It was quite an unnerving sight even in the darkness, being almost up to bridge level. He set off again, but at Milepost 21 he found that the track was flooded and some of the ballast had been displaced. After that he proceeded even more cautiously, not knowing what he might find, then just

Below:
Fowler LMS Standard 2-6-4T Class 4P, of the type used on the Central Wales line. Side cab windows were fitted to the last 30 of the class, Nos 2395-2424.

Left:
Stanier Class 5P5F 4-6-0 No 45190 awaits the 'rightaway' at Swansea Victoria on 20 April 1949 with the 12.30pm stopping train to Shrewsbury. LNWR ownership can be traced in the design of the signalbox and the signals. *H. Daniel*

Below left:
Stanier Class 8F 2-8-0 No 48354 sets off from Llandovery on 10 August 1963 with the 12.25pm from Shrewsbury to Swansea Victoria. Within a few minutes it will pass over the Glanrhyd bridge. *Gerald T. Robinson*

Below:
More recent motive power on the Central Wales line. A two-car DMU halts at Pantyffynnon with the 12.25 from Swansea to Shrewsbury on 18 November 1978. *G. Scott-Lowe*

outside Llandeilo he saw that the floodwaters were actually above rail level. He reported the facts to the signalman by telephone and thought to himself that he had never seen such bad flooding on the Vale of Towy line.

The situation was reported to various 'on-call' staff and it was decided that the first train the next morning, the 05.27 Swansea to Shrewsbury, should be accompanied by the local permanent way supervisor so that he could look at the places where flooding had been reported and examine the track to make sure that it was safe for the train to pass over, and to assess any necessary repairs. He made his way by road to Llandeilo with some difficulty as the road also was flooded, then met the train there, having already examined the line just outside the station and decided that it was safe for the train to proceed over it at 5mph. The permanent way supervisor then joined the train and they set off towards the next reported trouble spot at Milepost 21. This also was negotiated safely at about 5mph; and the train went on its way towards the last of the three places where the driver of the previous night's light locomotive had reported flooding. En route they passed over the level crossing at the old Glanrhyd station, which was closed about 30 years ago, at the required speed of 10mph and headed towards the bridge. In the driving cab were the driver, the permanent way supervisor and an operations manager. They saw the grey steel girders of the bridge end-on, then just as they reached them they noticed that the twin ribbons of the rails did not stretch in a straight line across the bridge, but they dipped somewhat and were out of alignment to the right. The driver shouted 'Hang on', and pushed his brake handle straight through to the 'emergency' position. It was too late. Even though they were only travelling at 10 to 15mph the front coach dipped and plunged into the swollen, raging torrent. It righted itself and settled down horizontally, with water up to chest level inside. The second coach came to rest on the sloping bridge deck.

To add to the sudden terror and confusion the lights in the first coach went out, although they remained on in the second. Dawn was just breaking and, when it was discovered that it was possible to clamber through the gangway connection into the second coach, and into relative safety, the few passengers and the railwaymen started to make good their escape. It was not at all easy; the two coach-ends were at an angle to each other and a torrent of water was surging through the gap. Three of the passengers and two railwaymen had crossed through safely to the second coach, and they were struggling to pull through an elderly lady when, with a loud crack the coupling between the two coaches snapped and the stricken coach swung away to become almost totally submerged. It became a tomb for the 58-year-old driver and a 14-year-old

Above left:
Llwyn Jack Bridge, between Glanrhyd and Llandovery. The width and strength of the River Towy can be gauged from this photograph. The bridge is supported by metal tubes, unlike the Glanrhyd bridge, which was supported on masonry piers. *Author*

Left:
End view of Llwyn Jack Bridge over the River Towy. *Author*

Below:
The Glanrhyd bridge over the River Towy on 19 October 1987. The first coach of the two-car DMU is almost completely submerged at this stage. *South West News*

schoolboy who had bravely stayed behind in the front coach to try to help everyone out. The elderly lady and her husband also lost their lives. Mr Alan Cooksey, Deputy Chief Inspecting Officer, subsequently held a Public Inquiry into the accident.

The bridge piers, of which there were four, all of the masonry type, dated from the opening of the railway, but in the 1950s the original box girders of the bridge itself were found to require replacement, and a new steel girder bridge was constructed, resting on the old piers. The bridge had been examined regularly, and from time to time repairs had been carried out to the piers and to remedy the effects of scouring round the foot of the piers. So far as everyone knew, the bridge was perfectly sound and none of the railwaymen involved had the slightest qualms about travelling over it, as indeed they had had no fears about travelling over another bridge over the same river at Ffair-fach, about a mile on the far side of Llandeilo. No one locally had had any experience of bridge collapses, nor ever heard of one except for the Tay Bridge disaster over a century ago.

If four people are killed on the roads it excites little interest, but four people killed in a railway accident by drowning, in a train which has plunged off a railway bridge damaged by a fast-flowing river running at flood level, is a matter of great public interest. All the dramatic elements were there — the darkness, tinged with the first glimmer of daylight, the fear of being trapped in a coach with water rising over your head, the noise of the river in full spate, the terror that the coaches might be swept away at any

Above left and left:
Two views of the 05.27 Swansea to Shrewsbury after the river level had fallen by several feet. The ordeal of the passengers and train crew can be imagined from these photographs.
Tom Clift

Below:
Another bridge over the River Towy, near Carmarthen. Great Western 0-6-0 No 2200 is seen on the 3.20pm to Aberystwyth on 20 June 1951. *J. N. Westwood*

moment, and the sheer uniqueness of the situation. Questions began to be asked about the wisdom of running a train in such conditions, and particularly a passenger train. The Railway Authorities were severely criticised, as though they ought to have known that the Glanrhyd Bridge would collapse. And yet such an eventuality was totally outside anyone's experience or knowledge. There was absolutely no reason for any of the local BR staff to suspect the integrity of the bridge at Glanrhyd, nor of any of the other bridges on the line, even though conditions were described by some people as the worst they had ever seen. After all, bridges are always built with a wide margin of safety, and those four bridges over the Towy had easily withstood the worst that the weather had thrown at them for 130 years. Anyone saying that a train should not have crossed the Glanrhyd Bridge that morning was surely being wise after the event. But great emotions had been stirred, and passions roused. BR was negligent, people said; as though the local staff should have been able to divine the future. The inquest jury agreed and returned a verdict of 'unlawful killing'. They did not specify who had done the unlawful killing, and it is difficult to escape the feeling that it was simply an emotional swipe at BR; an easy target. What no one seems to have considered is the sequence of events that would have unfolded if the light locomotive had not run on the Sunday evening. It was purely fortuitous that it did run. It was purely fortuitous that the three areas of flooding were noticed and reported. It was purely fortuitous that the 05.27 Swansea to Shrewsbury was accompanied by a permanent way supervisor and an operations manager. Without all that, the train would have set off normally as on any other day. The driver would have noticed the flooding just beyond Llandeilo and he would have slowed down. Being an experienced man he would have known where he might expect flooding and he would have driven accordingly at what he considered to be an appropriate speed. He might well have gone on to the Glanrhyd Bridge a little faster — is there any reason why he should not have done? — and the result might have been even more serious. He would have had no reason to have doubted the stability of the bridge. Would the inquest jury then have found 'unlawful killing'? Perhaps not. It would not have wanted to have blamed a dead man. Was the inquest jury aware that the last time anyone was killed in a bridge collapse was over 70 years ago? That was at Carr Bridge on the Highland Railway, between Aviemore and Inverness, on 15 June 1914, when the 10.00am express from Glasgow Buchanan Street to Inverness became derailed as the train was crossing a flood-damaged bridge. The driver stopped the train with some coaches still on the bridge, and a few minutes later it collapsed. One of the coaches fell into the swollen river and five passengers were killed.

It was absolutely right that there should have been searching inquiries into the circumstances of the Glanrhyd Bridge collapse in order to see what went wrong and to ensure as far as possible that such an accident does not happen again. And yet, our views on road and rail accidents are quite unbalanced. Some time after the Glanrhyd accident the following note appeared in one of the daily newspapers:

> 'Four men were killed last night on a country bypass, the A350, near Chippenham, Wiltshire, during the rush hour. A mother and child were among five injured cut from the wreckage and were rushed to hospital with serious injuries.'

Was there a great outcry? No. Were the four men who were killed any less dead than the four people who died at Glanrhyd? No. Did their relatives grieve any the less? No. Was there a full-scale public inquiry lasting four days and headed by a senior inspector from the Department of Transport? There was none. Did the inquest jury return a verdict of unlawful killing against the operators of the road system and the drivers of the road vehicles? Were stringent measures taken to ensure that it could not happen again? No, in all cases. Why do we apply such double standards to road and rail safety? Either we are over-reacting when there is a railway accident, or under-reacting when there is one on the roads. We cannot have it both ways.

There have been rare instances of other trains being involved in bridge collapses but without any casualties to passengers. An LMS Compound 4-4-0 was involved in one on an early morning local train to Skipton on 12 April 1947 after the severest winter in living memory in those parts. The bridge over a tributary of the River Aire at Eastburn near Keighley had been damaged by floods a year earlier and was being repaired. Single-line working was in operation over the double-track bridge and the traffic inspector on pilotman's duties was anxiously watching the river, which was in spate. He decided, in conjunction with the Engineering Department watchman, that no further trains should be allowed to pass over the bridge, but the District Control Office 'persuaded' him to allow the early morning train to pass, as it conveyed the mails, newspapers and parcels. It was therefore allowed to proceed, but the bridge collapsed under the engine and tender.

During the enquiries into the Glanrhyd disaster it was suggested that trains ought not to run over river bridges during flood conditions, but that seems to overlook a number of points. The damage is likely to be to the foundations of the piers or abutments, and may not be apparent except to divers. The damage may still be hidden when the flood waters recede and the river level goes down, except to divers. Is it seriously being suggested that BR should stop running trains for several days every time a river is in spate, and employ an army of divers? The point is that bridges are designed and built to withstand the worst possible flood conditions, and provided that there are adequate inspection and maintenance procedures, those whose job it is to run the trains are entitled to do so whatever the weather conditions, so far as bridges are concerned, unless the Civil Engineer advises to the contrary. Flooding of the track is a different matter, because it can damage the trackbed, hidden beneath the water. In such circumstances it is necessary to take the special precautions that were adopted for the passage of the 05.27 DMU from Swansea to Shrewsbury. The train was accompanied by a permanent way supervisor to advise the driver about track conditions, and the driver was warned by the signalman to proceed cautiously. The actual instructions to the signalman are contained in Regulation No 9 of the Regulations for Train Signalling, as follows:

> 'When it is required . . . to ascertain whether a line is clear, the signalman may allow a train to enter a section, subject to the following conditions: [among which the relevant ones are]
>
> > A train conveying passengers must not be used during fog or falling snow (the reason being the reduced visibility).
> >
> > During darkness the driver must be accompanied by a competent person (for example the guard, another driver, or any railwayman with enough railway experience of a relevant nature. The purpose of this instruction is to assist the driver in keeping a sharp lookout in the darkness).

The driver must be informed of the circumstances, instructed to pass the section signal at Danger, and proceed cautiously through the section prepared to stop short of any obstruction.

(There are special instructions regarding tunnels.)

The text in brackets does not form part of the Regulation.'

These are the instructions to the signalman, and tell him what to do. So far as the driver is concerned, he is told by the signalman what he is to do, and he is informed of the circumstances. He is not issued with a copy of the signalling regulations but is guided by what the signalman tells him, and the instructions in the Rule Book (of which he does have a copy). The following are the relevant ones:

The driver must not pass a signal at Danger except . . . when the line is to be examined to ascertain whether it is clear (there are several other exceptions).
The driver must ensure that he clearly understands what is required and how far the movement may proceed.
The driver must proceed at such reduced speed throughout the section of line concerned as will ensure that he can stop safely and well clear of any train or obstruction on the line ahead. In determining the safe speed at which the train may proceed, the driver must be guided by the braking capability of his train and the distance ahead which he can see to be clear. He must take account of darkness, fog or falling snow, curvature of the line or any other feature affecting his view of the line ahead. THE DRIVER MUST ALWAYS BE ABLE TO STOP WITHIN THE DISTANCE HE CAN SEE THE LINE TO BE CLEAR.

The Railway Rules and Regulations use ordinary English words in a special way at times, for example, the words 'obstruction', and 'clear'. In the quotations from the Rules and Regulations just mentioned, the word 'obstruction' is considered to mean a physical obstruction, such as another train, a vehicle, or some wreckage or fallen rocks, literally something which would impede the free passage of the examining train. In that context, 'clear' means unobstructed. However, the examination procedure can also be used if there is a suspected track defect, in which case the word 'obstructed' takes on a new meaning and the staff concerned would proceed accordingly. This examination procedure would never be used if the structure of a bridge were suspected of being unsafe. In such circumstances no trains would be allowed to pass until the Civil Engineer had decided that it was safe for them do do so.

This special use of 'Railway English', that is the attaching of a specific meaning to a general word, can be confusing to the lay person. It can be particularly confusing to members of the legal profession, who of course use words as the tools of their trade and find themselves puzzled when a word or expression does not mean what they think it means.

Having mentioned lawyers, this might be an appropriate place to comment on what appears to be an undesirable trend in the conduct of public inquiries into railway accidents held by Railway Inspecting Officers of the Department of Transport under the provisions of the Regulation of Railways Act 1871. Section 3 of that Act states that:

'The Board of Trade (now the Department of Transport) may . . . appoint any person to be an inspector for the purpose of . . . making any inquiry . . . into the cause of any railway accident.'

It is customary for such inquiries to be held in public, but it should be noted that the public have no legal right to be present, and the Inspecting Officer may at his discretion hold part of the inquiry in private. The Inspecting Officer conducts the inquiry and hears the evidence, being assisted in this by the report of the railway internal inquiry conducted by a panel of railway officers. The Inspecting Officer has the following powers under Section 4 of the 1871 Act:

'He may by summons under his hand, require the attendance of any person who is engaged in the management, service or employment of (the railway undertaking) and whom he thinks fit to call before him and examine, and may require answers . . . as he thinks fit . . . (It should be noted that the Inspecting Officer has no powers to summon members of the public to give evidence, but he may invite them to do so, and they usually accept the invitation).
He may require and enforce the production of all books, papers and documents (of a railway undertaking) which he considers important (for the purpose of the inquiry).'

The Inspecting Officer's task is to establish the cause of an accident and to make recommendations to prevent a recurrence. The inquiry is not a court of law and it is not concerned with legal or criminal responsibility. He, and he alone, is entitled to ask questions, but it is customary to allow the senior railway officers who are present, to put questions to witnesses, but they will only do so where it will clarify points and aid him. The trade union representatives are also allowed, solely at the Inspecting Officer's discretion, to put questions to witnesses, but they are accustomed to public inquiries and do not normally abuse the courtesy extended to them. What is more, they are *au fait* with railway terminology and practice. A particular problem arises in that respect with counsel and solicitors attending the inquiry on behalf of clients, because members of the legal profession may have little or no knowledge of either railway terminology or practice. The Inspecting Officer may sometimes extend to them the courtesy of asking questions, which should be put through him, but the practice is growing of allowing them to put questions directly to witnesses. Because lawyers may not understand railway working they may ask questions which confuse the witnesses, and they may misunderstand the answers. They may have to waste the inquiry's time by seeking clarification to help them to understand. None of this assists the Inspecting Officer in any way in the task for which he has been appointed. Finally, under Section 7 of the 1871 Act, the Department of Transport is required to make the Inspecting Officer's report public.

The catalogue of bridge collapses caused by the action of flooded rivers is not a long one, despite the fact that there are thousands of such bridges. Starting about 50 years ago, the ones not already mentioned include:

21 June 1936 River Dulais
Between Newtown and Caersws, GWR Shrewsbury to Aberystwyth line (graphically described in O. S. Nock's book *Historic Railway Disasters*).

March 1947 River Wye Strangford Viaduct.
Near Fawley. GWR Hereford to Gloucester line.

August 1948 Several bridges
East Coast main line north of Berwick.

19 Nov 1951
Between Cocking and Midhurst, Southern Region. Engine of freight train fell into the gap.

Early 1960s River Ystwyth
Near Aberystwyth, on the line to Carmarthen.

Sept 1968 River Wey
Godalming, on the Woking to Portsmouth line, Southern Region.

Sept 1968 River Mole
Cobham, on the Guildford New Line, Southern Region.

Sept 1968 River Kennett
Between Kennett and Higham, Eastern Region, near Newmarket.

Sept 1968 Bridge 317
Between Diss and Burston, Norwich main line.

Bridge collapses are rare, but not unknown. However, none of the following involved a passenger train:

1. **Strangford Viaduct over the River Wye, Great Western Railway between Hereford and Gloucester, March 1947.** *GWR*
2. **East Coast main line Bridge No 133 between Grantshouse and Reston on 15 August 1948, with the rails suspended in mid-air over the gap.** *BR*
3. **East Coast main line Bridge No 133 after temporary repairs, being tested by Class D49 4-4-0 No 62706 *Forfarshire* and Class A4 Pacific No 60012 *Commonwealth of Australia*.** *BR*

4. **Cobham Bridge, September 1968,** *BR*
5. **Bridge No 1122 over the River Kennett, Eastern Region, September 1968.** *BR*
6. **Bridge No 317, between Diss and Burston, September 1968.** *BR*

Of all these incidents, the most spectacular must have been the East Coast floods of 1948, which were caused by torrential rain during 11 and 12 August. Between Reston and Grantshouse, over a distance of five miles, the Eye Water normally meanders along, being crossed repeatedly by the East Coast main line. It is generally little more than a stream, but following the unrelenting downpour it became a torrent with sufficient force to demolish no fewer than seven bridges. On the next section of line between Grantshouse and Cockburnspath long lengths of track and ballast were washed away. Five of the seven bridges which collapsed were of the masonry arch type and two had wrought-iron girders. The line was reopened for passengers on 1 November 1948, using military-type bridges as a temporary measure, with severe speed restrictions. Some of the branch lines inland also suffered damage.

Railway bridges over rivers are designed to be able to withstand the most severe weather conditions, and generally speaking the weather is no worse now than it was 100 to 150 years ago when most of them were built. Railway bridges over roads were designed for the road traffic of the period — perhaps high enough for the driver of a stagecoach to pass under safely, without having his hat or his head knocked off. Today those bridges are under relentless attack from lorries, the speed and weight of which are sometimes sufficient to cause physical damage to the bridges. The building of motorways and bypasses, with higher overbridges, has eased the problem somewhat, but it is still a matter of concern to BR, as two recent items in its house magazine *Rail News* show. The October 1987 issue

Right and below:
The bridge over the A5 London to Holyhead trunk road at Hinckley, on the Leicester-Nuneaton line, has regularly been attacked by lorries. These two photographs show the result of one of the more severe impacts from an overheight lorry or load. *Raymonds Photographers/Author*

Above:
A view of the bridge over the A465 Hereford to Abergavenny road, just south of Pontrilas, as seen in July 1988. The bridge, which carries the Shrewsbury-Hereford-Newport main line, has been shored up to allow trains to pass over, pending permanent repairs. Single line working is in operation for road traffic. *Author*

tells how the Anglesey town of Llangefni narrowly escaped disaster when a juggernaut lorry rammed a railway overbridge shortly after a train conveying dangerous chemicals had passed over it. The main girder of the bridge was pushed off the abutment on to the top of the trailer, making a kink in the line which was so severe that it would almost certainly have derailed a passing train. Local police reported seeing the driver make two attempts to drive his 14ft 1in vehicle beneath the bridge, which was clearly marked 13ft 8in, and one wonders why they did not stop him before he made his second attempt. Perhaps they thought that an apparently flimsy trailer could not possibly damage a big, strong bridge. Maybe the driver thought so too, but at least he was caught in the act, unlike the lorry driver who attacked the bridge over the A465 Hereford to Abergavenny road, just south of Pontrilas, on 6 March 1988. The impact was so great that it damaged the bridge, so the driver can hardly have been unaware of the fact, but he did not bother to report it to BR. Either he did not imagine that his lorry could actually have damaged the bridge and endangered trains, or he did not care. Fortunately, a BR inspector driving his car under the bridge noticed the damage and raised the alarm. Single line working had to be introduced, with a severe speed restriction, until the bridge was shored up.

The second *Rail News* item tells of a low-loader type of lorry, carrying an excavator, becoming jammed under a railway bridge near Westbury (Wilts). The force of the impact lifted the bridge girders by 8in. Some 24hr later engineers were dealing with two more incidents in which container lorries had become wedged under bridges in Bristol. Low-loaders carrying plant and machinery are probably the greatest hazard. In 1975 one hit and almost completely demolished an overbridge at Gorey in Ireland. A CIE express train attempted to jump the gap but failed, and scattered itself all over the area, several lives being lost. It is feared that one day the same thing will happen in Britain. Already there have been derailments.

Bridges are not only at risk on trunk roads, but also on minor and local roads, as was demonstrated on 12 May 1978 in the quiet Scottish countryside about 25 miles inland from Aberdeen, on the line to Inverness. The train concerned was the 07.43 three-car diesel multiple-unit (DMU) from Aberdeen, and it set off from Inverurie at 08.12, with 54 passengers on board, on its way to the next station, Insch. About two miles before reaching Insch the railway line crosses the B9002 road, a quiet country road which connects Insch with the A96 Aberdeen to Inverness trunk road. The bridge bears a sign showing its height — 15ft 3in. There is a plant hire firm in Insch, and that morning one of the drivers, on reporting for work at 07.30, was told to take an excavator on an articulated low-loader type of lorry to Peterhead. His route lay along the B9002 road. He had driven this vehicle, loaded with the excavator, on several occasions and he knew that the overall height of the lorry and the excavator, when properly loaded, was just 15ft. The total weight was 30 tons. Being a careful driver he had checked on the first occasion when he had driven under the

The results of bridge-bashing at Oyne, between Aberdeen and Keith, on 12 May 1978

1. **The excavator on the low-loader, which caused the damage. The trailer has broken in two.** *Author*
2. **The distorted track and the derailed train.** *Author*

railway bridge on the B9002 that there was adequate clearance, and he had actually stopped close to the bridge to check.

The driver had loaded the excavator on to the low-loader himself the previous evening, so he knew that it was safe to pass under the bridge. Having received his orders for the day he went to get ready for the journey and whilst he was away the excavator operator started up the machine to remove the blade from the bucket, leaving it with the boom vertical. It was now 16ft high. Just after 08.00 the driver set off on his journey and at about 08.15, 3min after the DMU had left the last station before the bridge, the lorry with its 16ft high load approached the 15ft 3in high bridge, at a speed of about 20mph. The boom of the excavator hit one of the bridge girders with a resounding crack and knocked it out of alignment by over 3ft, distorting the railway track as it did so.

The passenger train was still five miles away. Was there sufficient time to warn its driver, so that the imminent disaster could be averted? When the lorry collided with the bridge, its driver was momentarily stunned. A moment or two later, a passing motorist helped him from the cab and then went off to telephone for assistance. The lorry driver, upon seeing the damage to the bridge, realised that if there was a train coming it had to be stopped. Not knowing from which direction a train was due, and in an awful quandary, he started to run towards Insch. He had taken the wrong decision. After a few moments he turned and saw the train approaching from the other direction. It was now too late to do anything.

Below:
The bridge over the A68 road, on the Danderhall to Bilston branch, near Edinburgh, completely demolished by a lorry on 24 September 1977. *The Scotsman*

Below right:
It is feared that this scene will one day be repeated in Britain. This accident happened at Gorey on the Coras Iompair Eireann in 1975 and several passengers were killed. The remains of the bridge can be seen in the top right-hand corner of the photograph. *Author*

On board the train, the driver was sitting at the controls, quite relaxed as he coasted down the gently falling gradient at about 55mph. He could see the bridge clearly from some distance away, but the curvature of the line prevented him from having a good view of the track over the bridge until he was quite close to it. With a start he realised that the track was terribly distorted and he immediately pushed the brake handle straight through to the emergency position. It seemed like an eternity before the brakes started to bite but they had reduced the speed of the train to about 40mph when it hit the buckle in the track. The driver clung on grimly as the train bucked and reared, then his coach plunged down the embankment and rolled over on to its side. The second coach followed but remained upright, whilst astonishingly the last coach was not even derailed. There was comparatively little damage to the coach bodies, and most of the passengers were able to climb out with no more than cuts and bruises, thankful to be still alive and in one piece. Only five passengers received minor injuries.

Could the accident have been prevented in any way, or was it just the consequence of an unfortunate set of circumstances? The lorry driver knew the bridge and believed that his load would safely pass under it. There are then only three ways of protecting bridges in such circumstances:

1. To erect a massive steel beam across the road on both sides, set at about 3in below the bridge height. This would effectively prevent any overheight vehicle from reaching the bridge, but the consequences of the collision of the lorry or its load with the beam might endanger other road users, although no more so than a collision with the bridge. The Department of Transport has assessed the cost at £100,000 per bridge, because the beams would have to be of very robust construction. A cheaper and less robust beam might suffice because even though it would not physically prevent the lorry from reaching the bridge the shock of the collision would alert the driver. This solution is not favoured by the Department of Transport (DTp) because the dislodged beam might injure pedestrians or other road users, which might suggest that the DTp

Above:
Low bridge at Settle, on the A65 Keighley to Kendal trunk road. Maximum clearance is only 14ft 9in, and high lorries have to keep to the centre of the road between the white lines. The bridge arch has been struck a glancing blow on countless occasions. *Author*

considers the lives of road users to be more important than the lives of railway passengers. This is the classic 'horse and stable door' situation. No loss of life has yet resulted from a damaged bridge derailment in Britain, although each year there are several bridge-strikes which could have resulted in railway passengers being killed, and it is generally accepted that sooner or later such a fatal accident will occur.

2. To raise the height of the bridge, either by increasing the height of the bridge abutments or by lowering the road surface. This would certainly be effective, but would be very expensive and could only be justified at the few bridges considered to be most at risk. The B9002 bridge would certainly not fall into that category.
3. To install infra-red detectors and automatic signs. High vehicles passing through the detector beam would activate a sign with amber flashing lights to indicate to a driver that his vehicle was over-height. It is the most effective signing measure available, and would cost about £35,000 per bridge. Whilst the equipment would not physically protect the bridge, only a very reckless and foolhardy driver would proceed after such a warning.

For various reasons the scale of the problem has reduced in recent years, thanks partly to the measures which have already been taken, such as improved bridge marking and signing; improved road signing; marking the height in the cab; and various other measures designed to increase driver awareness; although new road construction, with bridges at a minimum height of 16ft 6in has probably had most effect. As long ago as 1972 Col Robertson, the Chief Inspecting Officer, was drawing attention to the problem in his Annual Report. He mentioned that there were about 500 cases a year of damage to railway bridges over roads, and gave his prophetic view that the most damaging type of road vehicle was the low-loader conveying a heavy piece of engineering plant. However, by 1987 the number of potentially serious 'strikes' at the 4,640 bridges considered to be vulnerable had gone down to just over 200, but it is still regarded as a serious hazard and the Minister asked the Bridge-bashing Working Party, which had been in existence since the 1970s, to suggest a strategy to reduce substantially the number of 'strikes' over the next five years. The Working Party produced its Report in 1988 with a comprehensive list of options and a proposed programme, so the prospects are good, but the accident on the B9002 road seems to make it likely that the danger will never be completely eradicated. However, if it can be substantially reduced it will be another step forward in the long quest to improve railway safety.

7
Death on the Line

Hellifield is a station of ghosts. It is impossible to stand on its dilapidated platforms, parts of which are roped off so that the few waiting passengers or curious visitors will not be decapitated by panes of glass falling from the platform roof, and not sense the hustle and bustle that was once a part of everyday life there. The Scotch expresses used to call, not for the convenience of Hellifield's small community, but for the Lancashire connections. There was a sizeable engine shed here too with the noise of engines clanking on and off the shed, or the rattle and clatter of the tubs on the coaling stage as they were wheeled out to tip their contents into waiting tenders. Little knots of locomen and guards would hang around waiting to relieve through trains in order to work them over the 'Long Drag' to Carlisle, or into Lancashire. One can still hear in the imagination the voice of the foreman calling out 'The Brindle Heath's just passed Settle Junction'. Few passengers use the station nowadays, and there are no longer any staff there. It is a station of ghosts. And now there are two more.

Snow is not uncommon at Hellifield, situated as it is almost in the shadow of the Pennine giants — Penyghent and Ingleborough. When the winter wind blows from the north or the east it often brings snow with it; then Hellifield lies under a white mantle. Railwaymen in those parts learned long ago how to cope with snow and it became part of the railway tradition that 'the trains must get through'. The winter of 1978/79 has gone down in history as the winter of discontent. Not only were there industrial relations problems, but the weather was more severe than usual. At Hellifield on 15 February 1979 it was bitterly cold and a keen northeaster was blowing the lying snow about. In the signalbox at Hellifield South the signalman was trying to keep himself warm as the wind whistled through every nook and cranny whilst he waited for the late-running express from Nottingham to Carlisle. It should have passed through Hellifield just after lunch but here he was, after eight o'clock at night and still no sign of it. The weather must be bad further south, he thought to himself,

Below:
Hellifield — scene of former splendours. Now a station of ghosts.

Left:
Hellifield — the Lancashire connection. LMS Class 4P 2-6-4T No 42491 draws out of the bay platform with the 4.10pm to Blackburn on 3 September 1962. *L. Sandler*

when finally, at 20.46, his signalbox block bell rang to announce that the train had just left Skipton, 10 miles to the south and the next signalbox open. He sent the bell signal 'Is the line clear for an express passenger train?' to the signalman at Settle Junction and when he received an affirmative answer he tried to clear his signals for the express. However, when he tried to pull the lever of his Down Home signal he found that it was still 'locked' in the lever-frame, and he noticed that the indication light for some points beyond the signal had gone out. The points were electrically operated because they were at the far end of the station, and when they were in their normal position for trains to travel along the Down main line this fact was indicated to the signalman by a small light on an instrument in the signalbox.

The signalman had had some difficulty with these points earlier in the day when he wanted to run a train from the Down loop on to the Down main line, because snow had blown into them; and when he moved the points the snow became squeezed and compacted into ice, preventing the points from fitting correctly. He had then sent for the Signal Department technicians, who had put the matter right. They had now gone home, therefore he telephoned the permanent way cabin nearby and asked the platelayers to attend to the points. A few minutes later he saw his points indicator light up, telling him that the points were now in their correct position and that the electrical lock on his Down Home signal lever should now be free, so he pulled the lever over and cleared the signal together with all the other signals, for the express to pass.

The express no longer called at Hellifield — the Lancashire connections had long since been withdrawn — and the train approached the station at about 60mph as it swung round the approach curve on the falling gradient from Otterburn and roared past the signalbox. At the far end of the platform the driver suddenly saw the shadowy outline of a man crouched over the points leading from the Down Loop, and directly in the path of the train. He sounded the horn and threw the brakes on. It was much too late. Almost immediately the driver heard the stomach-churning thud and realised that the man had not managed to get clear.

When the call to clear the points had been received in the permanent way cabin two men had gone out to do it. They had donned all their cold weather clothing and muffled themselves up, then they picked up their tools and, heads down, they went out into the howling wind, with the flakes of snow stinging their faces. They cleared the snow and ice from the points (which allowed the signalman to obtain a 'points correct' indication, and clear his signals), then started to put a clamp on the points (a clamp is a metal appliance, rather like a vice, which is screwed up to hold the points firmly in position), oblivious of the fact that death was approaching them at 60mph. With the wind whistling round their ears, and bent over their task, they heard nothing of the train's approach until the last second. They looked up startled but it was too late. A 60mph train is a very effective killer.

Perhaps the two unfortunate platelayers had not expected the signalman to clear his signals, nor expected the train to arrive so soon nor travel so quickly. However, the signalman was fully entitled to clear his signals, and there were no instructions in the Rule Book or elsewhere to tell him not to. Platelayers had always cleared the points during snowy weather and were accustomed to look after their own safety. If necessary, one of the men would act as a lookoutman whilst the other got on with the work. The Rules stated that:

> 'When work is to be carried out on or near lines in use for traffic and danger is likely to arise, the man-in-charge must appoint one or more men . . . expressly to maintain a good lookout and to give warning of approaching trains. Where, of necessity, men are working during fog or falling snow, the man-in-charge must post a lookout-man . . .'

The question to be considered was whether one of the two men should have acted as a lookoutman. They were both qualified to do so. The Rule says that a lookoutman must be appointed if danger is likely to arise. With the line still open to trains, it was evident that danger was likely to arise, especially in the wind and darkness. On the other hand, until the points were cleared of ice and snow danger was unlikely to arise, because the signalman was unable to clear his signals. This risk of danger then became active at the moment the 'points normal' indication appeared in the signalbox. The platelayers may not have known the precise moment when this took place, but they would know that it was likely to occur as soon as the points were fitting correctly, and from that moment on there should have been a lookoutman. What we do not know, of course, is whether one of the two men was already acting as a lookoutman but if he was, such action was ineffective. There is another point too. The Rule says that during falling snow there must be a lookoutman. At the time of the accident, snow was not actually falling but it was being blown about and the effect on visibility may have been the same.

Below:
Hellifield — freight trunk route. LMS 'Crab' 2-6-0 No 42899 of Carlisle Kingmoor shed draws slowly along the Goods line to wait a path, passing Midland Class 3F 0-6-0 No 43756 as it does so, on 3 September 1962. *L. Sandler*

Bottom:
On the same afternoon, sister engine 42798 of Holbeck shed hurries through on the Up main line with an express freight. Another reminder of the past are the cattle wagons next to the engine. *L. Sandler*

As has already been mentioned, there was nothing in the Rules to prevent the signalman from clearing his signals for the express. He had no means of knowing whether or not the platelayers were relying on him for their protection, indeed for their very lives, but to place such a responsibility on the signalman would have been grossly unfair. Supposing that the signalman had misunderstood an arrangement he had made with the platelayers to protect them, or had momentarily overlooked it, might he not then have found himself in the dock facing a manslaughter charge?

And yet, was it enough to have left it to the platelayers themselves to look after their own safety on such a night? The circumstances of the tragic accident at Hellifield focussed attention once more on the subject. If there was going to be a system of protection involving the signalman it had to be cast-iron. BR pondered hard over this. There were two main considerations — the avoidance of the possibility of any misunderstanding between the signalman and the platelayers, and the avoidance of a situation whereby the signalman might be loaded with an unreasonable and haphazard responsibility for other men's lives. BR's solution was essentially simple. It issued a new Regulation designed to remove any doubts or misunderstandings. It stated that when a signalman sent for platelayers or technicians, etc to repair or make workable some piece of equipment on the track the men concerned must come to an understanding as to whether trains were still running or not, and if not, when they could be allowed to resume running. Alternatively, if the work could not be carried out safely with trains running, they were to be stopped. Where trains were stopped the signalman would give an assurance that this was so and that he would not allow train running to resume until the platelayers agreed. The signalman would also place a metal lever collar over the appropriate signal lever, to physically prevent him from pulling the lever in a moment of forgetfulness, and he would record all the facts in his Train Register Book.

Hellifield was not the only railway location to be affected by snow and tragedy that winter. The following morning, at Rowley Regis on the former Great Western line from Stourbridge Junction to Birmingham, two platelayers were clearing snow from points when they were taken unawares by the 07.42 DMU from Worcester to Birmingham. One of them managed to jump clear when the driver of the approaching DMU sounded an urgent warning on his horn but the other one was knocked down and killed. They had no lookoutman, but at least it was daylight and not snowing. They had merely carried out the former practice of looking out for their own safety when engaged in snow clearance.

Fatal accidents to men working on the line have been occurring ever since railways began and still do so today, despite all the Rule changes, explanatory booklets and changes in procedures, etc. BR is very concerned that such tragedies still occur, as the front page headlines in the September 1988 issue of *Rail News* show — 'Board alarm as track death figures mount'. The article goes on to say that of 83 railwaymen killed on duty since January 1984 more than half have been struck by trains while crossing, walking or working on the line. The table below nevertheless illustrates the tremendous improvement which has taken place since steam days. 1986 was the best year ever.

	1957	*1971*	*1980*	*1985*	*1986*	*1987*
Total No of staff	597,000	261,000	232,000	181,000	178,000	179,000
Killed whilst working on the line	33	14	6	10	3	7
Killed whilst on the line, eg standing or walking	70	18	9	4	1	1
Total killed (all causes)	176	60	32	25	16	16

(The above figures are for all railways in Britain)

The figures for 1985 were inflated by a particularly appalling accident which occurred at Severn Tunnel Junction on 11 February. Once again there was snow and men were on duty specially to keep the points clear. There were no fewer than six men employed in a gang that night, keeping the points clear of snow and ice on the main line from Paddington to South Wales, to the west of Severn Tunnel Junction station. It had stopped snowing but there was a strong, cold easterly wind, which was blowing loose snow into the points. All the points and signals were operated from Newport power signalbox 10 miles away, and the points themselves were equipped with gas heaters to prevent them from freezing up, but heaters are prone to being blown out in strong winds and require periodic checking and relighting. There were 42 sets of gas point heaters in the area.

Two teams of men were used at Severn Tunnel Junction for snow clearance duties and each team worked a 12hr shift, changing over at 19.00. The night shift men on 11 February worked for a while then had a break, during which some of them went to a local public house. On their return the six-man gang set to work again. It was now approaching midnight. They worked progressively on the points comprising the 'ladder' at the Newport end of the yards, but they had no lookoutman, nor had they come to any understanding with the signalman; errors that were to prove fatal. Perhaps, being Sunday night, they thought (incorrectly) that there would be very few trains about. They had perhaps forgotten about one insignificant little train, the 00.25 DMU from Cardiff, which terminated at Severn Tunnel Junction. Approaching the station its driver had reduced his speed to about 45mph, when he suddenly caught a fleeting glimpse of a high-visibility vest and almost immediately heard an impact. He knew instinctively what it was, but he had no idea that that slight noise had signified the deaths of no fewer than four men. It was one of the worst accidents of its type which had ever happened. All six men had received training and had passed a skill test for carrying out lookoutmen's duties. In addition four of them had attended a special course on lookoutmen arrangements and had passed out as qualified to decide whether or not lookoutmen should be appointed.

Above:
In 1965 Standard Class 9F 2-10-0 No 92208 draws slowly along the Down Goods line at Hellifield with the empty anhydrite hopper wagons in circuit working between Long Meg Sidings, near Langwathby, and Widnes. *N. Gascoine*

At the inquest the Coroner said that the cause of the accident was the failure to appoint a lookoutman. He did not consider that consumption of alcohol played a prominent part and thought it was probably a case of familiarity breeding contempt. The jury's verdict was 'Accidental Death'. The accident was also investigated by Mr A. W. Froud, a Railway Employment Inspector of the Department of Transport, who recommended that the

Below:
A Class 45 diesel-electric heads through Severn Tunnel Junction station with the 06.14 Sheffield to Cardiff Central on 13 August 1977. *D. Kimber*

Above:
'Planlite' gas-operated point heaters. *BR*

provision of lookout protection during the hours of darkness for men working on lines open to trafffic should be made compulsory. This recommendation was accepted by BR and is now incorporated in the Rules. He also reiterated the Railway Inspectorate's oft-repeated recommendation that headlights should be fitted to all traction units, so that men working on the track could identify the approach of a train sooner and more easily. BR is working on this, but slowly, because of the cost involved. All new traction units are so equipped but BR have been reluctant to spend money on slower traction units which are approaching the ends of their lives.

The problem of the appointment of lookoutmen is a very long-running story. An official group, known by the somewhat cumbersome title of 'The Railway Industry Advisory Committee Working Group on Safety of Staff on the Track' (a joint body representing the DTp, BR and the trade unions — chaired by an Inspecting Officer) has spent many years deliberating this issue and gradually pushing BR into extending and improving the lookout arrangements. The question might reasonably be asked as to why BR apparently had to be pushed, when lives were at stake, and there are two main reasons — the difficulty in fixing a precise dividing line between those situations where a lookoutman was essential for safety and those where men could reasonably be expected to look out for their own safety; and the fact that every additional lookoutman employed means another man on the line and another life at risk. Lookoutmen themselves have been knocked down and killed by the very trains they were supposed to be looking out for. And whilst cost ought not to be a factor in the

Below:
The effectiveness of point heaters in keeping the points free from snow. *BR*

C514

Left:
The 11.02 Bristol to Cardiff service leaves Severn Tunnel Junction station on 7 October 1976. *L. Bertram*

Below left:
At Severn Tunnel Junction station on 31 March 1980, Class 46 diesel-electric No 46036 prepares to replace Class 47 No 47182 on the 14.30 Swansea to Manchester. *D. J. Smith*

reckoning where men's lives are concerned, it must be. It has to be. Cost is a factor in the reckoning of any safety precaution.

The main difficulty has been the fixing of the dividing line between those cases where a lookoutman was necessary and those where he was not. It would obviously be nonsense to provide a lookoutman for someone who merely needed to cross a quiet branch line in broad daylight, or who needed to do a little work on such a line where trains approached at low speed and could be seen a mile away. Equally it would be nonsense not to provide one, or even two, on a high speed multi-track main line, when a gang of men had to work on the track. Between those two extremes there is a judgement area where the decision is left to the man in charge. He was given some guidance — the time-honoured phrase being 'where danger is likely to arise a lookoutman must be appointed'. That sufficed for many years. It was embraced within the Board of Trade's 'Prevention of Accidents Rules 1902', made under The Railway Employment (Prevention of Accidents) Act, 1900, and was still in the Rule Book, though amplified somewhat in 1988. The Rule has been the subject of many court cases. In a 1942 case the Court of Appeal held that a lookout might not be necessary in the case of a branch line with only two or three trains a day. In 1958 Viscount Kilmuir said that the words 'any danger is likely to arise' must be given their ordinary meaning and import an estimate of likelihood not of what might possibly be foreseen, but of what should be expected to occur. The estimate must be made according to ordinary principles of common sense and experience in the light of all the relevant circumstances known.

The Health and Safety at Work Act 1974 gave a fresh impetus to the question of safety of men on the line and since then BR has found its Rules and methods and procedures under closer scrutiny. It has responded by issuing reams of instructions in an attempt to cover every contingency and situation, lest it should find itself in the dock facing a criminal charge under the Act; but the men who work on the track are employed for their manual skills rather than their intellectual capacity and there is a danger that, finding themselves bemused by floods of literature and continuous exhortation, they will revert to first principles. It is, of course, absolutely right and proper that BR should do all it sensibly can to protect the lives of its staff, regarding equipment, methods, Rules, procedures and training, but in the ultimate reckoning some regard has to be paid to the nature of the men concerned and how they will respond. There is a law of behaviour which states that 'the degree of observance of a rule is in inverse proportion to its complexity'. 'Keep it simple' should be every rule-maker's motto, and some regard must be paid to the common sense and experience of the men whose job it is to interpret and carry out Rules and instructions. After all, the volumes of Rules and instructions and the thousands of hours spent in learned discussion by eminent committees did not save the lives of four men at Severn Tunnel Junction on the night of 10/11 February 1985. Perhaps there is

Below:
On 15 October 1986 train No 6S75 sets off to Carlisle from Severn Tunnel Junction yards behind Class 47 No 47162.
Brian Perryman

another law in operation here — 'the bigger the committee, the less it achieves'.

The provision of a lookoutman does not in itself automatically guarantee the safety of the men at work. In an accident at Pear Tree public footpath crossing near Salfords station on the Brighton main line on 2 October 1983 two men, a father and son, were killed when they were knocked down by the 08.00 train from London Victoria to Three Bridges. The lookoutman himself was also hit by the train, which cut off his left leg. The men were part of a gang repairing the timber crossing and they appear to have been taken unawares by a train on the Down slow line. There are four tracks at this location and the line is busy, with train speeds up to 90mph. The accident happened in clear weather and daylight and the fact that the lookoutman himself was injured seemed to indicate to the investigating Inspector that he had failed to see the approaching train until the last few seconds, and in consequence had failed to warn those whose lives were in his hands. This underlines the heavy responsibility which lookoutmen carry.

In another case, on 7 May 1984, near Bushey, on the West Coast main line from Euston, a lookoutman was knocked down and killed by the very train for which he had already given a warning to the men he was protecting. They were unharmed.

Perhaps this would be an appropriate place to say a few words about the 1974 Health and Safety at Work Act. Its title sounds harmless enough, indeed it sounds entirely beneficial and a credit to a responsible and progressive society. In reality it is a burden and an encumbrance so far as the railways are concerned, BR being an innocent victim. It may well have been a necessary measure so far as certain industries were concerned, but it was almost entirely superfluous so far as BR were concerned, because the railways already had a very extensive safety organisation, in which the local staff representatives were already involved; and the Department of Transport already had extensive powers under the 1900 Railway Employment (Prevention of Accidents) Act. The 1974 Act was quickly discovered to be something of a bureaucratic nightmare, and it has absorbed enormous quantities of management time in its procedural complexities; time which would have been more usefully devoted to the practicalities of achieving a safer railway. It did not prevent the accidents at Polmont, or Severn Tunnel Junction, or Methley Junction, described in this chapter. In the view of many people the Act was ill-conceived, inadequately thought-out and badly drafted.

As train speeds rise and the use of noisy machinery increases, the difficulty of giving timely and effective warning to men working on the line becomes more pronounced. In an accident at Polmont, on the Edinburgh-Glasgow main line on 5 August 1983, inquired into by John Seager, the Principal Railway Employment Inspector, both these factors were present. The line at the site of the accident was sharply curved, and the maximum permitted speed was 90mph (100mph for IC125 units). A gang of men was employed in repacking the ballast under a dipped welded rail joint on the Down line, using Kango electric tamping hammers. Owing to the restricted visibility the man in charge had appointed an extra lookoutman to give advance warning of the approach of trains on the Down line before they could be seen by the normal lookoutman, who was posted at the site of work. When the advance lookoutman saw a train approaching he would wave a blue and white chequered flag, and upon seeing this the site lookoutman would switch off the electric power to the Kango hammers and sound a siren. These combined actions were sufficient to warn the workmen to stand clear of the tracks. Whilst the provision of an advance lookoutman enabled the men to be given an earlier warning than would otherwise have been the case (and without whom it would have been unsafe to have carried out the work at all without trains being stopped), the procedure suffered from an

Below:
One of the high speed push-pull services in use between Edinburgh and Glasgow. Class 47 diesel-electric No 47702 is seen near Linlithgow with the 08.30 from Glasgow on 20 September 1986. *W. A. Sharman*

inherent and dangerous defect — it was not fail-safe. If the site lookoutman for any reason did not notice the advance warning, the men at work would not receive a warning to stand clear until the train came into view from the work site, if then. That could be too late.

After the men had taken their breakfast they resumed work on the track. Then, according to the evidence given in Mr Seager's Report on the accident, a Down train approached and the advance lookoutman waved his blue and white flag. The site lookoutman saw this, switched off the Kango hammers and sounded the siren. The gang moved clear, and then restarted work after the train had passed. A few minutes later an IC125 unit came along the Up line. The warning was given and the men stood clear. They had very little time to do so because of the curvature of the line and the speed of the train, and the site lookoutman felt uneasy about this. He called across to the man in charge to discuss the problem with him, taking his eyes off the advance lookoutman as he did so. It was a fatal mistake. The advance lookoutman saw another train approach on the Down line and turned to wave his flag. To his consternation the site lookoutman did not respond. He waved his flag frantically and shouted, but got no response. The men on the Down line, directly in the path of the approaching train, carried on with their work, quite oblivious of the fact that they were living their last few seconds. The train struck them with appalling suddenness, and they probably never knew what hit them. Two men were thrown clear and killed, whilst the body of a third man became lodged below the nearside guard iron of the power car and was carried forward to where the train stopped. The fatal flaw in the system had been exposed. It is expecting a lot of human nature to rely implicitly for the safety of men's lives upon one man never taking his eyes off another for hours on end. There was, in fact, a better warning system available, known as the 'Pee Wee' system. This is a transportable electrical advance warning set of equipment which is used by the advance lookoutman to sound the siren at the worksite, and is a safer method of giving warning. Two sets of this equipment had been supplied to the local depot, but one had been unserviceable for some time prior to the accident and the other was missing, presumed stolen.

It might be thought that the only certain way to prevent men from being killed whilst working on the track would be to stop trains from running altogether. Such arrangements already exist when major items of work have to be undertaken, but even then misunderstandings can have fatal results. On Saturday night 6 November 1982 some work was programmed to be carried out at Denham station on the Bicester to Marylebone line. Accordingly, the Civil Engineer closed the Down line at 01.15 on Sunday morning and told a gang of painters that they could erect scaffolding on the Down line in order to paint the bridge at Denham station. He could not at that moment close the Up line because he had to wait until an empty DMU from Bicester to Marylebone had gone by. Through some misunderstanding the painters erected their scaffolding on the Up line instead of the Down line, before the empty DMU had passed. It ran into the scaffolding and three painters were killed.

One might imagine that an accident such as the one at Polmont on 5 August 1983 could not happen again; that steps would be taken, training improved, supervision intensified, new equipment devised and maintained in proper working order, and everything reasonable be done to ensure safety. And yet there was an accident at Methley Junction, near Leeds, on the former Midland Railway main line to Sheffield on 8 December 1987 that had many similarities with the Polmont tragedy. Once again a gang of men was working on the track with Kango hammers, which make so much noise that the machine operators cannot hear the approach of a train. Indeed, the equipment makes so much noise that the operators have to wear protective ear muffs, thus ensuring that they cannot hear trains approaching. In such circumstances, with the men so completely exposed to mortal danger, it is essential that the

Below:
The 13.17 Edinburgh to Dunblane train brakes for the Polmont stop on 20 February 1982. *D. M. May*

Left:
Men at work on the track using hand-held machinery. They are wearing ear protectors, which prevent their hearing from being damaged, but make them totally dependent on the lookoutman for their safety. The lookoutman is holding the switch which cuts off the power to the equipment and sounds a siren on the approach of a train.
John Rose Associates

warning system is foolproof and fail-safe. We have seen how the system in use at Polmont had a fatal flaw, but in fact the system in use at Methley was the same one, with the advance lookoutman with his same blue and white chequered flag, and the safety of the gang entirely dependent on the site lookoutman never taking his eyes off the advance lookout.

On the morning of the accident two trains had passed without incident. Each time, the site lookoutman had seen the chequered flag and had switched off power to the Kango hammers, which automatically sounded a siren. Each time, the gang had stood clear until the train passed and had then resumed work. Each time, whilst the men were standing clear, the site lookoutman had walked down the line about 60yd to move a marker board. It was not his job to do so; he should have had no other duties but it seemed safe enough at the time. However, and here was the fatal flaw, in order to stop the siren from sounding, the site lookoutman had to switch on the power to the Kango hammers. The consequences were revealed in the following evidence given at the Official Inquiry and at the Coroner's Inquest.

A little later, the 10.43 DMU from Leeds to Sheffield approached at 60/65mph. The advance lookoutman waved his flag. The site lookoutman acknowledged and gave his usual warning. The gang stopped work, then the site lookoutman walked down the line a little way to move the marker board. Power to the tools was now back on again. Suddenly he heard the Kango hammers working. Through some misunderstanding the gang had gone back on to the track and restarted work, but the train had not yet gone by. The site lookoutman ran back towards the gang shouting and waving his arms in desperation but they did not hear him. The noise of the hammers, and the protection of the ear muffs, ensured that they did not.

The DMU had just got into its stride after the Woodlesford stop when the driver saw the gang of men on the track with their backs to him. 'I was shocked when I saw what was in front of me,' he said at the Inquiry. 'It was unusual that they were still on the track as I approached. I blew the horn to warn them but I got no response. The men didn't appear to move so I started blowing the horn again and putting the brake on. There was no reaction from the men whatsoever. There was no movement from them before the impact. I hadn't a chance to stop. It was terrible. I was just transfixed.' Four men were killed.

The foreman of the Inquest jury criticised BR, saying that the warning systems were inadequate, the men lacked training, and there was insufficient supervision. The Coroner commented 'It seems inconceivable that in this day and age we still rely on 18th century methods of using flags to warn men on the track.' What would he have said, one wonders, if he had known that the flag system was of quite recent vintage, and introduced to enable the workmen to be given earlier warning of the approach of trains? A foolproof portable, fail-safe system, which relies as little as possible on human intervention, has still to be introduced for one-off use. On high speed lines there is a permanent automatic system which gives an audible warning, initiated when an approaching train occupies a track circuit. The system can be switched off when not required, because the noise it makes is not popular with local residents, but there is a danger that one gang could switch off the system, unaware that another was still depending on it. Work is therefore in progress to see whether an Inductive Loop Warning System can be devised for use on such lines. In this system, cables would be laid along each side of the track to form a loop which would transmit warnings to portable units carried by lookoutmen and others who need them. It would also be able to give warnings inside protective ear muffs when noisy equipment such as Kango hammers are in use. However, as long as human beings are capable of error or misunderstanding it seems likely that death on the line will continue to occur.

Almost as a postscript to this chapter it is sad to have to relate the death of yet another lookoutman, on 13 October 1988, near Attleborough on the line between Norwich and Peterborough. A 61-year-old leading trackman, with 31 years' railway experience, was acting as a lookoutman for a track maintenance gang of four men when he was knocked down and killed by the 13.43 Sprinter from Norwich to Blackpool. His was the 10th death on the line in 1988, emphasising that the problem of the safety of men working on the track is particularly intractable. The train is a most effective killer.

8
Trespassers and Suicides

In 1987 three passengers were killed in train accidents. Sixteen railway staff were killed in all types of accident. By contrast, in the same year 144 trespassers were killed, and there were 173 suicides. Ten years earlier the figures were:

Passengers killed in train accidents	Nil
Railway staff killed in all types of accident	34
Trespassers killed	101
Suicides	219

The distinction between trespassers and suicides depends on the findings of the Coroner, but the annual total of trespassers killed is running at a very high level, and in part it represents the increasing tendency of people to trespass on the railway by using it as a short cut, instead of going a longer way round by public road or footpath. But whatever the reasons are, trespass is much commoner than it used to be.

However, the problems of trespass were recognised at a very early stage in the development of railways, and it was considered such a dangerous practice that it was legislated against in the Railway Regulation Act of 1840. Section 16 of that Act imposed a fine not exceeding £5 (a hefty sum in those days) upon any person who wilfully trespassed upon the railway, or any of the stations or other works or premises connected therewith, and who refused to quit the same upon request by an official or agent of the company. Section 16 also provided a power of arrest to any officer or agent or any person called to his assistance. It will be noted from this that the offence of trespass arises anywhere on railway premises and not just on the railway line (which is where the danger arises), but only if the trespasser refuses to leave. The penalty is now £200.

The Regulation of Railways Acts of 1868 and 1871 laid down that 'if any person shall be or pass upon any railway, except for the purpose of crossing the same at any authorised crossing, after having once received warning not to go or pass thereon' such person would be liable to a fine of 40 shillings.

The individual railway companies made similar provisions under their own Acts, thus giving rise to those well known and wordy cast-iron signs to be found at stations and crossings, the wording of which many youthful train spotters could recite by heart, having read it many hundreds of times in the intervals between trains. Here is a typical one:

> Midland Railway
>
> 7 Vict Cap 18 Sec 238 enacts "That if any person shall be or travel or pass upon foot upon the Midland Railway without the licence and consent of the Midland Railway Company, every person so offending shall forfeit and pay any sum not exceeding Ten Pounds for every such offence."
>
> Notice is therefore hereby given that all persons found trespassing upon this railway or the Works thereof will be prosecuted.
>
> Alexis L. Charles
> Secretary
>
> June 1899

In the general sense, ordinary trespass, as is now well known, is not a criminal offence, and those notices which say 'Trespassers will be Prosecuted' are misleading. This is not to say, of course, that a landowner has no rights against a trespasser. He can, for example, claim damages in a civil court if he thinks he can prove that damage has been caused, and in general he owes a trespasser no duty of care, other than not to injure him intentionally or recklessly, but the legal position today is rather more complicated, particularly regarding children.

To understand the relatively new situation regarding children it would be as well to describe the legal position regarding fencing, which is largely governed by the Railway Clauses Consolidation Act of 1845. Section 68 lays down that:

> 'The company shall make and at all times thereafter maintain the following works for the accommodation of the owners and occupiers of lands adjoining the railway: Sufficient posts, rails, hedges, ditches, mounds or other fences . . . to protect from trespass land not taken for the use of the railway, and to protect cattle of the owners or occupiers of such land from straying thereout by reason of the railway . . .'

It will be seen, therefore, that the railway's requirement to fence is to protect adjoining land from trespass from the railway, and to prevent cattle from straying on to the railway. There is no duty on the railway to prevent the public at large from straying on to the railway, and the fences which are erected are not intended to keep people out, nor are they intended to be unclimbable. They are merely required to comply with the Act. First time travellers on the Continent are always astonished by the absence of fences, but those countries have no 1845 Act. (Note that there is a separate requirement to provide a 6ft unclimbable fence on lines electrified on the third-rail system.)

BR has tens of thousands of miles of fencing, and its maintenance is very expensive and labour-intensive. Local civil engineers, whose job it is, have customarily concentrated their resources on those locations which appeared to them to be the most important, but a legal action in 1970, known as the Herrington Case, altered the position substantially. The facts of the case are that a six-year-old child was playing in a meadow next to the railway line, a meadow which was sometimes used by children as a playground. Part of the railway fence was dilapidated and offered no barrier, and there was a hole in the fence opposite. People were using it as a short cut across the line. The child walked over the broken-down fence on to the line and was injured. About six weeks earlier the stationmaster had been notified that children had been seen on that stretch of line, but there was no evidence of any inspection of the fence. The judge awarded damages against the BR Board because he held that it was negligent for, among other things, permitting the fence to remain in a dilapidated condition. The BR Board appealed to the House of Lords on the grounds that since the child was a trespasser it owed him no duty in law to take any care for his safety, but the Lords dismissed the appeal, mainly on

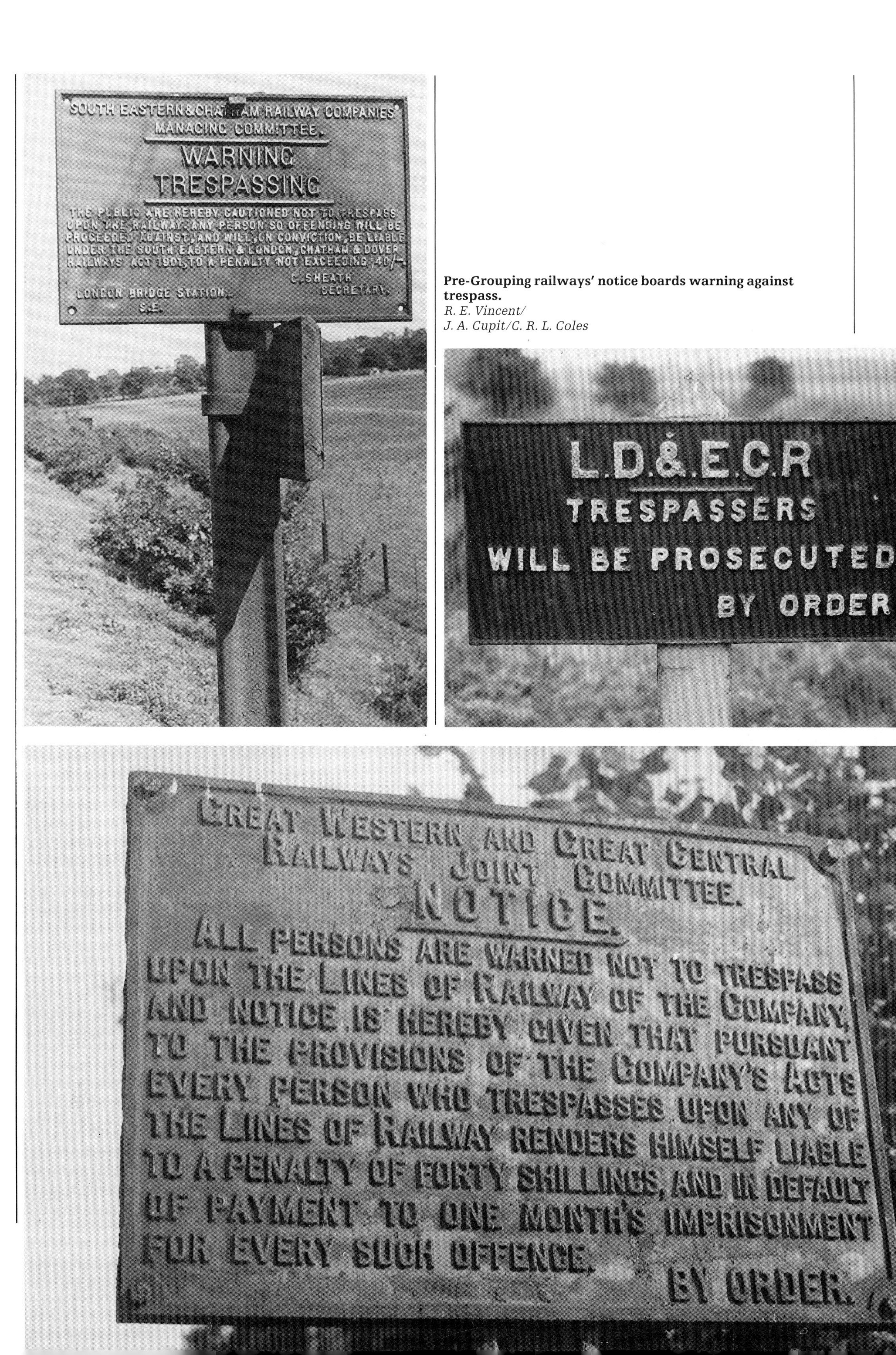

Pre-Grouping railways' notice boards warning against trespass.
R. E. Vincent/
J. A. Cupit/C. R. L. Coles

the grounds that if railway operators foresaw or ought to have foreseen the likelihood of such trespassers, common humanity should require them to take some reasonable steps for their safety.

This decision increased the Civil Engineer's burden considerably. He now had to maintain fences in good repair wherever children might be expected to play, no matter how frequently those fences were damaged or broken down, either by the children themselves or by adults seeking a short cut. However, he is not expected by the Courts to erect childproof fencing. Infants are expected to be under the control of an adult, whilst there are few fences which cannot be climbed by a determined child.

Local authorities and other developers often do not help the situation. For example they construct housing estates next to the railway line and leave an open area adjacent to the fence, which is an invitation to children to play there. Sometimes the school is on the opposite side of the line, which encourages children to take a short cut across the railway line. Often shops and public houses are on the other side of the line, so that adults are tempted to break down the fence so that they can use the railway line as a short cut. A few years ago one of the large metropolitan authorities in the north of England mounted a campaign against BR on the question of deaths to child trespassers. Discussions followed at national level with the Association of Metropolitan Authorities and when their own sins were pointed out to them by BR they quickly retreated. As a result of these discussions local authorities have a much better appreciation of BR's problems, whilst BR in return is able to demand the provision of a much sturdier fence when land alongside the railway is developed.

Coupled with the need to maintain fences is the need to take more positive steps to discourage child trespass. This takes two forms — education and deterrence. Specially selected drivers regularly visit schools to talk to children about the dangers of trespass, both from trains and from the electrified third rail or overhead wires. Police officers do the same, at least in those areas where there are sensible local authorities. So far as deterrence is concerned the practice started in the 1970s of runnning 'Q' trains in the worst affected areas. These carried a number of police officers and stopped wherever trespassers were seen. In some cases the officers were in radio contact with nearby patrol cars, who could be summoned if necessary. In the West Midlands, where the idea is thought to have originated, diesel parcels railcars were used. Elsewhere DMUs and EMUs have been used. The practice is very effective, but needs to be repeated at fairly frequent intervals. The desire is not to prosecute, but to educate and deter.

Suicides are a different matter altogether. Thirty years ago there were 123 cases in a year. In 1987 there were 173. The railway has always been and still is, a favourite place for committing suicide, as this recent newspaper extract shows:

> 'John Smith (not his real name), 18, jumped to his death in front of an express train near Reading after a row with his parents.'

It is quick and effective. In 1987 only 19 people failed in the attempt, receiving serious injuries instead of death. One of the worst effects of a person committing suicide is upon the innocent train driver. One moment he is quietly and happily sitting at the controls of his locomotive; the next moment he suddenly sees a figure step out from behind a bridge abutment and stand directly in front of the train. There is rarely time for the driver to do anything other than blow his horn and avert his eyes, then wait for the awful thud as the locomotive hits the person. It is far too late for the brakes to have any effect — even a suicide has enough presence of mind not to give the driver time to stop. Some drivers are able to shrug off the experience, but it haunts others for months or even years, to such an extent that ASLEF, the drivers' trade union is trying to obtain compensation for them. There are, however, certain areas, usually near mental hospitals, where suicides are not uncommon and railway staff in the area become hardened to them. On one occasion two railway officers had been visiting a stationmaster and as the three of them came out of his office they saw a terminating DMU arrive in the platform opposite, four tracks away. Whilst standing on the platform talking they noticed without much interest a man whom they took to be a carriage examiner crouch down and apparently look underneath the coach just behind the first bogie. They were interested only to the extent that if the DMU had some defect which could not be quickly rectified it would be necessary to make alternative arrangements for its next journey. As they stood there mildly interested, the DMU set off gently in the opposite direction in order to cross to the other platform, and as it did so the person who had mistakenly been thought to be a carriage examiner calmly laid his neck across the rail and his head was cleanly and noiselessly severed, without any fuss. The DMU continued on its way, because its driver had no idea of what had happened, but the three railway officers were momentarily stunned. Quickly recovering themselves they sent for a large sack in which to put the remains, partly to hide them from the horrified gaze of passengers on the platform which the DMU had just vacated, who were suddenly confronted with a severed head and a headless body, and partly to allow the London-bound express, already standing at the signal, to enter the platform. They were a hard-bitten trio, who had experienced too many suicides and knew how seriously trains could be delayed if the police arrived on the scene before the body was moved clear. Some police officers are under the impression that a body must not be moved until it has been photographed by the police photographer, which may mean the line being closed for up to 2hr, but this is not so. The instructions to staff as to what to do in the case of fatalities on the line, either from accident or suicide, are contained in the General Appendix and were revised some years ago in consultation with chief constables after several cases of serious delays to trains. The revision was done to clarify the situation and to explain to staff exactly what they were entitled to do.

The instructions say that the body should be moved clear of the rails immediately in order to prevent delay to trains, but the position in which it was found must always be carefully noted and marked out. After this has been done the police must be informed as quickly as possible, and normal train running must be resumed. Decisions on the running of trains are matters for BR staff and not the police. If the police arrive on the site before BR staff do so, as often happens, and have reasonable grounds for suspecting foul play they may request that the body remain on the line for a short time, and this should be agreed to, but such occasions are comparatively rare.

So far as the locomotive is concerned, it does not normally need to be taken out of service immediately, but the maintenance depot concerned must be asked to test various items of equipment. The police have to make a report to the Coroner and need evidence about the locomotive.

It might be mentioned at this stage that British Railways has its own police force, whose status is unique. In the early days of railways, when construction was proceeding apace, Justices of the Peace sometimes found it necessary to appoint special constables to keep the peace amongst the unruly navvies, and in due course railway companies obtained powers under statute to appoint their own constables. Upon nationalisation in 1948 these separate police forces were combined in the new force, the British Transport Police, which is a properly constituted police force the same as any other police force, and at one time was the largest police force in the country after the London Metropolitan Police Force. However, by virtue of the layout of the railway system BT police tend to be concentrated in the larger centres, therefore if an emergency arises in other areas it is likely that a member of a local police force will be on the scene first. Such constables may only enter railway property or land upon invitation or in certain specific circumstances of crime, and when they do so unaccompanied, difficulties can arise, particularly if they attempt to interfere with railway operations. They may also put their lives at risk if they stray upon the railway line. After some particularly unfortunate incidents following an accident at Luton on 25 June 1976, when staff were obstructed by police officers when carrying out protection procedures, Lt-Col Townsend-Rose, who inquired into the accident, gave the following views and guidance in his Report, and suggested that when the local police force is called to a railway accident it is mainly for the following reasons:

1. To escort and help passengers to safety.
2. To take charge of personal belongings left behind.
3. To note the names and addresses of killed or injured passengers, so that the next of kin, etc may be informed.
4. To control crowds of onlookers who may interfere with rescue operations.
5. To provide radio communication.
6. To evacuate surrounding property if dangerous chemicals have been spilt, or if there are other hazards, eg fire or explosion.
7. To co-ordinate rescue and restoration activities being carried out by the emergency services and voluntary bodies.
8. To retrieve, identify and remove bodies on behalf of HM Coroner.

Lt-Col Townsend-Rose also attempted to give some guidance as to what police officers should not do. He said that they should not delay traincrews in the protection of the lines after an accident; they should not interfere with a signalman's duties, and without good reason should not enter a signalbox unless accompanied by a competent railway officer, and should not interfere with any signalling equipment either in the signalbox or on the ground. One might go further and suggest that they should not interfere with any equipment, eg on the locomotive or in the train, or parts of the permanent way, because to do so might impede both the railway authorities and the Railway Inspectorate in the investigation into the cause of the accident.

Below:
The problem of maintaining fencing in good condition is well illustrated here. The fence had been erected at a cost of £9,000, only six weeks before this photograph was taken. *BR*

This timely warning has generally proved sufficient, but a railway employee going about his ordinary duties may feel intimidated when faced by a uniformed police officer making what appear to be urgent demands, as happened quite recently at Shippea Hill station on the Norwich to Ely line. The county police were following a suspect car, but after it went over the station level crossing the signalman closed his gates for a locomotive and brakevan. When the police car arrived at the level crossing and found the gates barring the way, a police officer insisted that the signalman reopen the crossing, despite being told that a locomotive was approaching. The signalman thereupon swung his gates across the railway to allow the police car to cross. Unfortunately the locomotive was too near the crossing to stop clear when the protecting signal was put back to Danger and it smashed its way through the gates.

One final case might be quoted, which emphasises some of the points already made. On 17 April 1969 a little girl of two years and two months, who lived on a housing estate next to a railway line, toddled off whilst her mother was hanging out the washing and obtained access to the railway through a gap in a broken-down stile leading to a level crossing, where she promptly sat down on one of the rails. When the driver of a single coach diesel railcar came round the bend he saw something on the line ahead which he took to be a piece of paper or litter. He sounded his horn as a precaution, and reduced speed, but then he saw some movement and he applied his brakes fully. He waved frantically at the little girl and hoped desperately that he would be able to stop in time. It was not to be. The front wheels of the railcar just ran over the little girl's legs.

When the railway was built in 1860, the railway company had bought a stretch of pasture land on which to construct its line, and there was a footpath across the pasture and across the railway line. In 1969 the local council developed a housing estate of nearly 200 houses on the pasture and it bought a strip of land along the railway, on which it erected a fence, and a new stile for people using the footpath. The stile was completed 16 days before the accident but it was not suitable for old or small people, or small children, and it was soon demolished, probably by vandalism, leaving an open gap.

The Court of Appeal allowed an appeal on the child's behalf in a claim for damages for negligence and breach of statutory duty against the British Railways Board for failing to maintain the stile. Fortunately the Board was entitled to recover the damages from the local council, because when the housing estate was built the council had entered into an agreement to maintain the fence and stile.

The points of interest to us in this case are:

1. When the housing estate was being developed the local council agreed to erect, and to be responsible for, a fence and a stile. This absolved BR from the responsibility for its maintenance and from the consequences of any negligence to do so.
2. The new stile was broken down within a week or so. The problem of maintaining gates and stiles in good condition in places where children play, or where adults find the gates or stile a nuisance, is a serious one.
3. The path was a well-used one. It linked the housing estate on one side of the line with shops and a school on the other, creating much more pedestrian traffic over the crossing. It is possible that the stile was broken down so that mothers with prams could use the crossing to reach the shops. If there had not been a footpath already in existence it is quite possible that the fence would have been broken down in order to make an unofficial one. This often happens in such circumstances, but it then allows small children to get on to the line, as happened in the Herrington case.

Trespassers and suicides represent by far the most common cause of death on the railway. In 1987 there were 317 of them, compared with 73 from all other causes (excluding the King's Cross fire), including railway staff and road users at level crossings. It is a figure which seems unlikely to decline.

Below:
Today's fast, silent motive power means that children playing on the line often do not have time to get clear. Nos 87024 and 87001 (the latter having failed) speed through Berkswell with the diverted 09.38 Liverpool-Euston on 14 October 1987.
John Chalcraft

9
Rush-hour Disaster at Clapham Junction

On Monday 12 December 1988 the 07.18 from Basingstoke to Waterloo, packed with commuters, came to an unscheduled stop at signal WF47, only a few hundred yards short of the platform at Clapham Junction station. It was not quite 8.10am.

The train was formed of 3×4-car VEP electric multiple-units, and had a seating capacity of 840. There were known to have been at least 700 passengers on board, but the actual figure may have been as high as 900. Certainly, some passengers were standing at the front of the train, but they often do so from choice, even though there may be vacant seats further back along the train, so that they can be among the first through the ticket barriers at Waterloo and so avoid the crush.

It is unlikely that any of the passengers felt uneasy that the train should be stationary on the line in the middle of the rush-hour. They may have been irritated at the delay, but they would hardly have felt unsafe. However, barely had they begun to wonder about how long the delay was going to last when their thoughts were shattered by a tremendous impact. The unthinkable had happened. Another train had come along and had crashed headlong into the standing train. The second train was the 06.14 Poole-Waterloo, also a 12-coach EMU, formed of a four-coach REP set, plus two sets of four unpowered vehicles. Its seating capacity was 610 and it was known to have carried at least 519 passengers, but undoubtedly there were more. (That morning it had started from Bournemouth at 06.30 owing to a previous accident, but that had no bearing on subsequent events.)

At this precise moment an empty EMU train was passing the other way on the next line. The Poole train tossed the last coach of the Basingstoke train up the bank, cannoned off, and hurled itself into the ever-narrowing gap between the two other trains, utterly destroying its first two coaches in the process. Some 35 people were killed in British Rail's worst disaster since the Hither Green derailment in 1967, described in Chapter 5, and 46 were injured sufficiently seriously to be detained in hospital. Altogether 130 people were treated in hospital, and it must be said at once that the response of the emergency services was rapid, efficient, and beyond praise.

Below:
The scene on the approach to Clapham Junction on 12 December 1988. On the left is the empty EMU which was travelling away from the camera. In the centre is the 06.14 from Poole (running towards the camera) which crashed into the rear of the stationary 07.18 from Basingstoke (right), tossing the last coach of the Basingstoke train up the bank. The first two coaches of the Poole train plunged into the narrow gap between the two other trains and were utterly destroyed. *Times Newspapers Ltd*

A fourth train narrowly avoided running into the rear of the Poole train. The driver of this train, a Waterloo to Waterloo circular via Weybridge, found that his train was losing power near Earlswood, about a mile from the wrecked trains, and as he coasted along hoping to reach Clapham Junction station he saw signal WF138 showing Yellow. Then, as he came round the corner he saw ahead of him, to his consternation, the rear of the Poole train. He threw on his brakes, hung on grimly, and screeched to a stop only 20yd clear. It was particularly fortunate that the collision between the Poole and the Basingstoke trains had caused the electric traction current to the third rail to be cut off otherwise the Waterloo circular via Weybridge train would have been travelling at the normal speed of a train preparing to stop at the next signal, WF47, and that may have been too fast for its driver to have stopped clear of the rear of the wrecked Poole train standing ahead of him.

There were now three trains in the 800yd section between signals WF138 and WF47, and signal WF138 was still showing Yellow.

The question to be asked immediately was how such an incredible series of events could take place on a busy suburban line. The safety of trains throughout the length and breadth of the country depends on the integrity of the signalling system; and on the simple principle of ensuring that the first signal behind a train is at Danger. In modern systems such as the one at Clapham this is achieved by a train detection device known as a track circuit. When a track circuit detects the presence of a train it reacts by switching to Danger the signal protecting that train. It is a simple device, and virtually foolproof. It has been in existence for a century or more. The track circuit between signals WF138 and WF47 should have detected the presence of the Basingstoke train and switched signal WF138 to Red. It did not do so. It should also have detected the presence of the Poole train and the Waterloo circular, and in due course we shall see why it did not do so, but first we must see why the driver of the Basingstoke train stopped at signal WF47.

As he approached signal WF138 (which was an automatic signal operated only by the passage of trains occupying track circuits and by the aspect being displayed by the next signal beyond it, and not capable of being operated by the signalman), it was showing Green, but when he was very near to it the signal suddenly changed to Red. That meant only one thing to the driver. Stop. He did so at the next signal WF47, which was showing Red when he first saw it, but then changed to Yellow.

The driver climbed down from his cab and telephoned the signalman at Clapham Junction 'A' signalbox from a nearby phone to find out what was going on. Sometimes, a malfunctioning track circuit will cause a signal to switch to Red, but the signalman replied that there was nothing wrong so far as he could tell. Perplexed, the driver turned to rejoin his train, but hardly had he gone two steps when he heard a tremendous crash and saw his train suddenly leap forward several feet.

The Poole train had been travelling at normal speed, but then it slowed down to about 50mph near signal WF138 (which was probably showing two Yellows — preliminary caution — but may even have switched to Green), in readiness for the 40mph speed restriction through Clapham Junction station. A driver who was travelling in the train saw the brake pipe pressure gauge suddenly go to zero and felt the brakes come on seconds before the crash. He estimated that the impact speed was about 35mph.

Nearly all the deaths occurred in the first coach of the Poole train, where 29 people died including the innocent driver. Sixteen passengers in it suffered only minor injuries or shock, and one incredibly fortunate passenger survived the crash quite unharmed. The other six passengers who died were in the seating portion of the second coach of the Poole train, which was a buffet car. The buffet was out of use but passengers who were standing in the buffet area were protected by the longitudinal bulkhead, which remained largely intact and saved their lives. The pattern of deaths did not seem to have been affected by whether people were sitting or standing.

We must now see why signal WF138 did not return to Danger behind any of the three trains which passed it, and which was still showing Yellow when the driver of one of the trains went back to look at it. Track circuits are designed in such a manner that if a malfunction occurs the equipment will react by switching signals to Danger, thus causing trains to stop, and ensuring safety. This is known as the 'fail-safe' principle, and is referred to as a right-side failure. What railwaymen fear most is the wrong-side failure which, though rare, has caused accidents in the past. However, it is almost unknown for a wrong-side failure to allow a signal protecting a standing train to show anything other than Red — Danger. Yet that almost unknown failure is what happened at Clapham Junction.

An examination of the signalling equipment in the Relay Room at Clapham Junction 'A' signalbox soon revealed the cause of the failure. In the signalbox a piece of wire, which should have been removed during signalling modernisation work, and which connected a power source to a piece of equipment known as a relay, was still in place, and was still connected to the power source. The other end was free, but continuously live. As long as the loose end did not touch any other terminal there was no danger, but it was a potential time-bomb.

The wiring was being renewed on a piecemeal basis over many weekends, and on 27 November 1988 a new wiring circuit was installed to control signal WF138, which was a new signal. The old wire already mentioned should have been removed at that time, but only one end (the relay end) was disconnected and moved away from its previous terminal. There it stayed, and as it was not at the time making any electrical contact its presence was not discovered during subsequent testing.

Two weeks later, the day before the accident, more work was being carried out in the signalbox relay room, this time on the adjacent relay. It is thought that this work may have disturbed the old piece of wire, which may then have resumed its previous shape and come into contact with its previous terminal, thus feeding current to the relay.

Track circuit equipment is designed so that when current is flowing, the track circuit is considered to be clear (ie unoccupied) and the signal approaching the track circuit will show 'Proceed'. (This may be one Yellow, two Yellows, or Green, depending on the indication being shown by the next signal.) When the Basingstoke train occupied the track circuit between signals WF138 and WF47 it had the planned effect of short-circuiting the electric current to the relay through the new wiring, which should then have caused signal WF138 to switch to Red, but the 'rogue' wire was still feeding current to the relay, therefore so far as that relay was concerned the track circuit was still unoccupied and signal WF138 did not revert to Red. The system 'lost' the train.

We must now consider why signal WF138 suddenly went to Red as the Basingstoke train approached it, and which caused its driver to stop at the next signal WF47. The standard signalling arrangements for the control of signals provide not only that a signal shall switch to Red when the track circuit beyond that signal is occupied by a train, but also that the signal shall remain at Red until the train has cleared a safety margin (known as an overlap and usually 200yd long) beyond the next signal. The safety margin had

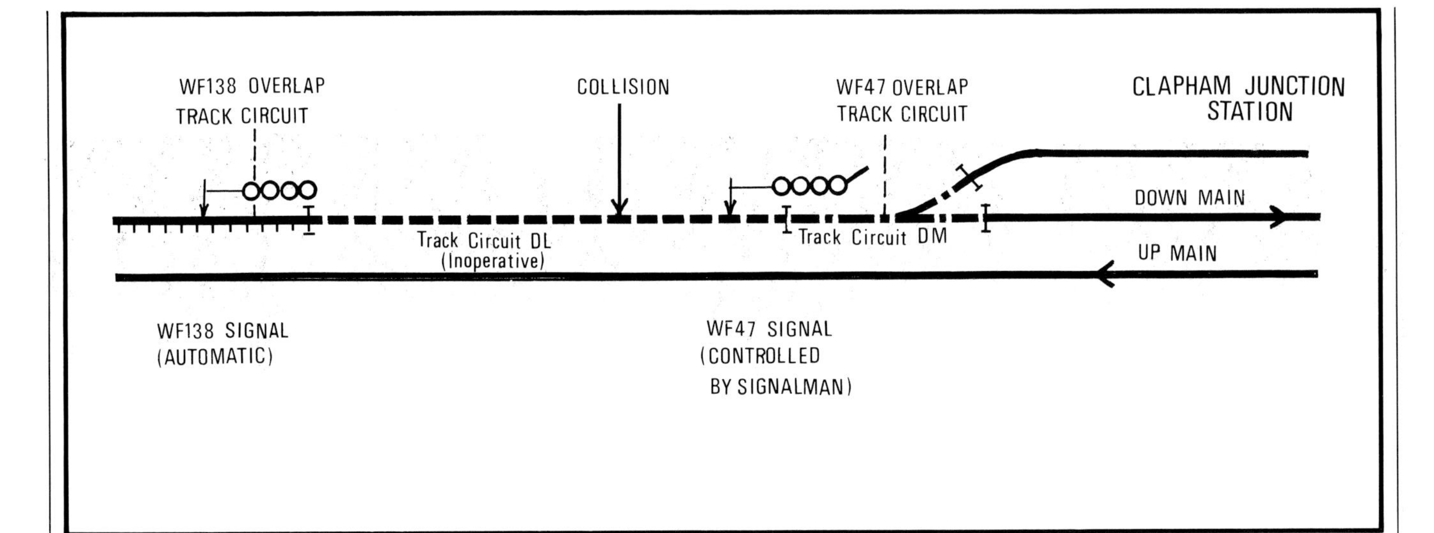

Above:
Approaching Clapham Junction from Woking (local lines not shown)

its own separate track circuit and the effect of this on WF138, with the 'rogue' wire feeding current, would be as follows:

As a train passed signal WF138 on to the bridged-out track circuit the signal would continue to show 'Proceed', and the train would disappear from the signalling system, but as soon as the train passed signal WF47 and occupied the 'overlap' track circuit it would be rediscovered by the signalling system and signal WF138 would immediately switch to Red. That is what the driver of the Basingstoke train saw, and that means that the train in front of him was not far ahead.

We may ask why the signal technician left the rogue wire in place. Was it tiredness, forgetfulness, carelessness, pressure of work? Human beings make mistakes. This sort of mistake was extremely rare. Almost unknown. Could any checking system or any amount of supervision guarantee to detect with 100% certainty such a rare error, year in and year out? There is no doubt that checking systems will be tightened up. Supervision will probably be intensified. Technicians' hours may be reduced (if BR manages to recruit more). But let us not delude ourselves. The Court of Inquiry may make a sacrificial lamb of the unfortunate technician, or the supervisor, or BR management, but errors of this nature by their very rarity may occasionally slip through the net. And let us not fall into the trap of believing that more supervision is necessarily the answer. We would do well to remember the old Latin tag *'Sed quis custodiet ipsos custodes'* which might be broadly translated as 'But who supervises the supervisors?' The causes of the Purley and Glasgow Bellgrove accidents, which occurred a few months later, were far more significant in safety terms, as we shall see in the next chapter.

The Court of Inquiry under Mr Anthony Hidden QC commenced in public on 20 February 1989, and the information given so far in this chapter is based on the evidence given at the inquiry. It would be inappropriate to make further comment until the inquiry report is published.

The Clapham accident was exceptional in its severity. Since the Hither Green derailment in 1967 there have been only three accidents on BR in which 10 or more passengers were killed. These accidents were:

1. West Ealing, 19 December 1973
   Ten passengers on the 17.18 locomotive-hauled train from Paddington to Oxford lost their lives when it was derailed at 70mph by points moving under the train. An unlocked battery box cover on the locomotive fell open soon after the train had left Paddington. It hit the platform at Ealing Broadway, breaking the chains supporting it and allowing it to swing down and smash into some lineside equipment which operated facing points in the line the train was travelling on. The points moved as the rear of the locomotive passed over them, turning the locomotive on to its side and derailing the coaches, which concertinaed together almost side by side. The locomotive had spent the previous night at Old Oak Common depot, where it had gone for repairs to a diesel engine, and the opportunity had been taken to recharge the battery. The battery box cover should have been locked when the locomotive left the depot, but it was not.
2. Taunton, 6 July 1978
   Twelve passengers were killed in a sleeping car fire. This accident is described in detail in Chapter 1.
3. Polmont, 30 July 1984
   Thirteen passengers were killed when the 17.30 Edinburgh-Glasgow push-pull express, being propelled, collided with a cow at 85mph and became derailed.

No pattern emerges from the causes of these three accidents and the Clapham accident, although simple human error is present in three of them. It is also significant that in those three cases the human errors involved people who had nothing to do with the actual operation of the train, and that in no case was either the driver or the signalman involved.

Wrong-side failures caused by errors of Signal Engineering Department technical staff have caused a number of accidents in recent years, some of which have occurred during signalling modernisation work, but none of them has resulted in passenger fatalities. All except one involved points operation irregularities, the exception being one of those very rare cases where a signal did not protect a standing train. This occurred on 7 March 1984 between Nuneaton and Water Orton (Birmingham) and is described in the Report for that year by the Chief Inspecting Officer of Railways. A freight train was brought to a stand at signal No SY326, which was showing Green, after the guard saw sparks coming from one of the wagons. A few minutes later a diesel locomotive running light (ie without a train) ran into the back of the standing train, causing considerable damage. The driver of the light locomotive had seen the signal in rear of the freight train at Green, and saw the train's tail lamp too late to avoid a collision. Investigation revealed that a Signal Engineering Department technician had attended a failure of the signal in rear of the freight train some months previously. He carried out repairs but failed to test the signal properly afterwards. Unfortunately a track circuit was omitted from the control of the signal, which consequently showed a clear aspect (Green) behind the standing train. This condition had existed undetected during those several months, because it was rare for a train to be stopped at signal No SY326, and the train in question was probably the first one which had done so since the wrong-side failure was built into the system by the technician.

Some of the other wrong-side failures which have caused accidents in recent years are shown in the appendix to this chapter. None of them has a direct parallel with the Clapham accident, although it is noteworthy that two of them occurred during the stage works of major resignalling schemes.

There were suggestions in the media after the Clapham accident that many lives might have been saved if the Poole train had been composed of more modern coaches of greater strength. This raises two questions. Were the coaches that were used on the Poole train that day unacceptably weak, and should they have been replaced by stronger ones? An examination of the behaviour of Southern Region coaches in accidents over the last 20 years shows that they have a very good safety record indeed. In that period there were 11 derailments and 21 collisions of sufficient severity to justify the holding of a public inquiry by the Railway Inspectorate. Six passengers were killed in those 32 accidents, but none of them were commuters. Before the Clapham accident, not a single commuter had been killed in a train accident on the Southern Region in the last 20 years — an almost unbelievably good record when one considers the intensity of the Southern Region commuter service, and the amount of resignalling work which has been done to commission the modern power signalboxes at London Bridge, Victoria and Three Bridges.

The second question, concerning the replacement of Southern Region coaches by more modern stock is really superfluous, because Southern Region stock has such a good behavioural record in accidents and its strength has been practically demonstrated. And even though the modern Mk 3 coach has a superb safety record it is impossible to say how it would have behaved in the Clapham crash. To put the proposition bluntly, should one replace all existing coaches or equipment immediately something safer is designed? Such a move could only be justified if the existing coaches were demonstrably unsafe and the new ones considerably better, which is not the situation in this case. It is not a new problem, but is as old as the railways themselves, as they progressed from four-wheeled coaches to six-wheelers and then to bogie vehicles; from wooden frames to steel frames; from wooden bodies to steel bodies; and from gas lighting to electric lighting. As is the case in so many other activities, the speed at which older designs of coaches are replaced by more modern and safer designs has to be set against the estimated degree of risk in allowing those older coaches to remain in service. In the case of Southern Region coaches, the experience of the last 20 years shows that it has been a very low level of risk.

We now come to the question of radio, and whether the provision of a radio link between the driver and the signalman would have avoided the accident, or at least have reduced its severity. On the morning of the accident the driver of the train from Basingstoke observed a signal behaving in an irregular manner, therefore he stopped his train at the next signal to report the fact to the signalman, using the telphone at the signal. He had no reason to suppose that the signal protecting his train would have done anything other than revert to Red. Nor had the signalman. The defective signal would have been dealt with in accordance with the Rules, and the drivers of all the following trains would have been stopped and warned about it by the signalman. If a train had already passed the point at which it could be stopped by the signalman, the driver of the train would have acted in the same way as the driver of the Basingstoke train, provided that the signal appeared to the driver to be acting irregularly. The Rules tell the driver that 'a signal imperfectly shown' must be treated as a Danger signal and reported to the signalman, which is what the driver of the Basingstoke train did. If radio had been provided he would probably have stopped his train and then reported the facts to the signalman by radio, it being undesirable, except in an emergency, for the driver to carry out radio conversations when his train is running at speed, owing to the obvious danger that his concentration on signals, etc, may be impaired. On the other hand, if an emergency arose the driver would make a special emergency contact with the signalman at once, but a defective signal would hardly be considered an emergency in those terms because it would be regarded as a Danger signal and could safely be dealt with under the normal procedures. When the signalman received such a report by radio he would put into operation the procedures designed to deal with it, and the radio would merely take the place of the telephone as a quicker and more convenient means of passing messages. However, if the next train had already passed the last signal at which it could be stopped, the signalman would send a radio message to that driver warning him of the defective signal ahead and giving him any necessary instructions. The vital point, so far as the Clapham accident is concerned, is whether there would have been sufficient time for the driver of the Poole train to have been warned about the defective signal and to apply his brakes before he saw the Basingstoke train standing on the same line ahead of him. It is at least possible that the Poole train might have been slowing down more than it did, when it hit the Basingstoke train. The driver of the Waterloo via Weybridge train could also have been forewarned.

The provision of radio communication between drivers and signalmen on BR did not start until comparatively recently, and then mainly as a by-product of other schemes, particularly in connection with a new signalling system on single lines, known as Radio Electronic Token Block signalling. However, radio communication between drivers and signalmen is also required if trains are to be operated without guards on suburban services. This already applies on lines from St Pancras, King's Cross and Glasgow, and is expected to be introduced on the Southern Region soon, but some years are bound to elapse before all the Southern Region commuter services are equipped.

The reasons for BR's dilatoriness in providing radio communication were not entirely financial, although the poverty-induced inertia of the late 1970s/early 1980s is a factor. Compared with the cost of electrification, or new power signalboxes, or new fleets of locomotives or rolling stock, the cost of a nationwide radio system is quite small. The fact is, that in order to survive, BR has had to concentrate on essentials, and radio was not considered to be essential. Also, BR had to cut its staff numbers to the bone, whilst the planning and installation of a national radio system is very labour-intensive in the use of planning and technical staff.

Serious accidents, especially where accompanied by loss of life, are normally followed by public inquiries held by an Inspecting Officer of the Railway Inspectorate of the Department of Transport. The legal authority for such inquiries, and the procedures for holding them, have already been discussed in detail in Chapter 6, but there is an additional provision in the 1871 Regulation of Railways Act, under Section 7, for the holding of a more formal investigation. Section 7 gives the Secretary of State for Transport the power:

1. To direct that a more formal type of investigation be held.
2. To appoint particular persons to assist the Inspecting Officer.
3. To appoint someone else to hold the investigation, assisted by an Inspecting Officer.
4. To hold the investigation in open court.

The court has all the powers of a court of summary jurisdiction and all the powers of an Inspecting Officer, plus:

1. They may enter and inspect any place or building which appears requisite (ie not confined to railway premises).
2. They may call any witnesses they think fit (ie, not just railway staff).
3. They may take evidence on oath.

So far as BR and its predecessors are concerned, this more formal type of inquiry has only twice been conducted by someone other than an Inspecting Officer since 1871 — once in connection with the Tay Bridge collapse in 1879 and once in connection with a collision between an express train and an abnormal load on a road trailer at Hixon level crossing (Staffordshire) in 1968. In each case the Railway Inspectorate had been previously involved; in passing as fit for use the Tay Bridge, and in drawing up in conjunction with BR the requirements for the installation and operation of automatic half-barriers at level crossings. In each of those cases it was necessary for the person holding the inquiry to be seen to be independent, and it was clearly an advantage to be able to call non-railway staff as witnesses, ie the designers and builders of the Tay Bridge on the one hand, and Department of Transport officials, road haulage people and the police on the other. In each of those cases, therefore, it was appropriate to hold the more formal type of investigation. It was also appropriate to do so following the fire at London Transport's King's Cross station on 18 November 1987, because it was expedient to consider the actions, responsibilities, and organisation of the emergency services. The King's Cross fire was not a train accident and there were many questions to be asked about materials used in the construction of the station, which involved calling non-railway staff as witnesses. These three accidents were exceptional in that they were not train accidents of a conventional nature, ie they were not collisions between trains, or derailments, or train fires. By contrast, the collision at Clapham was entirely conventional. One train running into the back of another has been a common occurrence throughout railway history. It happened at Harrow & Wealdstone in 1952, when 108 passengers were killed. It happened at Lewisham St Johns in 1957, when 89 passengers were killed. It happened at Winsford, near Crewe in 1962, when 18 passengers were killed. In each case the subsequent inquiry was held by an Inspecting Officer in the entirely satisfactory, thorough and competent manner which always has been the hallmark of the Railway Inspectorate.

Why, then, did the Secretary of State for Transport choose to order the more formal type of investigation for the Clapham accident, which was not in any way exceptional except for the death toll, and why did he appoint a QC, Anthony Hidden, to hold it? Is the Secretary of State suggesting that his Railway Inspectorate is no longer competent, or not independent? There can be no valid questioning of its competence or experience — one Inspecting Officer has served for over 20 years and two have served for between 10 and 20 years. Between them they have carried out dozens of inquiries. Any one of them could have carried out the Clapham inquiry without difficulty. Is it therefore the Railway Inspectorate's independence (presumably from BR's influence) which is in question? If so, the Secretary of State clearly does not know his Inspectorate. Even though it works closely with BR there has never been the slightest suggestion that it might favour BR in any way. The whole issue bears all the marks of a hasty reaction by the Secretary of State under political pressure on the question of the provision of public transport in the London area, and its financing. His ill-advised decision will provide a field day for the legal profession, but will not enable the cause and circumstances of the accident to be established any more clearly or accurately. It will certainly take a lot longer. But by far the worst feature is that it undermines the status and reputation of the Railway Inspectorate, which has been built up and enhanced over a continuous period of 150 years, and sets a lamentable precedent for the future. This dedicated body of men, never more than five or six strong, has performed services for railway passengers of a value quite out of proportion to its size; and it deserved better treatment.

Details of Accidents Caused by Wrong-Side Failures

1. Bletchley, 10 July 1974
   A special excursion train from Wigan to Euston was passing along a crossover from the Up Slow line to the Up Fast line opposite Bletchley signalbox at about 15mph, and just as the last coach was astride the facing points of the crossover they moved across, causing the trailing bogie to continue to run along the Up Slow line. The coach was eventually dragged into derailment and broke loose from the train. Lt-Col Townsend-Rose, who inquired into the accident, concluded that it was probably an irregular action by a Signal Engineering Department technician in the Bletchley power signalbox Relay Room that caused the points to move.
2. Hither Green, 6 November 1976
   As the 17.12 Margate-Charing Cross passenger train was approaching Hither Green on the Up Fast line, the driver observed two signals ahead of him revert from Green to Red. On telephoning the signalman he was instructed to pass them at Danger and to proceed at Caution. He had just passed the second signal at Danger and was travelling at about 25mph when his train was diverted at a facing connection, becoming derailed at switch diamonds in the adjacent Down Fast line, along which his train travelled until it came to rest some 20yd short of the Down Fast platform at Hither Green station. Control of the signalling in the Hither Green area had only just been transferred to the new London Bridge signalbox, and final testing had not yet been completed. Lt-Col Townsend-Rose also inquired into this accident, and found that the derailment occurred because of an error in the electrical connections to the points, which had remained undetected in spite of very thorough testing.

3. Farnley Junction, near Leeds, 5 September 1977
   Both a Down train and an Up train were stopped by signals near Farnley Junction, on the line between Leeds and Huddersfield. There were a number of failures in the signalling equipment, which had their roots in industrial action threatened by electricity power station workers, and Signal Engineering Department technicians were on the spot attempting to put things right. The 20.40 locomotive-hauled passenger train from Liverpool to Hull was standing on the Down line, and the 21.50 Mail from York to Shrewsbury, also locomotive-hauled, was standing on the Up line, with a facing crossover between them connecting the Up and Down lines. Maj Rose inquired into this accident and found that owing to a wiring error by the technicians the facing crossover moved to the reverse position (ie to take a train from the Up line to the Down, or vice versa) but still allowed the signals to clear to Green for movements straight along the Down line and Up line. There was some confusion as to whether the signalman was properly informed by the technician that the repair work had been completed and tested (which it had not). As soon as the signalman cleared the signals for the two standing trains the Liverpool to Hull train set off, but was diverted through the facing crossover into a head-on collision with the other train. Both drivers were killed.
4. Bushbury Junction, near Wolverhampton, 13 August 1979
   The 13.29 passenger train was derailed when passing over switch diamonds at Bushbury Junction, about 1½ miles north of Wolverhampton. Defective equipment allowed the signal to show Green even though the points were not fitting correctly. This accident was fully described in *Danger Signals*.
5. Chester, 9 June 1981
   The 13.48 DMU from Wolverhampton to Chester was running along the Up Slow line at about 15mph, when the trailing bogie of the first coach, followed by the remainder of the train, was diverted to a different line at a set of facing points. The first coach became derailed. Maj King inquired into this accident and found that the signalling was being converted from a mechanical system to an electrical system, as part of the stage works for the introduction of a new signalbox at Chester, and that earth faults in the equipment allowed the signalman to make an error and move the facing points whilst the DMU was just passing over them. The points should have been electrically locked but the earth faults rendered the safeguards ineffective.

Below:
Recovery of materials proceeds on 13 December, the day following the accident. *Brian Morrison*

10
Purley and Glasgow Bellgrove — Accident or Design?

On 4 March 1989, a perfectly normal Saturday, the 12.50 Southern Region EMU from Horsham to London Victoria, a four-coach set, approached Purley on the Up Slow line. The driver braked for the station stop, and as he did so the signal at the far end of the platform, T170, changed from Red to Yellow, and the junction indicator (a row of white lights) was illuminated to signify that the points ahead were set to take the train through the crossovers on to the Up Fast line. After the normal station stop the driver restarted his train at about 13.36, and took it steadily through the 20mph crossovers.

The signalling in the whole area is controlled from Three Bridges signalbox, and is very modern, being commissioned on 14 January 1984. On the main line from Brighton to London Victoria through Purley, four-aspect colour-light signals are used; the lines are track circuited throughout and are equipped with the BR standard Automatic Warning System. Many of the signals work automatically, and some of the ones which are operated by the signalman can also be set by him to work automatically, which means that they will change to Red as soon as a train passes them, then successively to one Yellow, two Yellows, and Green, as the train passes succeeding signals. The signal at the London end of the Up Fast line platform at Purley, T168, is such a signal. The signalman had set it to work automatically for a sequence of trains along the Up Fast line, but then he required to switch the Horsham train from the Up Slow line to the Up Fast line, so he restored T168 signal to non-automatic operation after the passage of a Gatwick Airport to Victoria express. This action held T168 at Red and prevented it from changing to Yellow etc. He then set the route for the Horsham train, which was a regular movement every half-hour and should have been perfectly safe provided any driver approaching along the Up Fast line ensured that he stopped his train at T168 signal, but the basic philosophy of BR signalling is that drivers do stop at Red signals and they have the Automatic Warning System to assist them. This system is operated by magnets in the track about 200yd before each signal, which send out an electrical message to be picked up by a receiver mounted

Below:
Purley 4 March 1989. The 12.17 from Littlehampton to Victoria cannoned off the rear of the 12.50 from Horsham (seen top left) and plunged down the steep tree-clad embankment almost into the houses below. The front of the train is shown circled, which indicates that the coach had turned through 180°.
Mail Newspapers PLC

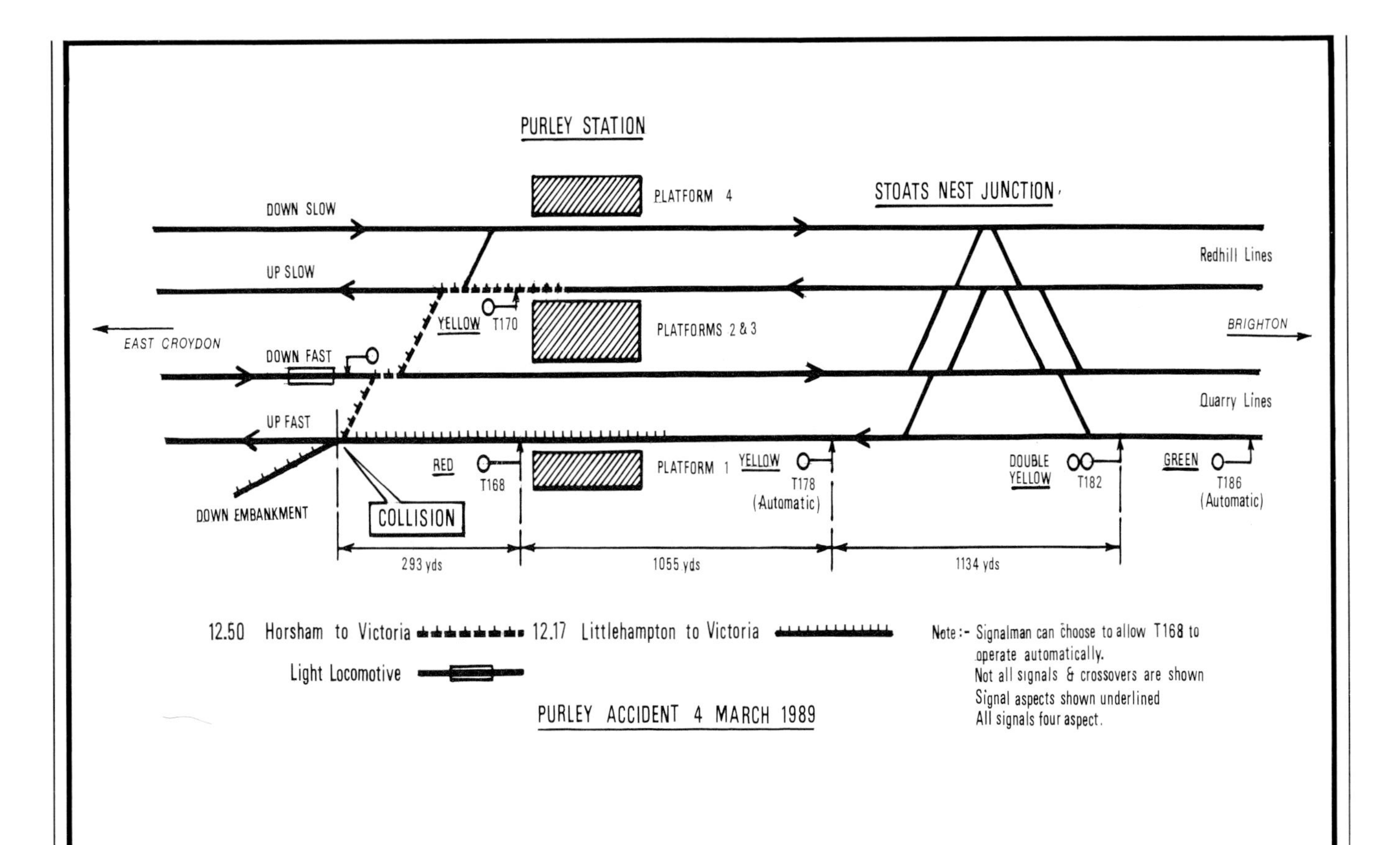

Above:
Purley accident 4 March 1989.

Left:
Purley. The battered first, third and fourth coaches of the 12.17 from Littlehampton. *Mail Newspapers PLC*

underneath the train. If the signal is at Green the message causes a bell to sound in the driving cab, but if the signal is showing any other aspect (ie two Yellows, one Yellow, or Red) a different message is sent, which sounds a warning horn. The driver then has 2-3sec to press a button to acknowledge receipt of the warning and if he fails to do so the brakes are automatically applied. It is a very valuable safeguard, but it is cancelled out as soon as the driver presses the acknowledgement button because he is then solely responsible for applying the brake and there is no equipment to check that he actually does so. This is now becoming widely recognised as a fundamental drawback, because in the course of a normal day's work drivers frequently require to press the acknowledgement button and then find that they have no need to brake, because they can see the next signal change to a less restrictive aspect (eg from Yellow to double Yellow or double Yellow to Green). This oft-repeated acknowledgement not followed by any action on the driver's part can lure him to disaster if he should subconsciously press the acknowledgement button and take no action at the very time he needs to do so. Collisions have resulted from this situation on a number of occasions.

When the signalman set the route for the Horsham train there was indeed a train approaching on the Up Fast line, the 12.17 from Littlehampton to London Victoria, an eight-coach EMU, and it was running at high speed down the favourable grade from Merstham Tunnel, four miles

Above:
Purley. The smashed-in front-end of the 12.17 from Littlehampton, in which the driver survived.
Mail Newspapers PLC

Left:
The Up and Down Fast lines through Purley, looking north towards signal T168 and London. The station buildings on Platform 2 obscure the driver's view of signal T168 owing to the curvature of the line, until he is within 300yd of the signal.
Author

Below left:
Purley. The view north from signal T168. At this point the driver of the 12.17 from Littlehampton would see the 12.50 from Horsham making its way through the crossovers, and realise to his horror that it was crossing on to his line. *Author*

away. The driver of a light locomotive (ie a locomotive without a train) which was standing at a signal on the Down Fast line just north of Purley, saw the Horsham train about to cross in front of him to the Up Fast line. At the same moment he saw the 12.17 approaching the station and realised in a flash that it was coming too fast to stop at signal T168. He was correct. The Littlehampton train ran by T168 and struck the last coach of the Horsham train, which was just coming off the crossovers, a glancing blow, at a speed said by an expert witness at the subsequent public inquiry to have been about 55mph.

The railway lines at this point are on a high embankment, with the Up Fast line on the outside. The Littlehampton train cannoned off the rear coach of the Horsham train and plunged down the tree-clad embankment, leaving only the last coach remaining on the track. Most of the other coaches were strewn at random, some upside down or on their sides. Five passengers died and 87 required hospital treatment, 32 of whom were detained, after being tossed around like peas in a drum inside the crazily tumbling carriages.

Public reaction, with the accident coming so soon after the Clapham disaster only a few miles away, was one of shock and astonishment. How could such a thing happen on a busy railway like the Brighton line with all its modern safeguards? This is what the Public Inquiry, held by Mr Alan Cooksey, Deputy Chief Inspecting Officer of Railways, was set up to establish. BR said that there was no evidence of any malfunction of the braking system or the AWS equipment on the Littlehampton train, nor any signalling operation malpractice, nor signalling equipment defect, and the cause of the crash was an error by the driver. The driver himself declined to give evidence in public, and until the report itself is issued it would be wrong to speculate about what might have caused the driver to pass the signal in error. However, from the evidence given it would seem that, after running on Green signals, he would then have received the normal sequence of signal aspects when approaching T168 at Red, ie two Yellows and one Yellow and that he would have received the normal AWS warning at each. Had he not acknowledged the warning the brakes would have been applied automatically. But in any case, the reason why he passed T168 signal at Danger, whilst interesting, is of no real consequence. The fact is that, for whatever reason, the signalling and AWS system in use failed to ensure that the train stopped at the Red signal, and that is what matters.

T168 signal is obscured by the station buildings and does not come into view from the driver's cab until the driver is within 300yd of it. That fact in itself should be of no consequence if a driver has correctly responded to the warnings at the previous two signals but, it assumes considerable importance if he has not done so, because by the time the Red signal at T168 comes into his view he is likely to be travelling at too great a speed to enable him to stop either at the signal itself or even at the crossover almost 300yd beyond. What is needed is a better Automatic Train Control system which will ensure that a train will stop safely at a Red signal irrespective of anything the driver does or fails to do. On the evidence available there is nothing new or unusual in the circumstances of the Purley accident and the whole subject was thoroughly explored in Chapters 1 and 8 of *Danger Signals*. Serious accidents of this nature are becoming an annual event, although not usually with so many deaths. The nearest parallel in recent years is perhaps the Wembley accident of 11 October 1984 in which a Euston to Bletchley commuter train passed a Red signal and collided sideways-on with a Freightliner train that was just leaving the sidings and was crossing over on to the same line as the commuter train. Three passengers were killed. The driver had received the normal Caution signals of two Yellows and one Yellow but had failed to react positively and had merely acknowledged the AWS warnings as a subconscious reaction. The driver, who was 63 years old, was subsequently examined by a specially constituted medical board who, on the balance of probabilities, believed that he had suffered from an episode of amnesia and confused behaviour which led him to ignore the signals at Caution and Danger, brought about by a rare but well recognised medical condition. Be that as it may, it is quite intolerable that drivers should have to carry such heavy responsibilities for the lives of hundreds of passengers, for which burden they are inadequately remunerated, with reliance upon a warning system which increasingly is showing itself to be ineffective when most needed. It is good to hear, therefore, that BR has decided at long last to install a better system. Let us hope that the work will be carried out with a proper degree of urgency. And in case it should be thought that such a better system is either a new idea or is not yet available, it ought to be pointed out that following a serious collision on the Midland Railway at Aisgill in September 1913 an eminent signal engineer wrote 'We believe we shall eventually develop a genuine speed control system which will in no way interfere with the driver's control if he does his work, but will check him if he exceeds the authorised speeds.' That was 75 years ago, and such systems have existed and have been in use on other railways for many years. And even while BR and the public were still recovering from the shock of the Purley and Bellgrove accidents there were two near misses within the next few days caused by drivers passing signals at Danger. One was at Worle Junction on the Western Region where a train from Weston-super-Mare overran a Danger signal and almost collided with a Penzance to Cardiff train on the main line. The other was many miles away in much more hostile country, where BR was engaged in one of its frequent diversions of West Coast main line services over the Settle-Carlisle line. The signalman had cleared his signals for a Down express to travel over the single line across Ribblehead Viaduct. An Up express came out of Blea Moor Tunnel. Its driver failed to stop at the Up Home signal, which was at Danger, and headed towards the single line and the approaching Down express. It would have made a fitting Wagnerian epitaph for Ribblehead Viaduct — two expresses colliding head-on and plunging to the valley below — but fortunately the signalman was on the alert. He immediately apprehended danger and pulled over his emergency detonator-placing levers, which laid detonators on the line. Their explosion caused the driver to make an emergency stop and there was no collision. On diversion weekends the Settle-Carlisle line attracts large numbers of train spotters, photographers, recorders and other enthusiasts, but they had all gone home. The incident happened during the night.

Emergency detonator-placing equipment was also used in the accident at Glasgow Bellgrove station, two days after the Purley accident, on 6 March 1989, but this time it was ineffective. Bellgrove station lies on the North Glasgow electrified line from Airdrie to Dumbarton and Helensburgh, and is the second station east of Queen Street Low Level station. There is a junction at Bellgrove to Springburn, which was formerly a conventional double-line junction but was remodelled in 1987 to a single-lead junction in preparation for the Yoker resignalling scheme. The question of these single-lead junctions and the safety problems they can cause was fully explored in Chapter 8 of *Danger Signals* but briefly they consist of a short piece of single line connecting the double track main line with the double track branch line. Their particular hazard lies in the fact that if the signal is cleared for a train to proceed off the

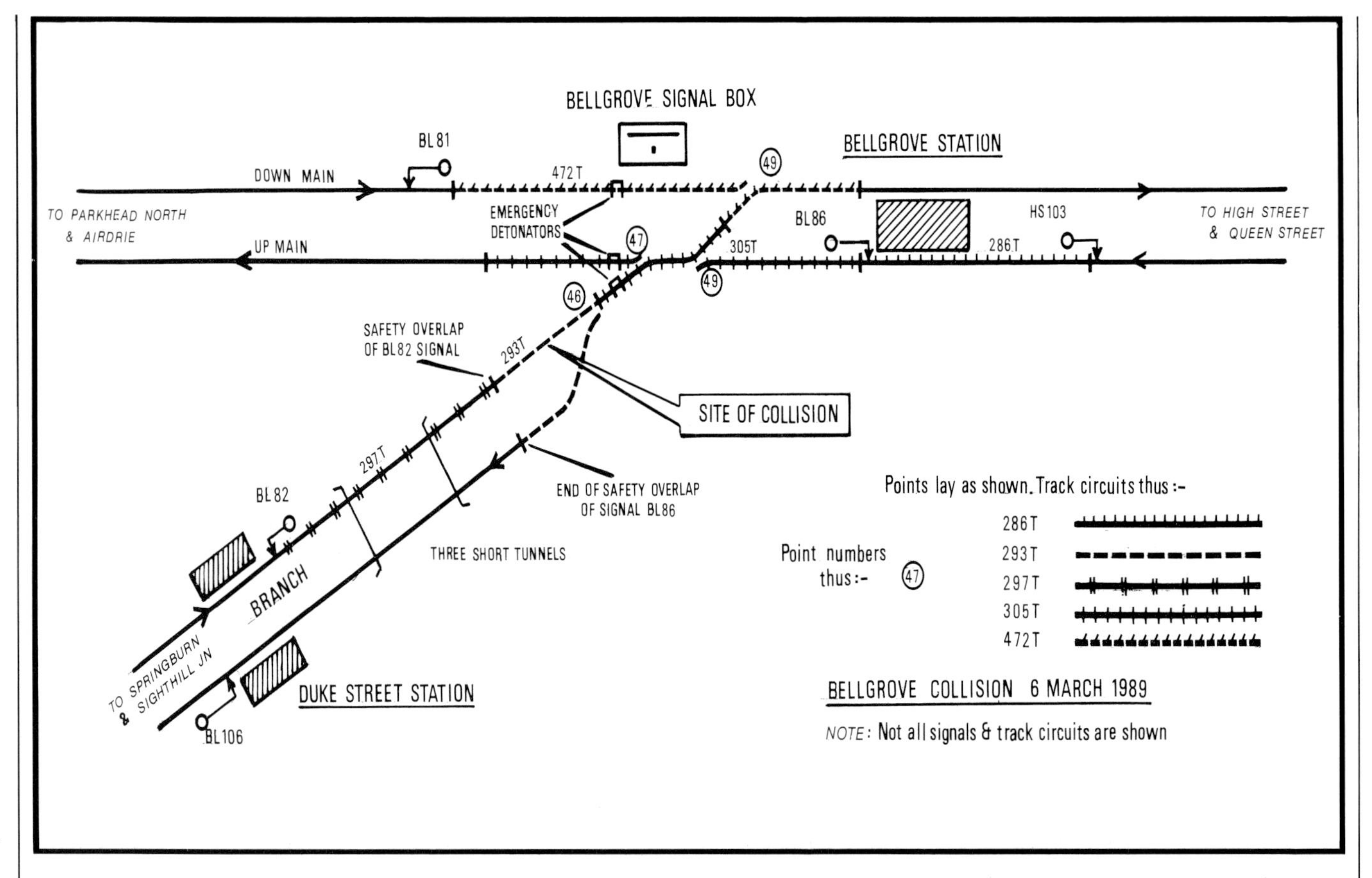

branch on to the main line the points will be set in such a way that if a train on the main line overruns the junction signal at Danger it will automatically be diverted on to the branch line and into a head-on collision with the train coming off the branch. This could not have happened with the previous double-line junction layout as the offending train would have been diverted out of harm's way on to the unoccupied branch line. Single-lead junctions therefore demand a higher standard of obedience to signals by drivers, and the identification and effective treatment of any special hazard at the junction signal.

There was just such a special and well known hazard at the junction signal at Bellgrove, which will become apparent from a description of the circumstances surrounding the accident. Two trains were approaching the junction at Bellgrove simultaneously — the 12.39 from Springburn to Milngavie and the 12.20 Milngavie to Springburn. Each was a three-car electric multiple-unit of 1960 vintage. Although the lines are track circuited throughout they are worked on the Absolute Block System. The signalman accepted the train from Springburn from the Sighthill Junction signalman, and cleared his signals for it to run as far as signal BL82 at Duke Street station. He also accepted the train to Springburn from the High Street signalman, after setting points 47 and 46 to the reverse position so that they lay towards the end of the safety overlap of signal BL86. When the train to Springburn had come to a stand in Bellgrove station, with signal BL86 at Red, the signalman normalised points 46 and reversed points 49 to take the train from Springburn through the junction to the Down Main line and into Bellgrove station. He then cleared BL82 signal and the train set off into the three short tunnels.

At this moment the Bellgrove signalman saw the train to Springburn start to leave Bellgrove station and to his consternation it passed BL86 signal, which, according to his signal lever, was at Red. He immediately pulled over his emergency detonator-placing levers and heard the bang as the train passed over the detonators and exploded them. However, the two trains were now very close to each other and they met head-on at a combined speed of about 30mph. The driver of the train from Springburn, and a passenger on that train, lost their lives.

The question at issue, therefore, is why the train to Springburn left Bellgrove station and passed signal BL86, which the signalling system should have held at Danger and with which no fault could subsequently be found. Events 10 years earlier, and only a few miles away, may provide the answer.

On Easter Monday 1979 the 18.58 from Ayr to Glasgow set off from Paisley Gilmour Street station, wrongly passed the platform starting signal at Danger, and collided head-on with the 19.40 Glasgow to Wemyss Bay, which was just crossing the junction. Seven people died. It was felt that the guard's bell signal to the driver that the train was ready to start had caused the driver to overlook the Danger signal at the end of the platform, and if that may sound strange it has to be said that it was a very well known and recognised situation which had caused many accidents in the past. Indeed, as long ago as 1957, following an inquiry into an accident at Staines, the Inspecting Officer, Brig Langley, had said that the great psychological effect of the guard's 'right away' signal had occasionally allowed drivers to be misled by it. The whole question was examined in detail in Chapter 5 of *Danger Signals*.

Following the Paisley accident, BR altered the Rules to require the guard to ensure, where practicable, that the platform starting signal (BL86 at Bellgrove) had been cleared before giving the 'Ready to start' signal to the driver. In his evidence at the Public Inquiry into the Bellgrove accident, held by the Chief Inspecting Officer of Railways, Mr Robin Seymour, the guard of the train to Springburn said that he could not remember looking at signal BL86. If he had done so, and if it had been at Red, he

Left:
Bellgrove collision 6 March 1989.

Above right:
Glasgow Bellgrove 6 March 1989. The 12.20 from Milngavie to Springburn and the 12.39 from Springburn to Milngavie meet head-on near the junction. *Mail Newspapers PLC*

Right:
Glasgow Bellgrove, showing the single lead connecting the Springburn Branch (left) with the Airdrie line (right). The collision occurred opposite the white hut (top centre). *Author*

Below:
General view of Glasgow Bellgrove station, looking towards Springburn and Airdrie. The signal at the far end of the platform, BL86, has been cleared for the Class 303 unit to proceed to Springburn. *Author*

should not have 'belled the train away', as he described it, because that would have been against the Rules. Was it practicable for him to see it? That is a matter for the Chief Inspecting Officer to decide. It is on the right-hand side of the line and clearly visible from part of the platform. Where difficulty arises in the visibility of such a signal, it is the practice to provide On/Off electrical indicators to help guards and station staff. There was no such indicator at Bellgrove. But in any event, the responsibility for obeying signals in such circumstances is entirely that of the driver. The Rules tell him that the 'Ready to start' signal indicates only that the station work is complete and that he must ensure before starting the train that the signal is cleared.

However, a wise and prudent management will learn the lessons of history; and, recognising that human beings make human errors, will take whatever steps it reasonably can to guard against such human errors, especially at those locations such as Bellgrove where there is an additional hazard. It is one thing to alter the Rules, but to be effective such alteration needs to be reinforced by training and supervision. How effectively is this Rule applied by guards in the Glasgow area, and how effective is the supervision? It seems that Bellgrove may not have been an entirely isolated case, for there was a near miss a few weeks later at, of all places, Paisley. And what action do drivers take when the Rule is not applied? Are either drivers or guards aware of the provisions of the Health & Safety at Work Act of 1974, Section 7(a), which says:

> 'It shall be the duty of every employee while at work to take reasonable care for the . . . safety of himself and of other persons who may be affected by his acts or omissions at work'?

Is there any equipment that BR can install to guard against a driver's wrongly passing, at Danger, signals such as BL86? The new Automatic Train Protection System which BR is proposing to install could include such a provision, but several years are likely to pass before the new equipment comes into widespread use. A quicker and cheaper alternative, to be installed at those places where train speeds may be quite high and where there is an additional hazard such as a single-lead or conflicting junction beyond the platform starting signal would be an AWS magnet located immediately beyond the signal. The equipment would give no indication at all if the signal showed anything other than Red, but whilst the signal was at Red the equipment would be de-energised and would sound a warning horn in the driving cab if a driver passed the signal at Danger — sufficient to alert him if he had passed the signal in error.

The 'system' (incorporating signalling, track layout, and operating methods) at both Purley and Bellgrove has been seen to be flawed. It failed to prevent the accidents of 4 and 6 March 1989. So it is reassuring for passengers to hear that BR now intends to take remedial action and install a better system, and if this sounds like closing the stable door after the horse has bolted, one can only retort that there are still plenty of horses inside the stable, whose safety is a matter of some importance, at least to them.

Below left:
A Class 303 unit stands in the platform at Glasgow Bellgrove. The guard is leaning out of the centre coach to make sure that the signal has been cleared for the train to proceed to Springburn. *Author*

Bottom left:
The guard on the Class 303 unit leaving Glasgow Bellgrove for Springburn appears to be making a final check that BL86 signal is still cleared for the train to proceed to the Branch. *Author*

Below:
A view of signal BL86 from the '3-car Stop' position. It is located just at the far side of the overbridge. The junction to Springburn is just out of sight to the left. *Author*

11
Conclusions

What are the impressions gained from the preceding chapters so far as safety is concerned? They fall, I think, into four main areas:

1. Technical Excellence

In 1948, when the railways were nationalised, their equipment and methods had changed but little in the previous half-century. The railwayman of 1900 would quickly have felt at home if suddenly transported to the railway of 1948, and vice versa. Since 1948, however, the railway scene has undergone a major change, whilst engineers and designers have achieved levels of safety standards in respect of the track and rolling stock that might have been thought of at one time as unattainable, especially when one considers the speed of today's trains. This particular area of activity must therefore be judged a resounding success in safety terms. However, it is impossible to guarantee that no more serious accidents will be caused by defective track or rolling stock; in fact history teaches us that one can almost guarantee that there will be further accidents and that some of them will be, in practical terms, unavoidable. To accept that situation is not being defeatist, but merely recognises the inevitability of accidents in the daily transport of millions of passengers and millions of tons of goods.

2. The Hidden Hazards of Technical Innovation and Change

The hidden hazards in this area are nowhere better illustrated than in the story of the development of continuously-welded rail, in which the main line became in effect an outdoor laboratory where experience was dearly bought by a process somewhat resembling that of trial and error. Then, just when engineers were beginning to think that they had at last reached a plateau of success, along came the Motherwell accident in 1986 to remind them of their fallibility. The development of CWR is a fascinating story, with engineers not only pushing at the boundaries of knowledge, but reaching beyond them; then reacting and adjusting as each new hazard revealed itself. Maj Holden's comments at the Public Inquiry into the Motherwell accident seem specially apt in this connection:

> 'This aspect of track design (ie the particular layout at Motherwell) is, perhaps, more of an art than a science and we may never come to a final mathematical conclusion. It is quite plain that a considerable amount of research needs to be done so that I can make some recommendations to the Secretary of State for Transport.'

3. Human Error

Many of the accidents described in this book confirm yet again that people, being human beings, make mistakes, or are careless. The range of human error is fascinating in its breadth and diversity, ranging from simple forgetfulness to errors of judgement; from lack of care to the jumping to wrong conclusions; and from the man at the bottom to the man at the top. Management, however, has a real responsibility here which it does not always recognise, or having recognised it does not always give it sufficient attention — and that is the responsibility to guard against the frailty of human nature. Technical safeguards are part of the answer, but another important area is that of training. There can rarely be too much of it, but sometimes there is insufficient. It is expensive, and an easy activity in which to economise when costs have to be cut. However, having said that, it must be pointed out that three of the worst accidents in the last 20 years (West Ealing 1973 — 10 killed, Taunton 1978 — 12 killed and Clapham Junction 35 killed) were caused by human errors that might seem almost trivial, but which had the most awful consequences and are exceedingly difficult to guard against.

The accidents at Purley and Bellgrove both demonstrated the still urgent need to do more to help the driver to avoid erroneously passing signals at Danger; a need which BR has at last accepted. Both accidents were clearly foreshadowed in *Danger Signals*, and even though BR is to take action, there are likely to be further accidents before that action becomes wholly effective. One hopes that more urgency will be shown than was the case with the existing Automatic Warning System. The decision to install AWS on the more important lines was taken in 1948. Design, development, testing and proving took 10 years. Installation took the next 30: the programme was not completed until 1988. Such snail-like progress would surely be unacceptable so far as the introduction of a modern Automatic Train Protection system is concerned.

4. Outside Influences

These are staggering in their diversity. They range from government action on the one hand, to lorry drivers bashing bridges on the other. Railways are, and have been for many years, a political football, and if management sometimes gives the impression that it does not know whether it is coming or going, is there any wonder? Furthermore, the situation does not improve. Privatisation, bus-substitution, sell-offs, reviews and inquiries, and fluctuations in capital investment are but a few of the BR Board's current problems. Each time there is a change of minister with responsibility for railways there are further upheavals, and as ministers change office so frequently, that is a major factor. Given Britain's political history, it was inevitable that the railways would be nationalised one day, but many of their problems have stemmed from the Transport Act of 1947, which brought them into public ownership. Prior to 1948 the four main line companies were basically well managed, each in its own particular way, but for historical reasons they were short of investment and their assets were not in a very good state, due to the war and its aftermath. By contrast, the nationalised railway cannot be considered to have been run as efficiently as the private companies were, because of the political interference to which it has been subjected; indeed, one would go further and suggest that BR has at times been virtually unmanageable, despite the considerable efforts of a lot of good managers.

Successive chairmen have come and gone, each one attempting to put things right according to his lights, and each one retiring, defeated. For 40 years BR has been struggling to get its organisation right and it has not yet entirely succeeded; which is a serious criticism because it has done nothing but reorganise since 1948 and it should be sufficiently expert by now. What is more, the railway of today is a much simpler affair than it was 10, 20 or 30 years ago. It must have seemed to the government many times over the last 40 years that the railways were a byword for waste and inefficiency, even though much of it was caused by the government's own policies, and it is hardly surprising that governments have imposed strict and severe financial constraints on the day-to-day activities. This has forced BR to cut its staff to the bone, and its margins below prudent levels in an almost desperate attempt to prove to the government that it deserves to be allowed to embark on a major capital investment programme. The downside of this daily struggle to exist within the government-imposed financial framework is that safety margins may become eroded, and this manifests itself in the long hours that staff have to work to increase their earnings to what they consider to be a reasonable level; in the shortages of key staff because BR cannot afford to pay the going rate in many parts of the country; in the upheaval of constant reorganisations, which distracts line managers from their job of supervising safety; and in the inability of BR to train its staff properly because training costs money which it has not got.

The Railway Inspectorate has voiced its concern over these issues several times in the last few years.

The public voice on railway safety has traditionally been the Railway Inspectorate, and it has fulfilled this role by holding Public Inquiries into accidents, and by publishing reports of those inquiries. Unfortunately the reports are often not published until many months, or even years, afterwards, which is much too late for them to serve their purpose. A more worrying trend in recent years has been the reduction in the number of Public Inquiries held. The average number of inquiries held in the 1970s was 11 per year. The average in the first half of the 1980s was eight. The average for the three years 1985-87 was five. In 1988, for the first time since the Inspectorate was formed in 1840, there was none. (The serious collision at Clapham on 12 December 1988 was followed by a formal inquiry headed by a QC.) This is not an indication that railway safety has improved so remarkably, but is caused by a shortage of staff in the Railway Inspectorate, due to the reluctance of the Department of Transport to pay the rate for the job and to recruit sufficient staff. Public Inquiries are very time-consuming, and in order that the Inspectorate can carry out its responsibilities effectively as the public watchdog on railway safety it needs to be properly staffed. The passenger has a right to know what is being done about his safety.

The Chief Inspecting Officer of Railways, Mr R. J. Seymour, concluded his Annual Report on Railway Safety for 1987 in the following terms:

> '1987 brought no grounds for complacency about the safety of railway travel'.

He tempered this remark somewhat by going on to say that a great deal of effort was devoted by the operators and their staff at all levels to maintaining the railways' traditionally high standards. The number of significant train accidents in 1987 was 200, the same as in 1986, and the figure has hovered around the 200 mark throughout the 1980s, after being halved during the 1970s mainly owing to changes in freight train operation. BR appears now to have reached a plateau so far as safety is concerned, and the following figures of passenger deaths in train accidents can only give rise to sober reflection:

Years	*No of Passengers killed in train accidents*
1900-09	169
1930-39	114
1960-69	134
1980-89 (June)	75

Much of the improvement in the 1980s can be attributed to the stronger coaches now in general use which prevent telescoping, a potent source of death in earlier decades, and it is difficult to see how the high standards of safety which have always epitomised Britain's railways can be greatly improved upon, given the multitude of causes of railway accidents, and the almost trivial but vital errors that caused some of the worst ones. Nevertheless, the unremitting struggle to achieve a safer railway must continue. The price of safety is eternal vigilance, but it would be unrealistic to pretend that we shall ever eliminate accidents altogether. They are the price of mobility.

Index

(Where only passing reference to an accident is made in the text, it is not included below)

Place	Near or between	Region	Details	Date	Page
Watford		LMR	Derailment of express	3.02.54	72
Wath Road Junction	Rotherham & Normanton	LMR	Derailment of express	18.05.48	54
Weaver Junction	Crewe & Warrington	LMR	Freight trains in collision	6.08.75	45
West Ealing	Paddington & Slough	WR	Derailment of express	19.12.73	114

Bibliography

Magazines & Periodicals

Modern Railways
Railnews (BR house journal)
Railway Gazette
Railway Gazette International
Railway Magazine
Railway Observer

Books

Biggs Clauses Consolidation Acts 1845-1866: James Biggs (1866).
British Railways Engineering: John Johnson and Robert A. Long (1981).
Danger Signals. An Investigation into Modern Railway Accidents: Stanley Hall (1987).
The First Principles of Railway Signalling: C. B. Byles (1918).
Gradients of the British Main Line Railways: The *Railway Magazine* (1936).
Historic Railway Disasters: O. S. Nock (1966).
Jubilees of the LMS: John F. Clay (1971).
The Law of Carriage by Inland Transport: Dr Otto Kahn-Freund (1965).
The Law of the Railway: Leslie James (1980).
Red for Danger: L. T. C. Rolt (1982).
Trains in Trouble: Vols 1 & 2: Arthur Trevena (1980/81); Vols 3 & 4: Ken Hoole (1982/83).

Reports & Pamphlets, etc

British Railways and Constituent Companies Books of Rules, Regulations & Instructions.
British Standard Code of Practice for Fire Precautions in the Design & Construction of Railway Passenger Rolling Stock (BS 6853: 1987).
The Carriage of Dangerous Goods by Rail: Paper delivered to CIT (Humberside Section) by G. W. Foulger (1978).
It Can Now be Revealed. More about British Railways in Peace and War (1945).
Railways of Central & West Wales: Neil Sprinks (1987).
A Strategy for the Reduction of Bridge Bashing: Report by a Department of Transport Working Party (1988).
Transport of CEGB Irradiated Nuclear Fuel: CEGB (1983).
Transportation of Radioactive Material: NUR (1987).